hotels • spas • resorts • villas

italychic

hotels • spas • resorts • villas

italychic

text leonie loudon • richard nichols • elena nichols • kerry o'neill

·K·U·P·E·R·A·R·D·

publisher'sacknowledgements

Finally la bella Italia has arrived! First of all, I would like to thank all of the fabulous properties that are featured in Italy Chic. As usual there are many others to thank, in particular, Massimo Bartolucci, Director of the Italian Tourism Board in Rome, and his colleagues in London; Mario Chessa, Regional Director of Sales and Marketing of Starwood Hotels and Resorts, Italy and Malta; Laura Pettazzi and Alex Fenzl; the Sales and Marketing team of Hotel Straf; Evelina Conti, Director of Sales and Marketing of the Rocco Forte Collection in Italy and Sue Heady, Director of Communications in London. And of course there's Paola Manfedi, for all her help.

From our own team, special thanks go to Isabelle du Plessix, Associate Publisher of the Chic Collection, who worked tirelessly to see the entire project through. As always, the team at Editions Didier Millet worked against the clock to meet the deadlines. Special thanks to Joanna Greenfield and Priscilla Chua, and the unsung heroes, KC Sin and Bobby Teh, who carried on the good work, got the book produced and delivered.

Finally, I thank you, the reader, for having bought this book, and for your support of The Chic Collection. Please register with us for some very special offers for your trip to Italy and I hope you find *Italy Chic* to be a wonderful resource to plan an unforgettable visit.

Nigel Bolding
editor-in-chief

executive editor
melisa teo

editors
joanna greenfield • priscilla chua

designers
lisa damayanti • felicia wong

production manager
sin kam cheong

first published in 2008 by
bolding books
121 telok ayer street, #03-01
singapore 068590
enquiries : nigel@thechiccollection.com
website : www.thechiccollection.com

©2008 bolding books
design and layout © editions didier millet pte ltd

first published in great britain 2008 by
kuperard
59 hutton grove, london n12 8ds
telephone : +44 (0) 20 8446 2440
facsimile : +44 (0) 20 8446 2441
enquiries : sales@kuperard.co.uk
website : www.kuperard.co.uk

Kuperard is an imprint of Bravo Ltd.

Printed in Singapore.

isbn: 978-1-85733-421-0

COVER CAPTIONS:

1: High up in the hills, the medieval Palazzo Viviani sits among the clouds.
2: Modern design and comfort at Charming House DD.724.
3: The view from the Hotel Gritti Palace.
4: Caffè Pedrocchi in Padua.
5: A luxury spa treatment.
6: The stunning glass dome at the Park Hyatt Milan's La Cupola restaurant.
7: A glimpse of Italy's café society.
8: Turin's Piazza San Carlo.
9: Gourmet cuisine at Hotel Giardino.
10: Rome's bustling Via Condotti.
11: Unrestrained glamour in Milan.
12: An amuse bouche from the Michelin-starred wonder Carlo Cracco.
13: Tuscan splendour at Montechiello.
14: Renaissance-style luxury at the gorgeous Ca Maria Adele in Venice.
15: The Vatican Museums' staircase.
16: Venice's canals, a landmark of Italy.
17: Enjoy a martini at the Hotel de Russie.
18: The stunning mosaics of Palermo's 12th-century Cappella Palatina.
19: Five-star dining, Italian style.
20 AND 22: The stylish L'Albereta.
21: Avant-garde detail at The Gray.

PAGE 2: Elegance abounds in the lakeside villas of Italy.

THIS PAGE: A Carlo Cracco creation.

OPPOSITE: First class al fresco dining.

PAGES 8 AND 9: The romanticism of Italy.

contents

italy by region

italy by chapter

**Milan +
Northern Italy**

**Venice +
Northeast Italy**

**Florence +
North Central
Italy**

**Rome +
South Central Italy**

**Naples +
Amalfi Coast +
Southern Italy**

**Island
Italy**

Island Italy

FRANCE

Bay of Biscay

Gulf of Lion

ANDORRA

SPAIN

*Mediterranean
Sea*

ALGERIA

introduction

picture perfect

Majestic peaks of the Dolomites towering over benign meadows; wheat fields full of poppies, distant cypresses vertical against the horizon; a riot of lemon trees on a precipice, the sea perilously far below; vast expanses of rice paddies merging into the twilight; a Greek temple silhouetted against an azure sky; a relentless sun beating down on a bleached-out square: each is a snapshot of an Italy, more or less familiar to all. An Italy that, as much as we think we know, always retains an irresistible enigma.

One of Europe's most visited countries, Italy's 20 regions are so different that no matter how many times you visit, there's always so much else to see. A giant assault on the senses, Italy gets under your skin, and lures you back again and again. And it's not just the natural beauty that attracts, it's also the staggering wealth of architecture. In recognition of this, Italy has more UNESCO World Heritage Sites than anywhere else in the world—over 40 in total. Naturally, Rome and Venice are the country's biggest draws, but individual attractions such as the Leaning Tower of Pisa and entire town centres are now protected as Italy's treasures—from Florence and Siena, to Verona, Ferrara and Urbino; from Naples, to the baroque towns of southeast Sicily. There's far more beauty than even the Italians can cope with and it's partly thanks to tourism that Italy's incredible heritage has survived so well.

an island of opportunity?

Almost an elongated island—other than its northern Alpine-locked frontier—Italy has enticed different civilisations to its shores since time immemorial. From the Greeks to the Saracens, from the Byzantines to the Normans, from the Spanish to the Bourbons and to the Austro-Hungarians, Italy has always been at the centre of the world in terms of trade and strategic importance. Furthermore, it's from the same coast that Italy's own seafarers left to make their mark—Marco Polo, Christopher Columbus and Amerigo Vespucci and, centuries later, thousands of impoverished Italians in mass migration to all four corners of the world.

THIS PAGE: *La dolce vita in action—Peter Sellers and his then wife, Britt Ekland, having fun in Rome in 1965.*

OPPOSITE: *Quintessential Italy, Venice attracts thousands with its romantic ambience and unique cityscape, seen here above St. Mark's Basilica.*

in extremis

A land of extremes with a north-south divide that's like no other, Italy remains one of Europe's wealthiest nations in the north, and one of its poorest in the south. It has endured and survived endless invasions, volcano eruptions, earthquakes and sustained bombings from both sides during World War II, only to resurge over and over again like a phoenix rising from the ashes. But while Italians are proud of their heritage, their heart is closer to their region than their country, for Italy as we know it now was only created in 1861. With the north begrudging the money that goes to the needy south, and the south saturated with organised crime and poverty, Italy's political world is another seat of discord divided from left to right with scant chance of ever really reaching agreement.

Dichotomies pervade the country's entire make-up: from the paganism of the Romans to the orthodoxy of the Roman Catholic Church; from the plotting and power-mongering of the Emperors and the Senate; from the feuding of the communes to the factions, which were split between the Guelph faction, with its allegiance to the Pope, and the Ghibelline faction, supporters of the Holy Roman Emperor. Even the Church split after the onset of Protestantism, only brought back together as a result of the Council of Trent. Yet, despite being so utterly rooted in its past and time-honoured traditions, Italy is the self-same country that coined the concept of futurism.

bella gente, bel paese

In spite of this constant push and pull and Italy's pushover tendency in international politics, it's testimony to the resilience, passion and prodigious talent of its people that Italy is the place it is. For the beauty of the landscape apart, it is the Italians who have created most of what makes Italy so special. Since the Romans, then the Renaissance and to the present-day, Italy has given the world some of its greatest writers, musicians and artists, not to mention its scientists, inventors and explorers. And it's not over yet. From fashion to football, from food to finance, Italy is a place to be reckoned with.

...beauty of the landscape apart, it is the Italians who have created most of what makes Italy so special.

made in italy: fashion

Synonymous with fashion, Milan arrived at the forefront of design in the 1960s and hasn't looked back since. While embracing the made-in-Italy tradition of tailoring, shoemaking and quality fabrics, the country's designers are firmly at the cutting-edge of the fashion industry due to their sheer sense of style; they are always leading with others following.

milan + northern italy

Although our word milliner comes from Milan's tradition of hat making, Milan is now renowned for its fashion houses. The golden triangle has the best of the designer shops: Via Montenapoleone for **Gucci**, **Versace**, **Prada**, **Salvatore Ferragamo**, **Fratelli Rossetti**, and **Valentino**; Via Sant'Andrea for **Fendi**, **Armani**, **Moschino**, **Gianfranco Ferré**, and **Trussardi**; and Via della Spiga for **Dolce & Gabbana**, **Tod's**, and **Bulgari**.

The **Spazio Armani** (Via Manzoni 31) is an all-Armani mall, also housing Milan's branch of Nobu. **10 Corso Como** is an ultra-trendy boutique, bookshop, gallery and restaurant in one. Firmly in touch with up-to-the-minute trends, this is an imperative stop for those in vogue. For other Italian brands, such as **Max Mara** and **Furla**, the longest shopping street of all is the Corso Vittorio Emanuele, which starts at Piazza Duomo. Head for the Navigli area for more off-the-wall fashion. As well as quirky Italian brands such as **Diesel** and **Miss Sixty**, there's a whole host of vintage shops and one-off boutiques featuring new talent.

venice + north east italy

Venice's designer clothes shops are all dotted around the web of streets around Piazza San Marco. **Vittorio Trois** (Campo San Maurizio, San Marco 2666) is the best place to buy Fortuny fabric. **Venetia Studium** (two branches in San Marco) sells fine Fortuny-covered items and fashion. Bologna's shopping heart is on Via Farini within the Galleria Cavour, which is home to **Versace**, **Gucci** and **La Perla** as well as the classic men's outfitters **Giusti**.

florence + north-central italy

There's a glut of designer legends in Florence. The city's main shopping streets are Via Tornabuoni and Via della Vigna Nuova, although less known designers and boutiques lurk around every corner. Local talent include the likes of **Gucci** (Via Tornabuoni 73r and Via Roma 32r) and **Roberto Cavalli** (Via Tornabuoni 83r) as well as less familiar names such as **Patrizia Pepe** (Piazza san Giovanni 12r). Both **Salvatore Ferragamo** (Via Tornabuoni 4r–14r) and **Emilio Pucci** (Palazzo Pucci, Via dei Pucci 6r), moved from Naples and made Florence their base. **SpazioA** (Via Porta Rossa 107r) is a stylish boutique that hosts various designers, from **Alberta Ferretti** to **Jean Paul Gaultier** to **Narciso Rodriguez** and **Moschino**.

rome + south-central italy

As well as being beautiful, Rome is one big shopping paradise of designer stores, boutiques and tailors or couturiers offering made-to-measure garments. The hallowed shopping streets are in and around Piazza di Spagna where the fashion gods are located. **Valentino** (Via Condotti 13, Via del Babuino 61 and Via

THIS PAGE (CLOCKWISE FROM TOP LEFT): Bulgari, a luxury Italian brand in business since 1905; Dolce & Gabbana is adored for its cutting-edge design; in the heart of Milan's glamour, Prada resides in the Galleria; a Tod's store in central Milan.

OPPOSITE: A model wearing a Gianni Calignano gown.

Bocca di Leone 15), **Fendi** (Via Borgognona 39 with a grand flagship at Palazzo Fendi, Largo Goldoni 415-421) and **Bulgari** (Via Condotti 10) are Roman designers through and through.

Nearby is **TAD** (Via del Babuino 155a), Rome's concept store and emporium of more eccentric designers. Described as achingly hip, **Degli Effetti** (Piazza Capranica 75, 79 and 93), with an interior designed by Massimiliano Fuksas, sells reworked vintage clothes from designers such as John Galliano and Comme des Garçons. **244 Via Panisperna** is another contemporary boutique for designer clothing, especially shoes. **Leam** (Via Appia Nuova 26 and 32) is a seriously stylish clothing shop with all the top designers. More mainstream fashion is on Via del Corso, Via Cola di Rienzo (near the Vatican) and Via Nazionale. Via dei Giubbonari, near Campo dei Fiori, has high-fashion boutiques intermingled with more run of the mill clothes shops. Nearby in the old Ghetto area are some of Rome's finest goldsmiths; there are dozens of ateliers to choose from. Via Veneto has its own prestigious shops too, **Brioni**, the gentlemen's outfitters, for one.

naples + amalfi coast + southern italy

Fashion in Naples is big business, both designer names and home-grown talent are spread along Via dei Mille and Via Filangieri, off Piazza dei Martiri. The tiny Via Calabritto, which ends opposite the sea by the Riviera dei Chiaia, is another haven for shoppers. **Eddy Monetti** (Via Dei Mille 45) is a byword for fashion for both men's and women's wear and is the place to come for bespoke suits. Presidents and princes shop for their ties in the historic institution of **E. Marinella** (Riviera di Chiaia 287) and nearby **Merolla e del'Ero** (Via Calabritto, 20) sells hand-made shirts, offering a vast range of buttons. Galleria Umberto I is home to the stylish boutique chain **Barbaro**.

Capri has a heavenly host of designer shops, competing with Rodeo Drive and Rome in terms of prestige and glamour. **Ferragamo**, **Fendi**, **Gucci**, **Cavalli** and **Prada** crowd around the central streets of Via Camerelle, Via Furlovado and Via Vittorio Emanuele. For bespoke Capri pants head for **La Parisienne** (Piazza Umberto I, 7). **Pucci**, their creator, opened his first shop on Capri in 1949. More recently, a shop has opened on Via Camarelle, selling beautiful bikinis and yachting accessories. **L'Arte del Sandalo Caprese** (Via Orlando 75, Anacapri) is where Antonio Viva makes the hand-made bejewelled sandals Capri's known for.

island italy

Palermo and Catania, on the island of Sicily, have their fair share of designers. Prime shopping streets are Via della Libertà or Via Vittorio Emanuele in Palermo and Via Etnea and Corso Italia in Catania. Here you'll find the top Italian names as well as Sicilian designers, many from third generation family firms. Local talent include **Di Maria** (Via F Bandiera 63, Palermo) for wedding gowns; **Roberta Lojacono** (Via Turati 17, Palermo) for one-off designs; and **Marella Ferrera** (Viale XX Settembre 25/27, Catania) for women's wear. Via Bara all'Olivella, near the archaeological museum, and parallel Via dell'Orologio are full of shops and home to **La Coppola Storta**, the trendy version of the Sicilian beret. The island of Lipari is famed for its made-to-measure leather sandals.

THIS PAGE (CLOCKWISE FROM TOP): **The Gucci handbag, a timeless classic; the exhibition for Valentino celebrating 45 years of style; a show at Milan fashion week; in 2007 Valentino showed about 64 dresses at a show in Rome to mark his anniversary.**

OPPOSITE (FROM TOP): **The Gucci store on Via Condotti, Rome; the TAD concept store, a sleek and eclectic department store.**

made in italy: design

Art and architecture are not the only areas in which Italians excel—applied design is yet another. While Italian craftsmanship is second to none, Italy is also one of the few remaining places where the artisan and small family business hold sway over the multinational and the production line. From high art to everyday object, it seems the Italians have the golden touch and whatever they make becomes highly desirable.

Italian designers have always been at the forefront of the international contemporary design scene, constantly innovating as well as adhering to fond-held, tried and tested traditions. Combining good looks with pure functionality is a skill that Italian designers thrive on. Take, for example, the Ferrari. It is known and loved not just for its powerful engine but for its sleek bodywork: think of the Testarossa of 1984, designed by Pininfarina, or his Alfa Romeo Spider of 1966. Simple run-arounds became the much-loved Fiat 500 by Dana Giacosa, the Vespa by Corradino d'Ascanio or the Lambretta by Ferdinando Innocenti. Even the humble Moka, the coffee percolator created by Alfonso Bialetti in 1933, entered the realms of historic Italian design and is ubiquitous across Italy and familiar all over the world. It's no surprise that Bialetti was the grandfather of another great designer: Alberto. As Italians would say, keep it in the family.

THIS PAGE (CLOCKWISE FROM TOP LEFT):
Poltrona Frau's classic Vanity Fair armchair, a replica of the 904 model that was part of the company's 1903 catalogue; a more recent creation, the Dezza, was designed in 1965; the flagship store in Milan.
OPPOSITE: Arper's finely crafted Duna chairs and the Leaf Lounge chair, both designed by Lievore Altherr Molina.

From Giò Ponti to Ettore Sottsass (and the Memphis Group), Achille Castiglioni and his two brothers, Tobia Scarpa and countless others, Italian design seems one step ahead of the rest of the world. Many classic designs from back catalogues are recreated today and appear as modern now as they were then.

italy

Founded in Turin but now based in Le Marche, **Poltrona Frau** (www.poltronafrau.com) is Italy's best-known chair manufacturer. Trading since 1912, it won the royal seal of the Savoy's, creating the seating ever since for the grandest of transatlantic ocean liners, car and airplane interiors, concert halls and parliament buildings as well as the humble home. Offering a vast range of fabric colours and finishes, Poltrona Frau has always combined tradition with technology, using cutting-edge designers such as Giò Ponti and more recently Frank O Gehry. In 2004 the firm bought up **Cappellini** (www.cappellini.it) and, in 2005, **Cassina** (www.cassina.com) became part of the group. Both are members of Italy's design aristocracy. Cappellini has long been making objects of desire and lighting while Cassina, started out in 1927 with tables and graduated to armchairs. Like Poltrona Frau, Cassina has created upholstery and chairs for hundreds of prestigious projects, from 1950s liners, hotels and casinos to Giò Ponti's legendary Leggera and Supper Leggera chairs.

Three other sought-after furniture firms are **Minotti** (www.minotti.it), **Il Loft** (www.illoft.com) and **Arper** (www.arper.com). Minotti has 60 years' experience in making armchairs and sofas, with designs in 2007 by Rodolfo

THIS PAGE: Murano glass artwork at the Casa Angelina.

OPPOSITE (CLOCKWISE FROM TOP): Barnaba Fornasetti is keeping his father's workshop running and creating new designs such as this curved cabinet named 'Zebra' and stool 'Bocca'; Arper's Catifa 70 and Leaf Chair, both designed by Lievore Altherr Molina; a stylish Zucchetti bathroom.

Dordoni. Il Loft makes award-winning chairs and fabrics by Giorgio Saporiti, entirely made in Italy. Arper, set up in the late 1980s, creates finely crafted chairs and tables, including the best-selling Duna and Catifa collections, designed by Alberto Lievore. Prize-winning designer bathroom and kitchen taps are made by **Zucchetti** (www.zucchettionline.it) while **Ceramica Flaminia** (www.ceramicaflaminia.it) is famed for its covetable bathroom suites.

Piero **Fornasetti** (www.fornasetti.com), Milan-born painter, sculptor, interior decorator, engraver and designer, was one of the most prodigious and imaginative talents of the 20th century. His son Barnaba has continued production, reviving his most popular pieces and creating new ones under licence.

Artemide (www.artemide.com), founded in 1958 by Ernesto Gismondi and Sergio Mazza, specialises in the manufacture of lighting designed by famous international designers and architects. Best known is the Tizio desk lamp designed by Richard Sapper in 1972 and the Tolomeo desk lamp, designed by Michele De Lucchi and Giancarlo Fassina in 1986, both of which have become icons of Italian modern design. Another lighting company, **Flos** (www.flos.com), was founded in 1962, employing such luminaries as the Castiglioni brothers and Tobia Scarpa. Flos is particularly known for its 1950s cocoon lamps, a spray-on plastic coating used in a variety of creative ways. In 1988 they produced the first lamp designed by Philippe Starck, named the Arà.

Still family-run, **Alessi** (www.alessi.com) is famous for its playful design of objects and appliances for the kitchen, created in colourful plastics and stainless steel. In business since 1921, it became particularly sought-after in the 1980s when Alberto Alessi took over. Alessi collaborated with designers such as Ettore Sottsass, Richard Sapper, Achille Castiglioni and most famously Philippe Starck. More recently Alessi has worked with Zaha Hadid and, in 2006, the company reclassified into three lines—Officina Alessi is its limited edition and the most experimental.

milan + northern italy

E De Padova (Corso Venezia 14) is Milan's main furniture store with six floors selling furniture and objects by designers such as Achille Castiglioni and Pierluigi Cerri as well as new talent. Before he died Achille Castiglioni often dressed the windows. Another showroom for top talent is **B&B Italia** (Via Durini 14). Founded in 1966, also offering furniture by top designers, their catalogue is tempting to say the least; it features many re-issued design classics as well as brand new desirables.

For collectible originals there are several galleries selling the decorative and applied arts as well as furniture. The **Galleria MK** (Via Pietro Maroncelli 2) and **Galleria Rossella Colombari** (Via Pietro Maroncelli 10) are good places to start. There are also auction houses, which can be a better bet for certain designers. A piece by Carlo Mollino, the design maverick from Turin, set world records for 20th-century furniture in 2005—a 1949 oak and glass table sold for $3.8 million. **Danese** (Piazza San Nazaro in Brolo 15), an archetypal design firm founded in 1957, has limited edition reissues and old stock at somewhat more accessible prices; much of their catalogue was created by Enzo Mari and Bruno Munari.

venice + north-central italy

Nowadays, Murano glass is Venice's best-known export. On the island of Murano itself **Carlo Moretti** (Fondamenta Manin 3) sells stylish contemporary pieces, as does **Domus Vetri d'Arte** (Fondamenta Vetrai 82). Back on dry land, **Pauly** (Calle Larga San Marco) sells classic glassware while **San Vio** (Campo San Vio) in the Dorsoduro is more design-focused.

rome + south-central italy

As well as individual firms' showrooms, there are contemporary design emporiums in Rome. **Spazio Sette** (Via dei Barbieri 7) has three floors of furniture inside the Palazzo Lazzaroni. Two stores to aim for are **Magazzini Associati** (Corso del Rinascimento 7) or **Benedetti** (Via Marmorata 1341), which has seven branches, each with different stock. For state of the art kitchens, there is **Arclinea** (Lungotevere de'Cenci 4b) or **Odorisio** (Via Tomacelli 150).

For vintage design, try Rome's antique shops. **Babuino Novecento** (Via del Babuino 65) sells furniture and objects of desire; **Maurizio de Nisi** (Via Panisperna 51), specialises in 1930s and 1940s design, while both **Retrò** (Piazza del Fico 20-21) and **High Tech d'Epoca** (Piazza A. Capponi 7) sell work from the 1900s onwards.

For glass—contemporary and antique—visit **Murano Più** (Corso del Rinascimento 43/45) or **Archimede Seguso** (Via dei Due Macelli 56). And for kitchen accessories, the luxurious **Fornari & Fornari** (Via Frattina, 133) is a must. **C.u.c.i.n.a.** (Via Mario d'Fiori 65) and **Gusto** (Piazza Augusto Imperatore 9) also have plenty to choose from. **TAD** (Via del Babuino 155a) also has a selection of household goods.

italy's restaurant scene

Enjoyed in every corner of the globe, there is more to Italian food than the ubiquitous pizza and pasta. Although a time-honoured tradition and a deep-rooted part of Italian daily life, dining in Italy remains a truly dynamic experience with new talent constantly emerging and keeping the restaurant scene firmly at the cutting-edge.

milan + northern italy

Cracco (Via Victor Hugo 4) showcases the creativity and orchestral finesse of talented chef Carlo Cracco. It is undoubtedly Milan's best restaurant, with no less than two Michelin stars and a super-star following. In the trendy Navigli area is Milan's other top chef, Claudio Sadler of **Ristorante Sadler** (Via Ascanio Sforza 77) who is renowned for his technical brilliance and immaculately sourced ingredients. Fish is his particular speciality, and his signature dishes include Lobster with Rosemary and Baked Fish with Pernod and Fennel. Just outside Milan, on the way to Turin is **Caffè Groppi** (Via Goffredo Mameli 20) with young Fabio Barbaglini at the helm.

Located outside Turin, in Rivoli, the Michelin-starred **Combal.Zero** (Piazza Mafalda di Savoia) boasts the avant garde talents of Chef Davide Scabin. Housed in a 13th-century castle beside a museum of contemporary art, Scabin's futuristic menu encourages diners to play with their food as much as eat it, with presentation key to their enjoyment.

In Turin itself, **La Pista** (Via Nizza 262/294) is dramatically sited at the top of Lingotto's fabled parabolic ramp. Stylish and tasteful décor combines with intriguing menus. The desserts are especially good. Other landmarks in the city include chef Piercarlo Bussetti's **Locanda Mongreno** (Strada Comunale Mongreno, 50), and Alfredo Russo's **Dolce Stil Novo** (Via San Pietro 71/73). Both are Michelin-starred.

Just south, in Alba, is Enrico Crippa's **Piazza Duomo** (Piazza Risorgimento 4). Also in the Langhe region, one of the most beautiful views, and traditional Piemontese cuisine, is at the **Locanda nel Borgo Antico** (Via Boschetti 4) in Barolo. Further south, on the coast in San Remo is **Paolo e Barbara** (Via Roma 47).

The two-Michelin-starred **Villa Crespi** (Via G. Fava 18) is an enchanted spot by Lake Orta. Right in the middle of Lake Como is some old-fashioned charm at the **Locanda dell'Isola Comacina** (Ossuccio). The restaurant serves a fixed menu and bewitches one and all with its simplicity, friendliness and fabulous views. One of Lake Garda's Michelin-starred offerings is Riccardo Camanini's **Villa Fiordaliso** (Corso Zanardelli 132).

Nadia Santini's elegant antique-filled restaurant **Dal Pescatore** (Loc. Runate 17) is located in an oasis of green just outside Mantua. Her simple cuisine and perfectly sourced ingredients find favour with the likes of Gordon Ramsay.

The highly rated **St. Hubertus de l'Hotel Rosa Alpina** (Fraz. San Cassiano) near Bolzano has two Michelin stars and attracts many famous diners. Chef Norbert Niederkofler offers an excellent tasting menu of seven courses with accompanying wines from Alto-Adige's fine vineyards. Right on the Wein Strasse is the **Castel Ringberg** (San Giuseppe al Lago 1), a 17th-century castle overlooking Caldaro with a creative and eclectic menu.

venice + northeast italy

One of Venice's top restaurants is the **Met de l'Hotel Metropole** (Riva degli Schiavoni Castello 4149), awarded with a Michelin star. A beautiful dining room, and a garden in summer, Chef Corrado Fasolato offers exciting cuisine, with the fragrance and spice of Venice's exotic past. **Il Vecio Fritolin** (Calle della Regina) in the Rialto—with a branch in the Palazzo Grassi—is run with passion by Irina Freguia, who serves traditional Venetian fare. There's another top female chef at **Laite** (Via Hoffe 10) in Sappada. Run by a husband and wife team in a beautiful wooden chalet, Fabrizia Meroi prepares exquisite dishes with the local game—venison, partridge and hare—and fish.

Young Massimiliano Alajmo is one of Italy's finest culinary talents. He runs **Le Calandre** (Loc. Sarmeola, Via Liguria 1) in Padua with his brother Raffaele, and serves clever, intriguing twists of a family-learned art. The youngest chef to win two Michelin stars, he has been described as the Mozart of cooking. Verona's classic enoteca and restaurant is the beautiful **Bottega del Vino** (Via Scudo di Francia 3), open since 1890. Expect excellent wines and classic local dishes such as polenta with gorgonzola or risotto all'amarone.

In Modena, Massimo Bottura's **Osteria La Francescana** (Via Stella 22) offers modern avant garde creations each presented with the chef's flair and talent.

THIS PAGE (FROM TOP): *Piercarlo Bussetti's version of sushi; Chef Enrico Crippa; Le Calandre restaurant.*

OPPOSITE (FROM TOP): *Carlo Cracco and two of his creations. The Oyster Accentuated with a Crisp Wafer of Smoked Sage-Infused Milk (below) is a recent addition to his highly inventive menu.*

THIS PAGE (CLOCKWISE FROM TOP): Paolo Lopriore in Il Canto restaurant; the rustic yet luxurious interior; his Calamari in Zimino, a modern take on the classic Italian stew.

OPPOSITE (FROM TOP): An amuse bouche from Moreno Cedroni; Chef Ciccio Sultano's innovative creation and unique ingredients.

San Domenico (Via Gaspere Sacchi 1) in Imola is one of the pillars of Romagnolo and Italian cuisine. Chef Gianluigi Morini has 30 years' experience at the top, combining balanced ingredients and a traditional repertoire with elegance. Valentino Marcattilii is his chosen protégé, promising an exciting future. The pretty **Caminetto d'Oro** (Via de'Falegnami 4) in the heart of Bologna serves classic local fare. A simple and pure menu, the chef uses mainly Slow Food producers.

florence + rome + central italy

Regularly voted Italy's best restaurant is the **Gambero Rosso** (Piazza della Vittoria 13) in San Vincenzo. Run by Chef Fulvio Pierangelini and his wife Emanuela it is a gourmet's paradise: his simple, almost essentialist dishes are described in poetic terms, his style and skill in execution are without peer.

Surrounded by some of the best grapes in the world, dining at the **Castello Banfi** (Loc. Sant'Angelo Scalo) in Montalcino is a pleasure. The sublime views aside, the seasonal Tuscan food is excellent and so is the wine. Some of Florence's finest steak Fiorentina is served at **Il Latini** (Via dei Palchetti, 6r) tucked away on a little street. Opened in 1950, the original owner Narciso is still in attendance, tables are communal and the food is exquisitely simple. A stark contrast is the **Enoteca Pinchiorri** (Via Ghibellina 87) run by an Italo-French husband and wife team with three Michelin stars.

In Siena, **Il Canto** (Hotel Certosa di Maggiano) is run by Chef Paolo Lopriore who is known for his reinventions of Italian classics. Further south in Maremma, **Da Caino** (Via Chiesa, 4) serves pure Tuscan fare in its cosy setting.

Vissani (Fraz. Civitella del Lago) is in a secluded position by a lake midway between Todi and Baschi. Using rich and complex combinations, Chef Vissani's take on local cuisine is highly innovative.

Rome boasts several top chefs and Heinz Beck of **La Pergola de l'Hotel Rome Cavalieri Hilton** (Via A Cadlolo 101) is one of the best. With three Michelin stars, his creative dishes, the elegant surroundings and fabulous views make for a winning combination. **Baby dell'Aldrovandi Palace** (Via Ulisse Aldrovandi 15) is run by Alfonso Iaccarino who is famed for his restaurant Don Alfonso in Massa Lubrense. A stone's throw from the Spanish Steps is the **Palatium Enoteca Regionale** (Via Frattina 94), a stylish but low-key centre of excellence. In trendy Trastevere is the **Enoteca Ferrara** (Piazza Trilussa 41). Run by two sisters, it's a highly-rated wine shop and restaurant with a weekly changing menu and stylish décor.

Le Marche's most notable restaurant is the Michelin-starred **Madonnina del Pescatore** (Lungomare Italia, 11). Chef Moreno Cedroni has been described as one of Italy's most modern with his experimentation and creativity.

southern + island italy

Near Brindisi, at **Osteria Già Sotto l'Arco** (Corso Vittorio Emanuele II 71) Teresa Buongiorno combines authentic ingredients with tradition and innovative touches. In the Capri Palace hotel is the Michelin-starred **L'Olivo** (Loc. Anacapri, Via Capodimonte 2b), run by young German chef Oliver Glowig. Opulent Mediterranean cuisine served in beautiful surroundings, recently restyled by Loro Piana. The ice cream trolley is a firm favourite.

Vico Equense hosts the **Torre del Saracino** (Loc. Marina di Seiano, Via Torretta 9), a Michelin-starred restaurant, with views over the Bay of Naples. Chef Gennaro Esposito, who trained under Vissani and Alain Ducasse, combines regional traditions with a magic touch.

Naples is the home of the pizza and even Neapolitans agree that **Da Michele** (Via C Sersale 1/3) makes one of the best. There are only two types to choose from: the classic Margherita or the classic Marinara. Just off the Corso Umberto I, expect to queue and share a table. There's top cuisine and arguably the best views in Naples at **La Terrazza dei Barbanti** (Corso Vittorio Emanuele 328), set on the rooftop of the Hotel San Francesco, offering classics from the Neapolitan repertoire with an elegant twist.

In downtown Palermo the **Antica Focacceria San Francesco** (Via A Paternostro 58) is an old favourite. Established in 1834 inside a former chapel, it serves excellent street food and classic cuisine in its elegant dining rooms. One of Sicily's top restaurants is the **Ristorante Duomo** (Loc. Ibla, Via Capitano Bocchieri 31). Ciccio Sultano's original flavours and perfectly-sourced local ingredients, such as Black Nebrodi Piglet in Caramelised Marsala with Roasted Cocoa Beans, have taken the culinary world by storm.

Cagliari is home to Sardinia's top restaurant, **S'Apposentu** (Via Sant'Alenixedda) inside the city's theatre. The mainstay is seafood, which is combined to delicious effect with mountain herbs. For rustic charm, traditional cuisine and some of the island's finest scenery, head for **Su Gologone** (Loc. Su Gologone, Oliena) in the heart of the Barbagia, famed for its pasta, spit-roasted meats and local cheeses.

the treasures of italy

A trip to Italy is guaranteed to be filled with artistic awe. At every corner there is inspiration from not just past masters of Italy's esteemed alumni but from new dynamic heroes of the art world. From the ancient Romans to Leonardo Da Vinci, the collection of treasures in Italy is without peer. Much to every visitor's delight, Italy has continued its creative traditions with aplomb and the country's contemporary art scene is as buzzing and as exciting as it always has been.

northern italy

Milan has a vast collection of art and the **Pinacoteca di Brera** (Via Brera 28) has its finest. Inside an imposing palazzo, treasures range from Raphael and Bellini to Modigliani and Carlo Carrà. The **Studio Museo Achille Castiglione** (Piazza Castello 27) gives an insight into one of Italy's most prodigious and respected design talents; for more exhibitions of design classics there's the **Milan Triennale** (Viale Alemagna 6).

Like Venice, Genoa's wealth came from the sea. Head for the exciting **Museo del Mare** (Calata de Mari 1), its impressive 21st-century design is inside a converted 17th-century shipyard where Genoese galleys were once built.

Turin is renowned for its Egyptian Museum, the second most important in the world. More fun, however, is Italy's finest **Museum of**

Cinema, inside the fabulous Mole Antonelliana (Via Montebello 20). Appropriately located inside the home of Fiat, Italy's best car collection is in the **Museo dell'Automobile** (Corso Unita d'Italia 40). Renzo Piano's specially designed space, **Lo Scrigno** (Pinacoteca Giovanni e Marella Agnelli) in the Lingotto, Fiat's legendary car factory, houses the Agnelli family's finest art: from Matisse to Modigliani.

Just outside Turin are two of the country's most dynamic temples to modern art: the **Fondazione Sandretto Re Rebaudengo** (Via Modane 16), and in Rivoli the **Museo di Arte Contemporanea** (Castello di Rivoli). In Rovereto the **MART** (Corso Bettini, 43) houses work by Fortunato Depero and holds major international exhibitions. Its satellite museum is in Trento, a Renaissance palace with Futurist art.

northeast italy

The apogee of Renaissance art can be seen at Venice's **Accademia** (Campo della Carita) but it also hosts breathtaking work spanning five centuries. Rare paintings by Giorgione are one of the highlights. Also in the Dorsoduro is the impressive **Peggy Guggenheim Collection** (Palazzo Venier dei Leoni), though less well known are the **Ca'Pesaro International Gallery of Modern Art** (Santa Croce 2070) and the **Palazzo Fortuny** (San Marco 3780). Both Renaissance palazzi, the first has contemporary international art from Klimt to Klee; the second shows the finest work of legendary designer Mariano Fortuny within his former home.

Bologna's **Pinacoteca Nazionale** (Via delle Belle Arti 56) boasts paintings by some of Italy's finest artists, especially those of Vitale da Bologna, Guido Reni, Guercino and the

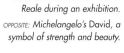

THIS PAGE (FROM TOP): Located in a 17th-century palazzo in Venice, Ca'Pesaro houses masterpieces from the likes of Chagall and Klee, to name just two; just one of Italy's treasures, Caravaggio's Coronation of Thorn on show in the Palazzo Reale during an exhibition.

OPPOSITE: Michelangelo's David, a symbol of strength and beauty.

Caraccis, all local-born. **MAMbo** (Museo d'Arte Moderna di Bologna), located in the renovated Renaissance riverside, is a museum to modern art, hosting important exhibitions; under the same umbrella is the **Museo Morandi** (Piazza Maggiore 6).

Faenza is home to the **International Museum of Ceramics** (Viale Baccarini 19), which exhibits a wonderful collection from Roman to the Renaissance to present-day. In Ferrara, the **Palazzo dei Diamanti** (Corso Ercole d'Este 21) hosts major contemporary art exhibitions and a fine collection of Renaissance paintings; next door is a museum to filmmaker Antonioni. The **Palazzo Massari** (Corso Porta Mare, 9) houses museums to De Pisis, Boldini and 19th-century art.

central italy

Florence's **Uffizi Gallery** (Loggiato degli Uffizi 6) scarcely needs an introduction. It is home to the world's greatest collection of Renaissance paintings, and to one of the world's most reproduced images, Botticelli's *Birth of Venus*. The **Bargello** (Via del Proconsolo 4) hosts Italy's finest collection of Renaissance sculpture, with masterpieces by Donatello and Michelangelo. Two of his best works—*David* and the *Four Prisoners*—are in the **Galleria dell'Accademia** (Via Ricasoli 58–60), however. Less familiar is the **Museo Salvatore Ferragamo** (Piazza Santa Trinita 5r), which is housed in the cellar of the firm's Renaissance headquarters.

Rome's **Capitoline Museums** (Piazza del Campidoglio 1) are the world's oldest and house incredible collections of paintings and classical sculpture. The sculptural overflow is at the **Centrale Montemartini** (Via Ostiense 106), within a turn-of-the-century power station. The new Esedra in the Capitoline's Palazzo dei Conservatori houses the collection's pièces de la resistance: three colossal bronzes, including that of Marcus Aurelius.

The **Vatican Museums** (Viale Vaticano) boast the world's most valuable art, without taking account of the Raphael Rooms and Michelangelo's Sistine Chapel. From the Pinturicchio-frescoed Borgia apartment to the Gallery of Maps, the Egyptian museum and the classical sculpture collection, the labyrinth of rooms is immense and their beauty astounding.

Probably Rome's finest private palace is the **Palazzo Doria Pamphilj** (Piazza del Collegio Romano 2). Still owned and lived in by the family, it boasts an exquisite art collection, from Velazquez to Caravaggio. The Villa Borghese houses the **Galleria Borghese** (Piazzale Scipione Borghese 5), complete with sculptural masterpieces by Berniniand and more paintings by Caravaggio, Titian and Botticelli. Nearby is the huge **Galleria Nazionale d'Arte Moderna** (Viale delle Belle Arti 131), with arguably Italy's best contemporary art, from Futurism to Modigliani and beyond. Highlights at the impressive **Galleria Nazionale Umbria** (Corso Vannucci 1) in Perugia are works by local artists Perugino and Pinturicchio.

southern italy

The biggest finds from Roman Pompeii and Herculaneum are on show at Naples' **Archaeological Museum** (Piazza Museo Nazionale 19). Its collection includes the incredible Farnese marbles, originally from the Caracalla Baths in Rome. The Farnese's fine collection of paintings is on show at the **Museo**

Nazionale di Capodimonte (Parco di Capodimonte); it includes work by Titian, Raphael and Caravaggio. **MADre** (Via Settembrini 79) is a contemporary gallery set in the convent of Donna Regina near the Duomo with work from Warhol to Gilbert & George, from Damien Hirst to Francesco Clemente.

The best finds of mainland Magna Graecia are in Taranto's **Palazzo Pantaleo** (Corso Vittorio Emanuele II). In Palermo, Sicily, the **Museo Archeologico Regionale** (Piazza Olivella 24) is small but equally impressive, especially the beautiful monumental artefacts from the temples at Segesta and Selinunte.

For an insight into Sardinia's Nuraghic culture head for the archaeological museum in Cagliari's **Cittadella dei Musei** (Piazza Arsenale). A brand new building to house it is currently being built by Zaha Hadid. Up in Nuoro, in the heart of the Barbagia, the well-presented **Museo della Vita e delle Tradizione Popolari Sarde** (Via Mereu 56), shows off its folk art, costumes and explanations of mysterious local rites.

THIS PAGE (FROM TOP): Part of Michelangelo's legendary work on the ceiling of the Sistine Chapel in the Vatican City; a reclining statue in the Vatican Museum courtyard.

OPPOSITE (FROM TOP): An exhibition opening at the Museo Salvatore Ferragamo in Florence; the Colossus of Constantine exhibits its staggering size at the Capitoline Museum courtyard in Rome.

italy's café society

The café is sacred in Italy; there's always a cool portico with a welcoming bar to shade you from the midday sun. Fundamental to Italian society, the piazza café has been the regular meeting place for generations. And, with Italy's distinct style, more and more chic establishments are cropping up all the time.

northern italy

The **Park Bar** (Park Hyatt Hotel) is a stylish mecca for Milan's most beautiful and is perfect for watching the passeggiata while sipping cocktails. The **Armani Privé** (Via Alessandro Manzoni 31), downstairs from Armani Nobu, is also where the high Milan society go. The **Martini Bar** (Corso Venezia 15), created by Dolce & Gabbana and just behind their store, is a black lacquered fantasy with a red dragon floor mosaic, trim leather banquettes and a courtyard. **Cova** (Via Montenapoleone 8), a 200-year-old gem in the heart of the golden triangle, is a beauty in its own right. The Belle Epoque **Caffè Zucca** (Galleria Vittorio Emanuele II) is filled with mosaics and marquetry, popular with tourists, but ideal for breathing in the city's old glamour. The nearby **Peck Bar** (Via Spadari 9) is as popular as the homonymous restaurant. Crowded with businessmen at lunchtime, it is quieter in the evening. **Caffeteria Leonardo** (Via A Saffi 7), designed by local Pupi Solari, has a stylish interior and a pretty outside space, with fine cakes, croissants and coffee on offer. In the

Parco Sempione, the art centre Triennale (Viale Alemagna 6) hosts the **Fiat Café** and **Coffee Design**. With 50 designer chairs to sit on and admire, it is an oasis in the city, with late opening in summertime and many cultural events.

In Turin, the **Caffè Al Bicerin** (Piazza della Consolata 5) serves its famous drink of coffee, cream and chocolate—queues form outside. Chocolatier **Baratti & Milano** (Piazza Castello 27) is one of Turin's grandest cafés. **Mulassano** (Piazza Castello 15) is another gem, a tiny place with a wood-coffered ceiling, filled with boiserie, brass and marble and a famous water fountain. The perfect neighbourhood bar is the **Caffè Marconi** (Corso Marconi 3) with its fine coffee, complete collection of Illy cups and selection of beautiful gifts. The **Ciak Bar** (Via Montebello 20) is one of the city's trendiest.

north-central italy

Venice's grand cafés are legendary: the **Caffè Florian** (Piazza San Marco 56) opened 300 years ago, and attracted the likes of Goethe and Stravinsky. Beautiful inside and outside, the views are second to none. Arch rival, the **Ristorante Gran Caffè Quadri** (Piazza San Marco 121), filled with mirrors, paintings and stuccoes, was the first place in Venice to serve Turkish coffee. It holds gastronomic events in winter. For a quieter and more exclusive time, head for the enchanted world of the **Bar Dandolo** (Hotel Daniele). Perfection reigns: in the coffee, club sandwiches, range of teas and cakes and the cocktails and fine wines. Elsewhere the city is filled with quintessential bacaros, tiny, old-fashioned places with nibbles or cicheti in the evening. **Bacaro Jazz** (San Marco 5546) near the Rialto is a good lively choice.

In Florence, **The Fusion Bar** (Gallery Hotel Art), designed and owned by Ferragamo, is largely a sushi bar where east meets west, open all day and late into the night. For old-fashioned elegance, head towards **Donatello** (The Westin Excelsior). Locals like antique-filled **Caffè Cibreo** (Via del Verrocchio 5r) for its excellent coffee, cocktails and fine food, while literary fans favour the old-fashioned **Giubbe Rosse** (Piazza della Repubblica 13/14r). It has its own publishing house and was once full of intellectuals and artists. On the other side of the river is **Negroni** (Via de'Renai 17r), named after the inventor of the famous 1920s cocktail. In Montalcino, **Alle Logge di Piazza** (Piazza del Popolo 1) is the perfect bar to taste fine wines and take in the view over the Tuscan hills.

rome

Not far from Termini is the **Tazio Champagnerie** (Hotel Exedra). On Piazza Republica, it's named after the original paparazzo, Tazio Secchiaroli. Rome's top cocktail bar is the **Stravinskij Bar** (Hotel de Russie); it boasts fabulous martinis, delicious snacks, stylish service and a beautiful courtyard in summer.

In the centro storico, an old-fashioned stand-up bar is the **Tazza d'Oro** (Via degli Orfani 84) near the Pantheon, serving its own blend of coffee. Near the Spanish Steps, the **Museo Atelier Canova Tadolini** (Via del Babuino 150 a/b) serves tea, cakes, light meals and cocktails surrounded by marble sculptures by Canova's favourite protégé, Tadolini.

Over in Trastevere, the pretty tearoom and garden of **Bibli** (Via dei Fienaroli, 28) is a bookshop with literary readings and other events. It's an oasis serving delicious cakes and jasmine

THIS PAGE (FROM TOP): A waiter serves at Venice's famous Caffè Florian on St. Mark's Square; the chic Stravinskij Bar lounge in the Hotel de Russie in Rome.

OPPOSITE: A favourite place for Milanese, the eminently stylish Park Bar at the Park Hyatt Hotel in the centre of Milan.

italy's café society

THIS PAGE (FROM TOP): Al Bicerin's famous drink consists of espresso coffee, bitter chocolate and freshly whipped cream; the art of coffee-making, a skill the Italians excel in; the romantic ambience in one of Rome's cafés.

OPPOSITE: The quintessential café experience in Italy, outdoors and in a scenic piazza.

tea, and there is a fine buffet at aperitif time. **Freni & Frizioni** (Via del Politeama 4-6) is a trendy spot for coffee in the daytime. It gets very lively in the evenings when the fabulous buffet is served and people spill out on to the streets.

For late night action, Ostiense is the liveliest area, although in the centre near the Pantheon is the **Supperclub** (Via dei Nari 14). Created by the same people as Amsterdam's equivalent, it's housed in Nero's former baths. With cabaret, DJ sets and a giant baroque bed, it became an instant favourite with the locals.

naples + around

Naples is renowned for its coffee—it's dark, strong and already sweetened. Ask for amaro if you want it without sugar. Most bars are stand-up affairs. Fans of kitsch will adore **Bar Mexico** (Piazza Dante 86). **Gran Caffè Gambrinus** (Via Chiaia 1-2) is one of Naples' few remaining grand old cafés. Just opposite the royal palace and Teatro San Carlo, there are tables outside and a beautiful art nouveau interior. The **Gran Caffè Cimmino** has two branches (Via Filangieri and Via Petrarca 147); both are popular with Naples' well-heeled. For Milan-style high-tech, head to **Culti Spa Café** (Via Carlo Poerio 47), it's set inside a former cinema and serves fine cocktails and nibbles.

The **Quisi Bar** (Grand Hotel Quisiana) in the heart of Capri is the island's trendiest bar—its Krug Champagne Bar and Sushi Bar are ideal for people-watching. In Amalfi, the historic **Caffè Pansa** (Piazza Duomo 40) has the best view of the Duomo. On Ischia there's **Dal Pescatore** (Piazzetta Sant'Angelo) in the tiny pearl of Sant'Angelo. It serves homemade cakes with fine coffee and offers the perfect view.

island italy

Sicily is famed for its cakes and ice cream. To taste the best, head for the southeast of the island. In Ragusa, **Pasticceria Di Pasquale** (Corso Vittorio Veneto 104) serves wonderful cakes and granitas all made from local produce. Try the Etna-grown wild strawberry, mulberry or pistachio. Over in Noto, the **Caffè Sicilia** (Corso Vittorio Emanuele 125) is renowned for its wondrous concoctions, many of which combine sweet and savoury.

Palermo has the award-winning **Spinnato Antico Caffè** (Via Principe di Belmonte 107/115). It's a family-run place with delicious coffee, cakes, cocktails, ice cream and sandwiches. In the Kalsa, the **Kursaal Kalesa** (Foro Umberto I, 21) has a gorgeous courtyard with fig trees on the first floor and a cool stone-walled interior filled with art and velvet sofas. It's open night and day.

In Sardinia, Cagliari's **Antico Caffè** (Piazza Costituzione 10/11) is a historic café, open from dawn to dusk. Alghero's **Caffè Latino** (Bastioni Magellano 10) is high over the port with picture-postcard views, perfect for early morning coffee and late drinks on a summer night. Arzachena hosts the **Ojster's Bar** (Villagio Poltu Quatu) in the port of Poltu Quatu, serving aperitifs, champagne and oysters as well as good breakfasts. Porto Cervo is not all glitz and glamour, **Caffè du Port** (Molo Vecchio) is an old-fashioned bar located on the marina. Perfect both day and night, it's open 24 hours in high season. For serious cocktails, Italian-style, head for San Teodoro and the **Buddha del Mar** (Villagio Gallura 2). A bar with DJ set, it has giant and mini orange buddhas left right and centre and a fun atmosphere.

the best markets

Just about every village, town and city has a market in Italy. Food markets are daily affairs in cities, often held under cover in purpose-built buildings. Others are held once a week in the main square, where traffic is diverted and parking is a nightmare. Flea markets are held monthly. Some towns are famed for antique markets, which attract people from all over the country and further afield. Food and flea markets generally wind down by 1.30 in the afternoon.

northern italy

The main flea, clothes and antique market in Milan is in the **Navigli** on the Ripa Ticinese, held on the first Sunday of the month. **Turin** has a vast covered market, open daily; Saturday sees a flea market and once a month there's the **Grand Balôn**, a giant antique market, all held around Piazza Borgo Dora in the Quadrilatero Romano. **Savona** is famed for its ceramics—a good market is held on the first weekend of the month while two of the biggest antique markets in Italy are held in **Chiavari** (second Sunday of the month and following Saturday) and **Sarzana** (the first Sunday of the month). Aosta in Valle d'Aosta is famed for its **Sant'Orso fair**, held at the end of January. The oldest market in Europe, it was established in 1000, and sells local arts and crafts. Trieste hosts a grand flea market on the third weekend of the month, specialising in Austro-Hungarian antiques.

central italy

In **Florence** a popular flea market is held on the second Sunday of the month, while **Arezzo** holds one of Italy's best antique markets over the first weekend of the month.

One of Rome's prettiest squares, the **Campo dei Fiori** hosts a daily morning food and flower market, which is especially lively at the weekend. For clothes, head to **Via Sannio** on weekday mornings. **Bracciano** also has a flea market that's held on the second Sunday of every month.

L'Aquila has held a market in Piazza Duomo since 1304. It sells food from Monday to Saturday and holds a flea market on the second weekend of the month. Umbria is particularly known for its markets: there's a big flea market in **Perugia** over the first weekend of the month while **Todi** hosts another major antiques market in the last week of March.

southern italy

The first Sunday of the month is market day in Puglia: **Brindisi** hosts a big furniture market in Piazza Teresa, while **Lecce** and **Gallipoli** have flea markets. **Naples** hosts the biggest antique fair in the south, in the Villa Comunale, held on the third and fourth weekends of each month.

Sardinia is great for craft markets. The biggest of all is the carpet festival at **Mogoro** held in late July early August. On the second Sunday of the month, **Cagliari** hosts a large flea market; **Sassari**'s is always on the last Sunday of each month. In Sicily, **Giardini Naxos**, near Taormina, hosts a market on the third weekend of every month. But, without a doubt, **Palermo** and **Catania** have the best food markets of all, and are quintessentially Sicilian.

THIS PAGE (CLOCKWISE FROM TOP LEFT):
Amalfi lemons and local chillies,
mainstays in Italian cooking;
a display of Italian cheeses;
food markets are daily affairs;
porcini mushrooms, a
famed Italian ingredient.
OPPOSITE: Mainly housed in
permanent covered buildings,
markets are a social gathering.

italian indulgence

Not one to be left behind, Italy is at the forefront of the spa industry. Making good use of its surroundings, spa-goers will find a wealth of choice, from resort spa to remote mountain spa, to pampering in an opulent city day spa. Modern treatments and traditional therapies are on offer across the country and of course, the Italian spa enthusiast can do it in supreme style.

northern italy

Milan's **Bulgari Hotel Spa** (Via Privata Fratelli Gabba 7b) is one of the most glamorous spas to be found—all teak, bronze and stone with a gold mosaic pool, it has a Turkish bath set inside gleaming emerald glass. Suntrap Merano has two mountain spas, the **Terme Merano** (Piazza Terme 9), a giant glass cube with fabulous views by architect Matteo Thun, and the **Vigilius Resort** (Vigiljoch Mountain) in nearby Lana. Merano's is in the heart of the city, flooded with light and a vast range of pools; Vigilius is more exclusive. Reached by a chairlift, with its own hotel and restaurant, it's in the heart of the mountains and offers hay baths and mountain herb treatments, peelings with apple, corn and honey, and lots of mountain air.

In Valle d'Aosta are the Roman thermal spas of glamorous **Terme Pré-Saint-Didier** (Allée des Thermes Pré-Saint-Didier), near Courmayeur. Over in Sondrio are the **Bagni di Bormio Spa Resort** (Via Bagni Nuovi 7) with pools of hot spring water from nine mountain sources.

In the Lakes is the beautiful spa **Henri Chenot's Espace Vitalite** (L'Albereta) in the Franciacorta. In an area renowned for its wine, there's a fine restaurant and top golf course too. Designed by Ettore Mocchetti, the director of Italian AD magazine, the spa is colourful and tranquil—neither minimalist nor old-fashioned.

In the heart of Venice the **Casanova Spa** (Hotel Cipriani) uses La Prairie products. The spa offers couples' massage in a room with Dolby surround sound and aquatic fibre optics.

central italy

Perhaps Tuscany's most famous spa, and Italy's most awarded, is the **Terme di Saturnia** (58014 Saturnia, Grosseto). Offering a vast range of treatments, the centre is set amid a complex of beautiful natural pools with rich thermal waters and the waterfall of Gorello. Further north is the **Grand Hotel Tombolo** (Via del Corallo 3). Seawater therapy is administered in the olive groves and vineyards beside a family beach. The vast array of treatments includes the unique chocotherapy.

The **ESPA at Castello del Nero** (Castello del Nero Hotel & Spa) is in the heart of the Tuscan hills. Designed by Alain Mertens, the glass and olive wood interior merges with the stunning views outside. Of the treatments on offer the aromatic caldarium is particularly relaxing. **Borgo La Bagnaia** (Strada Statale 223 Km 12) near Siena is filled with Chinese and Indian antiques, in a beautiful verdant estate where deer roam.

Right in the heart of Rome's centro storico, near the Pantheon, the **Acanto Benessere Spa** (Piazza Rondanini, 30) recreates the rituals of the ancient Romans on the site of Nero's old

baths. The focus is on hydrotherapy and the treatments are administered in a mix of ancient-futurist interiors with acanthus leaf mosaics, candles and rose petals in abundance.

southern italy

The **Capri Beauty Farm** (Capri Palace Hotel & Spa) is an award-winning spa with a famous leg school. In a beautiful location, it is popular with celebrities. Over on Ischia is the most radioactive thermal water in Europe—the luxury **Spa at Mezzatorre** (Mezzatorre Resort & Spa) has one of the island's most privileged views, over the beautiful beach of Montano.

The **Furore Inn Resort & Spa** (Via dell'Amore) on the Amalfi Coast offers a day spa with a pool and a full range of treatments, including chocolate body wraps and several romantic day packages for couples.

In Puglia, located midway between Bari and Brindisi, is the **Masseria San Domenico** (Strada Litoranea 379). Surrounded by orchards and olive groves, there's a private beach, golf course and thalassotherapy. The seawater here is particularly rich in minerals and plankton. Products used are La Prairie, Thalgo and the hotel's own biological olive-sourced range.

In Sicily, the luxurious **Daniel Steiner Beauty Spa** (Kempinski Hotel Giardino di Costanza Sicily) is a hideaway south of Trapani. Set on a private beach, many of the treatments use Trapani salt as well as volcanic clay, alongside local citrus fruit, almonds and olives.

In Sardinia, the **Villa del Parco and Spa** (Le Méridien's Forte Village Resort) is set in lush rainforest-like vegetation. There are six pools with thalassotherapy on offer and a pool filled with aloe vera.

THIS PAGE: Offering the best treatments available, Italy's spas promise total relaxation in stylish surroundings. Hot stone therapy is just one example.

OPPOSITE (FROM TOP): The comfort of the luxurious Bulgari spa in Milan, where the décor is effortlessly chic; Bulgari's stunning hammam, encased in emerald green glass, a modern take on a time-honoured spa tradition.

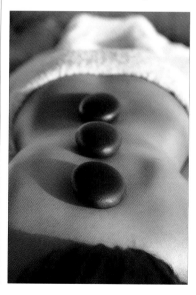

the best views of italy

Even with the latest camera, finding the perfect shot is not a certainty. Finding the perfect spot from which to take sublime pictures of is the fun part. The following is a taster of the views that enable you to get the best pictures of Italy.

milan + northern italy

The **Dolomites** have heart-stopping views. Head towards the Sella Ronda, or drive along the legendary **Great Dolomite Road** from Bolzano to Cortina d'Ampezzo. The mountains here are particularly haunting.

In downtown Turin get the lift to the top of the **Mole Antonelliana** for great views over the city to the snow-capped Alps beyond. The view over **Bergamo Alta** from the top of the chairlift on to one of Italy's most beautiful squares, the Piazza Vecchia, competes with sitting on the rooftop of Milan's cathedral for sheer glamour. By the water's edge, there's manicured **Portofino** or the wilds of the **Cinque Terre**. And of course sublime **Lake Como**, best seen from a boat.

venice + northeast italy

The **campanile** and **Doge's Palace** of St. Mark's Square are best seen from the tip of the Dorsoduro or on the Giudecca. **St. Mark's Basilica** is at its most glorious face on.

Over in Verona there's the splendid **Arena** and pretty frescoed **Piazza dell'Erbe**, quite possibly the Veneto's most photogenic square. Around Vicenza and Padua there are dozens of Palladian villas: **Barbaro at Masèr**, near picturesque Asolo, is a particular beauty.

Bologna offers superb photo opportunities with its red-brick towers and **Piazza del Nettuno**, while Ferrara has its honeyed cathedral and moated **Castello Estense**. Parma's **Duomo** delivers a rhapsody in pink marble.

florence + north-central italy

For budding photographers in Florence, the view over the city is particularly breathtaking from the gardens of **Boboli**. Alternatively, you can go high up towards **Fiesole**, just outside the city. A climb to San Miniato al Monte rewards with views over the **Arno River** and the city but this time around the **Ponte Vecchio** area.

The towers of medieval **San Gimignano** give way to the definitive Tuscan landscape complete with cypresses, and up high again in the **Torre del Mangia of Siena**, privileged views create the perfect shot over the town's circular Campo and beyond. For wilder scenery there's the spectacular white clifftops of the **Conero**, just south of Ancona, in Le Marche or the snow-capped **Monte Sibillini**, seen at their best from Castelluccio in Umbria.

rome + south-central italy

In Rome, for the big picture, head towards **Pincio**—just beyond the Spanish Steps—or the rooftop of the **Hotel Raphael** near Piazza Navona. For views over the **Forum** towards the Colosseum, go to the balcony by the Piazza Campidoglio. To see all **seven hills of Rome**, climb to the top of **Via Garibaldi** in Trastevere: the city is right at your feet.

Assisi affords beautiful views, especially at sunset. The essence of Abruzzo is its mountains: head into the **Gran Sasso** near L'Aquila for the best photo opportunities.

amalfi coast + southern italy

The **Faraglioni** stacks are quintessential Capri, and a must for visiting photographers. For the best panoramic views head for **Villa Krupp** or Marina Piccola. The terrace of the **Villa San Michele** in Anacapri also gives one of Capri's best views.

Ravello is home to two of southern Italy's most familiar snapshots of the Amalfi Coast: from the balcony over the sea at **Villa Cimbrone** and the umbrella pine framing the coast on a steep staircase beside **Villa Rufolo**. Colourful **Positano** seen from the beach is another favourite, as is Amalfi's beautiful **Duomo**.

Seen from the calm of Sorrento, the **Bay of Naples** shows off its simple beauty; while the view from the top of the **Castel Sant'Elmo** in Naples reveals just how vast and impressive the city and its setting really is.

Further south, **Matera** has a tragic beauty, best appreciated from the panoramic terraces of the upper town, while the Greek temple complex at **Paestum** during the magic hour of sunset is photographic gold dust. Other favourites in the area include capturing the **golden stone of Lecce's baroque cathedrals** and the picturesque **trulli** located around Alberobello.

island italy

The view of the Greek theatre over to Etna and the sea from **Taormina** is staggering—as are the temples of **Agrigento** in springtime when they are surrounded with fresh blooms. On Sardinia, the quintessence of the island can be appreciated from the beauty of **La Maddalena** by boat, the mountains of the **Gennargentu** around **Bitti** and the **flamingo-filled salt marshes** near Cagliari during the winter.

THIS PAGE (FROM TOP): The Dolomites; the stunning sea views from Villa San Michele in Anacapri; the Tuscan Hills near Florence; the unique trulli houses of Alberobello, a UNESCO site that does not disappoint.

OPPOSITE: The absolute must for visitors to Venice, a picture of St. Mark's Basilica, best taken face on—in any weather.

milan+northernitaly

FRANCE

GERMANY

SWITZERLAND LIECHTENSTEIN

AUSTRIA

Palace Merano Espace Henri Chenot <
Seiser Alm Urthaler <
Hotel Milano Alpen Resort, Meeting + Spa <
Villa Lake Como <
Hotel Giardino <

Merano

Bolzano
Caldaro
Appiano

Cortina d'Ampezzo

Dolomiti

Trento

Ascona

Lago
Maggiore

Lago
di Como

Rovereto

Gulf of
Venice

4634
Mte Rosa

4478
Mte Matterhorn

Omegna

Como

4808
Mte Bianco

Arona

Bergamo

Courmayeur   Aosta   St. Vincent

Verrès

Brescia

Desenzano

Novara

Milan

Vercelli

Cremona

Pavia

Bardonecchia   Susa

Turin

> L'Albereta
> Palazzo Arzaga Hotel Spa + Golf Resort
> Grand Hotel et de Milan
> Park Hyatt Milan
> The Gray Milano
> The Straf
> Portofino Paradiso

Sestriere

Asti

Torre Pellice

Bra   Alba

Saluzzo

Acqui Terme

Cuneo

Genoa

MONACO

Albenga

La Spezia

Lerici

Gulf of Genoa

Imperia
San Remo
Bordighera

N

Legend

= Highway
— Main Road
— Other Road
⊕ Airport
○ Lake

4000–5000 m
3000–4000 m
2000–3000 m
1500–2000 m
1000–1500 m
500–1000 m
200–500 m
100–200 m

0 km   25   50   75 km

milan + northern italy

Northern Italy's natural beauty is its prime attraction for many, but its principal cities, Milan, Turin and Genoa—renowned champions of taste—offer some of the country's finest art, architecture and design, as well as superb food and wine. Historically the regions vary hugely and were long fought over or annexed in and out of neighbouring nations. Its proximity to France and the former Austro-Hungarian Empire has created a historical melting pot, making Northern Italy different from the rest of the country.

It's easy to combine city action with forays into the wilds—the roads are excellent here. You can drive from Milan to a mountain spa and be back in your hotel by nightfall. From Turin it's easy to go for a day or two's skiing in the Val di Susa or head south for the peaceful hills of the Langhe. From Genoa there's a vast choice of beaches and pretty inland villages to explore in the hills that fringe the narrow coastline. Further afield, the mountains and small towns of Valle d'Aosta and Trentino-Alto Adige have less urbane delights on offer—but no less pleasurable for that.

moneyed milan

Milan has always been a strategic city, first for the Romans, then the Lombards and, finally, on its own with the establishment of the Lombard League in the 12th and 13th centuries. Ruled by the Visconti and Sforza families, Milan was at the forefront of the Renaissance: Tuscan Leonardo da Vinci chose Milan over Florence in his quest for patronage. Today Milan and the North act as Italy's economic backbone, home to manufacturing and the Borsa (the Italian Stock Exchange), affording it the distinctly well-groomed look of prosperity. Milan is now the base for many of the world's finest and most influential fashion designers—due in no small part to the fact that there's money to burn here. But, as well as splashing out, there's plenty to explore in the city. Its gothic cathedral on Piazza del Duomo is one of the largest in the world; it took 500 years to complete. Gorgeously elaborate, with gargoyles galore and 135 spires, it's fitting that the city, itself a temple of fashion, has such a show-stopper of a cathedral.

PAGE 42: Turin's noble Piazza San Carlo, guarded by the equestrian statue of Emanuele Filiberto di Savoia.

THIS PAGE: Made in Italy: cutting-edge fashion meets design classics head on.

OPPOSITE: The breathtaking gothic rooftops of Milan's Duomo.

From the cathedral rooftop, views include the square and the grand entrance of the Galleria Vittorio Emanuele II. Known as Milan's salon, the Belle Époque Galleria is the archetypal shopping mall. A giant wrought iron and glass pavilion, built in 1877, it is lined with two four-storey arcades with a giant cupola at its centre, above glorious floor mosaics that include the symbols of the zodiac. Locals believe it brings good fortune to stand on the genitals of the Taurean bull—and there's no harm in trying your luck. A recent renaissance has brought the big names in fashion back to the Galleria, interspersed with elegant bars, such as the new Gucci café, and the nearby ultra-luxurious Park Hyatt Hotel. At the far end of the Galleria is the legendary opera house, the Teatro alla Scala. Opened in 1788, it has always attracted the world's finest performers. Sumptuous red velvet and gilt boxes line the theatre: once lit by candlelight, glittering in a myriad of mirrors, it is a spectacle in itself.

West of the centre on Piazza Castello is the Visconti's Renaissance Castello Sforzesco. Inside are unfinished works by Michelangelo and Leonardo frescoes. Back around the cathedral are two other art venues, the Pinacoteca Ambrosiana with paintings by Leonardo da Vinci, Botticelli, Giorgione and Caravaggio. Close by is the

THIS PAGE: Shopping in style in the Galleria Vittorio Emanuele II.

OPPOSITE (FROM TOP): Minimalist panache at the Emporio Armani offices in the Navigli district; colourful buildings of the Ripa di Porta Ticinese, also in Milan's canal district.

Civico Museo d'Arte Contemporanea, which, after some major restoration, will display its staggering collection of 3,000 contemporary works, ranging from post-Impressionist to abstract schools, including Van Gogh, Cézanne, Modigliani and De Chirico. But the Pinacoteca di Brera is perhaps the most impressive. Housed in the city's 17th-century Accademia di Belle Arti, the collection ranges from early art to contemporary. Particularly memorable are Mantegna's The Dead Christ, Raphael's Marriage of the Virgin, and one of the 19th century's most romantic paintings, *Il Bacio*, by Francesco Hayez. Rooms X and XI show contemporary art amid some fine Cycladic heads and figurines.

The word ambrosial came from Milan's patron saint Sant'Ambrogio, his honeyed tongue so eloquent it is said to have attracted the bees. His beautiful basilica, built between 4 and 10 AD, is a real eye catcher although most make a beeline for Santa Maria delle Grazie, the 15th-century convent housing Leonardo da Vinci's masterpiece fresco, *The Last Supper*. Booking ahead to view is mandatory.

Art of a different kind is around the golden triangle of Via Montenapoleone, Via della Spiga and Via Sant'Andrea. For it is here that the great names of fashion have their headquarters, and it is here that those in the know come to shop till they drop, as well as party and dine in legendary style. Milan's up-and-coming area is away from the centre though, amid the industrial chic of the Navigli canals, also the oldest part of the city and the place to be. Design pioneer, Achille Castiglioni, who died in 2002, has a new museum showcasing his work in Piazza Castello. Not far away is the Triennale on Viale Alemagna, which houses a permanent collection of Italian design as well as prestigious temporary exhibitions and two ultra-cool cafes. Modern architecture fans can wander the streets admiring trailblazing works: the 1935 Villa Figini, Italy's earliest building in the Rationalist style; the Torre Velasca of 1957; Giò Ponti's 32-storey Pirelli Tower and his

Chiesa di San Francesco of 1964. In the suburb of Pero and Rho, in a former oil refinery, is the new Fiera di Milano by Massimiliano Fuksas, part of an exciting new project of urban renewal involving Europe's leading architectural talent.

lombarding you with art

Milan aside, Lombardy has other treasures. Cremona, a stylish city, all curls, volutes and rosy hues, has Italy's tallest campanile and a masterful medieval astrological clock. It was home to one Antonio Stradivari, the 18th-century violin maker par excellence. Violins are still big business here and there are some beautiful examples in the city's ateliers and museums. Mantua, an impressive city on the banks of the River Mincio, is renowned for its fine food and grand squares—the 13th-century Piazza dell'Erbe, Piazza del Broletto and Piazza Sordello are the city's hub. Visitors flock here to see the Palazzo Ducale, once Europe's largest palace, and famed for its Renaissance frescoes and trompe l'œil. The most sumptuous are by Andrea Mantegna in the Camera degli Sposi—assorted figures and cupids peer down from the ceiling, cornucopia, animals and fantastical landscapes adorn the walls. Elsewhere in the town Palazzo Te has equally striking artwork. High drama has always marked Mantua's existence: Virgil was born here; Shakespeare sent Romeo into exile here; Rigoletto was set here.

Bergamo's upper town, built largely in the Renaissance and backed by mountains, has the Piazza Vecchia, which was praised to the skies by both Le Corbusier and Frank Lloyd Wright. The funicular up to the castle at San Vigilio gives superb views. Bergamo's lower town was designed by realist architect Marcello Piacentini in the 1920s, no less of a feast for modernists. The art collection in the Accademia Carrara is one of Italy's finest. Opposite is the Galleria d'Arte Moderna, which hosts top temporary exhibitions as well as housing a fine permanent collection.

North of Brescia, the Val Camonica is famed for its beautiful rock carvings, like a giant graffitied wall, with markings from the neolithic era to Roman. Nature's own hand can be admired at Cislano where fabulously eroded stone pillars, nicknamed the fairies of the forest, sit beside the magical glaciated lake of Iseo. Pavia—south of Milan and once capital of the Lombard kingdom—witnessed the coronations of Charlemagne and Frederick I Barbarossa. Filled with beautiful Lombard architecture, the nearby Certosa di Pavia, which took 200 years to complete, is the icing on the cake.

turin: under the gaze of the alps

Once the capital of the French-speaking principality of Savoy, Turin has a red-brick staidness in its elegant arcades, piazzas, palaces and museums. But it's also flamboyant and baroque, home to a café society, where people partake in the finer pleasures of life. In the Quadrilatero Romano, Turin's funkier side is let loose. Boasting bars, restaurants and clubs as well as boutique shopping, Turin's bohemian edge defies its traditional reputation. The landmark Mole Antonelliana is home to the stylish museum of cinema, while elsewhere on the River Po, the boathouses of the Murazzi, offer a more underground scene—one concerning artists' happenings and clubs.

At the heart of the old town is the Piazza San Carlo, leading to Via Roma and its arcades, and the splendid Palazzo Reale. The Palazzo Carignano (the site of Italy's first parliament in 1861), the Palazzo dell'Accademia delle Scienze (home to the Egyptian Museum and Galleria Sabauda), the Royal Chapel of San Lorenzo and the Cappella

THIS PAGE: Sunset over Turin, with a view of the distinctive dome of La Mole Antonelliana and the lure of the Alps beyond.

OPPOSITE (FROM TOP): Andrea Mantegna's brilliant trompe l'oeil in the Palazzo Ducale; images of praying women at Val Camonica, just one of scores of neolithic rock carvings.

della Sindone are all by genius architect Guarino Guarini. Geometric domes are fundamental in his idiosyncratic style. The Duomo, where the Turin Shroud is sometimes on show, is Turin's only Renaissance building, although heavily baroqueified inside. A pleasant stroll from Porta Nuova, the main train station, is the Parco del Valentino on the banks of the Po River. Created for the 1884 Exposizione Universale, it is home to a botanical garden and the Borgo Medioevale.

The lively Quadrilatero Romano neighbourhood has a strong community feel. Turin's trendiest area, it is home to Lavazza coffee, as well as Il Bicerin, a charming café in existence since 1763 that's famed for its trademark coffee, cream and chocolate drink. Opposite is the Santuario della Consolata, which runs non-stop masses; and around Piazza Repubblica there's the city's market, housed in a glass and metal art nouveau structure. Saturdays see a flea market on the streets all around, while the prestigious Gran Balon, is a monthly antiques market. Nearby, the Galleria Civica d'Arte Moderna e Contemporanea (GAM) is dedicated to 20th-century art.

Turin was the first Italian city to boast an exhibition of modern art back in 1863 and it's still innovating. Winter sees Turin lit up in a spectacular light festival called Luci d'Artista while ManifesTO brings poster art to the streets. Artissima is a giant contemporary arts fair held in the Lingotto, the former Fiat factory. Now home to Lo Scrigno—a gallery containing priceles pieces by Modigliani and Picasso—the Lingotto was built between 1916 and 1926. Hailed by both the Futurists and Le Corbusier, it was a triumph of the production line. Raw materials on the ground floor emerged as a finished car on the top floor straight onto a rooftop test track, reached by a helical ramp. This ramp was shown in all its splendour in *The Italian Job*.

Other notable buildings in the city are by Pier Luigi Nervi, whose 1949 Exhibition Building was temporarily transformed into the hockey stadium for the Olympics; and the Palavela, a reinterpretation of the 1961 Palazzo a Vela by Annibale and Giorgio Rigotti. Its striking sail structure and interior were also seen in *The Italian Job*.

piemonte: mountains of food

All around Turin are hunting lodges, or one-time stomping grounds of the Savoys, the Stupinigi Palace is the most splendid example. Other highlights are the Lombard Abbey of Novalesa in the Val di Susa—where there is also superb skiing in the Milky Way—and the Sacra di San Michele, high above Avigliana. The Forte di Fenestrelle, built to keep the French out, is worth seeking out. The picturesque Val Pellice was once a safe-house for the persecuted Waldensian community, who protested against the Catholic Church long before Luther. At Colle Vaccera, near Angrogna, there is an extraordinary rock formation nicknamed the Face of the Prophet. And at Torre Pelice, the Galleria Civica d'Arte Moderna, Filippo Scroppo, houses works by Italian post-war artists.

South and east of Turin is where Piemonte's renowned food and wine grow. Towards Vercelli and Novara is a checkerboard landscape of fields of rice. In the heart of the Po valley, shared with Milan and frequently shrouded by fog, the scene is one of melancholy, unless you contemplate the delicious risotto it goes on to make. Far more Dionysian is the Langhe region to the south, legendary for its white truffles from Alba, and the world-famed wines of Barolo, Nebbiolo, Barbaresco, Dolcetto and Barbera. The best time to come is during the autumn harvests when countless food fairs take place.

The landscape is peppered with feudal castles, lush vineyards and pretty towns. The town of Asti, famed for its spumante, holds a palio in September, a celebration of medieval pageantry as well as full-on banqueting. Alba—Asti's traditional rival—holds its own palio where donkeys are ridden by clowns, in mockery of the real thing. Beyond Alba is Bra, the headquarters of the pioneering and incredibly influential international movement, Slow Food, which was established to preserve gastronomic

THIS PAGE (FROM TOP): Undulating vine terraces on a Barolo hillside in Piemonte; white gold, tartufi bianchi.

OPPOSITE: The original Fiat factory, the Lingotto, with exciting additions by Renzo Piano.

traditions. Alba is also home to the headquarters of Ferrero Rocher, makers of diplomats' favourite chocolate and Nutella. Pessione is where Martini are based and where they host a museum of wine and aperitifs. There's also Aqui Terme, an ancient and delightful Roman spa town, known for Brachetto, a delicious sweet wine.

keeping up with the joneses

Though Milan and Turin are today's economic mainstays, it was Genoa that dominated for most of the last millennia. The Genoese Republic controlled some of the world's wealthiest colonies in the Middle East and North Africa and dominated the Tyrrhenian Sea. Christopher Columbus brought the Republic even more fortune and the city's Bank of San Giorgio at one time bankrolled most of the military campaigns across embattled Europe. Genoa saw its zenith under the redoubtable condottiere, Andrea Doria, in the mid-16th century.

Genoa has a rugged edge to it. A vast commercial port, seemingly a far cry from its glorious past, it has two distinct faces: the kasbah quality of the port and the dazzling wealth of the palazzi on the Strada Nuova. One side was where the money was made; the other was where the money was spent. Janus, the Roman two-faced god, is even perched above the city's emblem. A port of hope and sadness, it's from Genoa that Garibaldi set sail with his thousand men to unify Italy but it's also where hundreds of thousands of Italians left for America in the early 20th century, praying for a better life. Once run down, Genoa received much needed fund injections in recent decades and it's all paid off: tourism is booming and the city won UNESCO World Heritage status in July 2006 for the Strada Nuova.

The Rolli system of the 16th and 17th centuries saw the city's palaces detailed according to size, beauty and importance. From this list the governing body decided where visiting nobles would stay according to rank. Hence the Genoese nobility's keeping up with the Joneses mentality, which saw every aristocrat vying with his neighbour for a more beautiful palace, boasting better art, bigger statues and more floors in the hope of better social standing. The finest palazzi, where the Pope or Holy Roman Emperor could stay, were on Via Garibaldi, the city's top address. Palazzo Bianco, Palazzo Rosso and the Palazzo Reale on Via Balbi each have incredible art collections and are now open to the public.

Around the port there's a somewhat salty, seedy air: the narrowness of the old town's carrugi (alleyways) lends an air still tinged with excitement. Not far from the Bank of San Giorgio is Genoa's world-class aquarium, built for Expo '92, key to Renzo Piano's regeneration project. There's also the Bolla, a hothouse for exotic plants, and the Bigo, a crane with a panoramic lift, as well as lots of restaurants and bars to sit in and admire the view. Beyond, is Genoa's lighthouse, the trans-Atlantic maritime station and the splendid Museo del Mare, which recreates the thrill of Genoa's Golden Age.

The Palazzo Ducale, on Piazza De Ferrari, is the city's real centre. The former home of the Doges of Genoa, it's now a huge cultural centre where major art exhibitions are held. Nearby are the twin towers of the Porta Soprana, dating from 1155. Once part of the old walls, Columbus' father was a gatekeeper here; his former house is said to be nearby.

San Lorenzo, the city's cathedral with its black and white striped Gothic façade, is a short walk away. The treasury claims to hold the Holy Grail as well as the platter used to serve St. John the Baptist's head to Salome. Piazza De Ferrari leads to the Teatro Carlo Felice. Heavily bombed by the Allies, the theatre was given new life by Aldo Rossi. Maintaining the old façade, it is entirely new inside.

THIS PAGE (FROM TOP): Inside a castle in Genoa, showing the beautiful architecture of the 19th century; keeping guard at San Lorenzo.
OPPOSITE: Taking it slow, the passeggiata alla Genovese.

good things come in small packages

South of Genoa is one of Italy's finest coastlines. First ports of call should be Nervi, then Camogli, a beautiful fishing village and naval centre. Portofino is a tiny treasure chest with a handful of hotels, restaurants and bars adorning the harbour. At weekends and high season the road in gets gridlocked with day-trippers; the stylish way to arrive is by boat. It has great diving opportunities and is part of a dolphin and whale sanctuary. Just around the promontory, a visit to the San Fruttuoso abbey is a must. Founded in 711, it has a pretty little beach and trattoria. Further around the coast is the fashionable and much livelier 19th-century resort of Santa Margherita Ligure. Several other resorts jostle for your attention along this coast—Rapallo, Sestri Levante and Moneglia are the best.

The Cinque Terre have become legendary over recent years: five tiny villages, medieval in origin, sited on a rugged and, until now, very inaccessible coastline. Although fishing villages, wine is really the main livelihood, and vines grow on impossibly steep stone walled terraces now protected by UNESCO. Many people come here for the beautiful coastal walk that connects the five villages, but visitors can also travel between them by boat or train. Pretty Monterosso is the largest, boasting two fine beaches; Vernazza is a stylish beauty, its little church perched above the waves; Corniglia, the quietest, is also the least accessible; multicoloured Manarola tumbles down from a big black rock to its postage stamp beach while lively steep Riomaggiore has the best diving.

western liguria: of olives, caves and casinos

The coastline west of Genoa is relatively tame compared to that of the rugged south. There are strings of beaches, the umbrellas and sunbeds forming delineated tracts of colour on the golden sands. In between are little treasures, well worth seeking out. Tiny Noli, a maritime republic between 1192 and 1796, is a medieval town with a pretty beach. Imperia is famed for its olive oil trade. Pretty Dolcedo, just inland, is home to

THIS PAGE: Dining at Portofino.
OPPOSITE: One of Italy's most beautiful bays—dolphins love tiny Portofino too.

some of Italy's finest olive groves. Cervo hosts an international chamber music festival each summer, in front of its baroque Corallini Church, named after the local coral fishers. San Remo shows off her Stilo Liberty elegance with a flourish. A grand old lady of the Riviera resorts, it has beautiful villas and graceful hotels, the onion domes of its Russian Orthodox church (the town once had a sizeable Russian émigré population) and its biggest attraction, the splendid Casino. There's also a medieval old town hidden behind Piazza San Siro, while the palm-lined Corso dell'Imperatrice and steep panoramic Corso degli Inglesi are the places to promenade. Further west are Dolceacqua and Bordighera, beloved of the painter Monet. Then almost in France at Roman Ventimiglia are the Balzi Rossi caves with pre-Iron Age finds, dating from 200,000 BC. Back towards Albenga are the equally impressive Grotte di Toirano with etchings, prehistoric footprints and spectacular stalactites.

the lakes

Sheltered by a range of steep snow-capped mountains, each lake in the Italian Lake District has a gentle, sunny microclimate, and each has its own distinct attraction. Maggiore is a sedate beauty, with the sobriety and fastidiousness of a dowager aunt; Garda is a vision of loveliness, like a wholesome au pair who wins everyone over with a welcoming smile; Como tantalises, dressed to kill like a gorgeous hussy bedazzling a bevy of suitors and annihilating the opposition.

Lake Maggiore, the closest lake to Milan and Turin, stretches all the way up to the Swiss border. The second largest of the lakes, it's surrounded by lush botanical gardens and grand old villas owned by local bigwigs. Stresa is a pretty town and gateway to the Borromean Islands, home to architectural follies and landscaped parks. Also at Stresa is a cable car to the summit of Monte Mottarone—on a clear day there's a fantastic view of the Alps and all seven lakes.

Lake Garda, the largest and liveliest, is a heavenly shade of blue—you would be forgiven for thinking you were at the seaside. Shared by three regions, the north is in Trentino, the west is in Lombardy and the south and east are in the Veneto. Sirmione, in the southeast, has been a pleasure dome since Roman times, when Catullus stayed there writing torturous love poetry. The crenellated castle of the Rocca Scaligera dominates the pretty harbour and the town's cobbled squares, where the beautiful people cluster over aperitifs and dinner. The lake's largest town, Desenzano, has some of the region's best nightlife, while Riva di Garda, in the far north, is popular with windsurfers. In the northeast, spectacular views may be had from the lake's highest peak, Monte Baldo. Salò, on the west shore, is a beautiful town, where Mussolini set up his ill-fated republic in 1943.

The sapphire waters of Lake Como curve into a narrow wishbone beneath snow-capped Alpine peaks, the perfect setting for weekenders from Milan or escapees from the Hollywood hills. Its romantic shores and luxurious houses have featured in films such as *Casino Royale*, *Star Wars*, *A Month in the Country* and Hitchcock's *The Pleasure Garden*.

THIS PAGE: Isola Bella, one of Lake Maggiore's Borromean Islands.

OPPOSITE: One of the many Scaligeri castles and historic towns on beautiful Lake Garda.

...the perfect setting for weekenders from Milan or escapees from the Hollywood hills.

While the stars have only discovered Como's charms fairly recently (George Clooney, Sting, Tom Cruise and Richard Branson to name a few), the Italians have long known about its Unique Selling Point. Luciano Pavarotti and Gianni Versace both owned houses here and before them came generation after generation of royals and others in the know. It's where both Pliny the Elder and Younger are from, where Bellini, Rossini and Verdi sought inspiration, and where the trio of poets, Wordsworth, Byron and Shelley stayed.

Just an hour's drive from Milan and just east of the Swiss canton of Ticino, Como is one of the deepest lakes in Europe but only 35 km (22 miles) long and 4.5 km (3 miles) across at its widest point. All around its shores are pretty towns with sublime architecture and charming little houses with cascading geraniums, cobblestone streets, piazzas and promenades housing cafés and restaurants with views to die for. Though overlooked by the Alps, Como has a sunny Mediterranean climate. Verdant and vibrant, citrus and palm trees run riot with bougainvillea and hibiscus; terraced gardens complete with statues tumble down to the lakeshore, where private jetties and beaches await. The best way to see the lake is from the water; visitors can rent their own boats, with or without a skipper. Como's western shore is quieter, more exclusive and more sophisticated—the towns of Como, Cernobbio, and George Clooney's villa at Laglio are here. The eastern shore, with Varenna as a highlight, has a railway line and is more accessible. Further north the lake becomes much quieter and decidedly less jet-set—windsurfers adore Domaso. The southeastern tip meanwhile has Lecco. Dramatically set on a deep fjord with waterfalls, Leonardo da Vinci used the landscape as the backdrop for two of his masterpieces, *The Virgin of the Rocks* and *The Virgin and St. Anne.*

THIS PAGE: *The exquisite Villa Carlotta at Tremezzo, originally bought as a wedding gift for Princess Carlotta of the Netherlands, is filled with frescoed rooms and fine art, and is renowned for its superb landscaped gardens.*
OPPOSITE: *Mareccio Castle (Schloss Maretsch) in Alto-Adige, a romantic region of castles and vines.*

mountain chic

Valle d'Aosta, in Italy's northwestern corner, has Roman and medieval treasures aplenty, stylish ski resorts and wine from Europe's highest vineyards. The region teems with fortified castles, many of them Renaissance gems such as at Issogne, Fénis and Verrès. For fabulous skiing and unsurpassed après-ski there's Courmayeur. And for thermal spas, there's Pré St. Didier and St. Vincent. Come summer the mountain scenery is equally mesmerising; the flower-filled meadows at Val Ferret near Entrèves are the perfect antidote to the high living at Courmayeur.

The town of Aosta has the oldest continuous market in Europe, Sant'Orso (going strong since 1000), a famous bullfighting festival—with just the bulls locking horns—and some fine Roman and medieval architecture. The Tour Fromage houses the city's collection of modern art. Cogne is the pretty gateway to the magical Parco Nazionale del Gran Paradiso, a former hunting reserve of the Savoys. Skiers at La Thuile in the Colle del Gran San Bernardo may well witness one of the world's favourite dogs—the St. Bernard—in action. The breed hails from the 11th-century monastery located on the summit of the pass. Now in modern-day Switzerland, you'll need to bring your passport to visit. The mythical Courmayeur, set at the foot in Mont Blanc, is one of the Alps' top resorts.

trentino-alto adige: a split personality

Trento and Alto-Adige are a little different from the rest of Italy. The northernmost province of the region was once part of the Austro-Hungarian Empire, only absorbed into Italian territory in the last century. The province of Trento in the south is Italian-speaking; the province of Bolzano, to the north, is largely German-speaking, with towns bearing names in both languages. The Dolomites are mainly in Alto-Adige (also known as the Süd Tirol), and both the architecture and feel are very much more Austrian than Italian, as is the cuisine.

The whole area is renowned for its skiing and walking, although Italians also come here for its fine wine. There's a wine route starting south of Bolzano, through a valley with beautiful vineyards and castles galore. The best places to stop are Eppan (or Appiano) and Kaltern (or Caldaro), where there's a wine museum in Castel Ringberg. One of Italy's wealthiest areas, this is also one of its most picturesque. Meadows, forests and the majestic Dolomites with precariously positioned castles open on to pretty old world towns, perfect for those looking to escape the rat race.

Bolzano, the capital of the Alto-Adige, is set against the beautiful Rosengarten mountains, whose limestone peaks turn pink at sunset. A market town since the middle ages, its main attraction is a mummy called Ötzi, dating from 5,300 years ago. Found in near perfect condition in a local glacier in 1991, he is now housed in an archaeological museum. South of Bolzano the Val Gardena is well worth a stop, while the drive to Cortina d'Ampezzo is incredible, if not for the fainthearted.

Merano is famed for its spa, which is housed entirely in glass, boasting fabulous views. Popular with walkers, Merano has splendid castles—Trauttmansdorff, beloved holiday home of the Empress Elizabeth I of Austria, and the Castello Principesco are two of the finest. There's also a contemporary art gallery and a prestigious racecourse.

Rovereto, just south of Trento, is equally pretty. There's a charming museum here to futurist artist, Fortunato Depero, showcasing his vibrant paintings, tapestries and puppets. Next door a shop sells beautiful reproductions of some of his work. More Depero and futurist artwork can be seen at the MART, a new arts centre in the town centre on Corso Bettini. In addition to exhibitions it hosts a major international dance festival in summer. Southeast of the town, you can follow in the footsteps of dinosaurs: dating from 200 million years ago, there are dozens of them. Stretching into Austria and Slovenia from the Venezia Friuli-Giulia region are the little-known Julian & Carnia Alps. The most densely forested region in all Italy and home to bears, eagles and lynxes, there is fine skiing at Sella Nevea near Tarvisio, and the town of Tolmezzo leads the way to other treasures, which are all well worth seeking out.

THIS PAGE: In Valle d'Aosta there is year-round skiing on the Toula glacier, Mont Blanc.

OPPOSITE: A mirror image in the Dolomites—the crystalline Lago di Misurina and the impressive Gruppo del Surapis.

...precariously positioned castles open on to pretty old-world towns...

grand hotel et de milan

...experience Milan at its most stylish and sophisticated...

THIS PAGE (FROM TOP): The Grand Hotel's opulent suites have played host to many distinguished guests, including the great composer Verdi; rooms exude a stylish charm.
OPPOSITE (CLOCKWISE FROM TOP): Don Carlos is known for its innovative Italian dishes; the lobby's majestic interior; the atmospheric Gerry's Bar sets the mood for a relaxing drink.

As the capital of Lombardy, Milan was historically a trading centre between converging trans-Alpine routes. Today it is a bustling metropolis, thriving in business, fashion and finance; it is cosmopolitan and chic, offering a wealth of diversions from world-class opera to stunning art treasures and the ultimate in high-fashion shopping.

Those looking to experience Milan at its most stylish and sophisticated might stay at the Grand Hotel et de Milan, whose fascinating history has been inextricably entwined with that of the city for over 100 years. Inaugurated in 1863, the Grand Hotel was a favourite with Giuseppe Verdi, given its central location and proximity to La Scala opera house. In fact, it virtually became an annex to this unrivalled musical establishment as Verdi's successes were celebrated at the hotel, with arias sung from its balconies. Caruso, Callas and a string of other operatic legends—not to mention visiting royalty and dignitaries—enjoyed its extraordinary hospitality and continue to do so to this day.

The hotel lobby's vast, glass-domed roof filters natural light over an elaborate tiled floor decorated with rich oriental rugs, while the intricately carved marble fireplace is complemented by glorious antique pieces.

Rooms are lavish and supremely comfortable, decorated in classical 18th-century Liberty or Art Deco style. Polished wooden floors and rich, brocaded drapes provide the backdrop for sumptuous furnishings. Some suites even boast original artefacts relating to the legendary

patrons of the hotel. Bathrooms, on the other hand, are palatial, bedecked in Italian marble with deep tubs and boutique toiletries. What better than to unwind at the end of the day with a long, hot soak to shake off the stresses of Milan's busy streets.

Opportunities for fine dining abound at the Grand Hotel, be it at the cosy and atmospheric Don Carlos—every inch of its wall space is covered in intriguing paintings and prints—or in the gracious dining room of the Caruso. Highly acclaimed Chef Angelo Gangemi adopts an innovative approach to classical Italian cuisine, while the exceptional wine cellar offers countless prestigious labels to accompany the tantalising menus. For a luxurious stay in Milan in a uniquely historic setting there is no match for the Grand Hotel.

ROOMS
95

FOOD
Caruso: Italian • Don Carlos: Italian

DRINK
Gerry's Bar • wine cellar

FEATURES
gym • personal trainers

BUSINESS
banqueting rooms • meeting rooms

NEARBY
Duomo • La Scala opera house • Galleria Vittorio Emanuele • Via Montenapoleone

CONTACT
Via Manzoni 29, 20121 Milan • telephone: +39.02.723 141 • facsimile: +39.02.8646 0861 • email: reservations@grandhoteletdemilan.it • website: www.grandhoteletdemilan.it

hotel giardino

...the latest modern conveniences in a relaxed and luxurious environment.

Although technically located within Switzerland, the Hotel Giardino has an inherent Italian quality in every sense. After all, the town of Ascona in which it sits is well known for its very Italian character. Then there's the climate that is more Mediterranean than Alpine. Even the language spoken by the locals is Italian. So in many ways guests of the hotel get to enjoy the best of both worlds—Swiss standards of efficiency and management coupled with Italian standards of hospitality and character—not a bad combination by any means.

Perhaps it is this clever blend of influences that has made the hotel such a renowned success in the years since it opened in 1986. A member of the much-esteemed Relais & Chateaux group, the Hotel Giardino is a five-star establishment that is regularly recognised as the best holiday hotel in Switzerland and has simultaneously earned an enviable reputation for providing the very highest standards of service, hospitality and cuisine.

Set within its own well-maintained and landscaped Mediterranean-style gardens, the Hotel Giardino offers 72 generously-sized rooms, suites and residential apartments, all of which offer the latest modern conveniences in a relaxed and luxurious environment. It's a careful balance of style and comfort that extends to the public areas which are characterised by lavish furnishings, exotic tiles and bold Italian colours. Throughout, there is an attention to detail and to a guest's well-being that is rare even by the high standards of a Relais & Chateaux establishment.

In addition, the Hotel Giardino offers two of the finest dining establishments to be found in the region. In the newly opened Ristorante ECCO, Chef de Cuisine Rolf Fliegauf has combined the accumulated knowledge of a career at the cutting-edge of modern cuisine to create radical new dishes that are as joyous to behold as they are to consume. The Ristorante Aphrodite, on the other hand, has Head Chef Urs Gschwend at the helm, serving contemporary Mediterranean and Italian specialities that have acquired no fewer than 16 Gault Millau points for excellence, as well as numerous other national and international awards.

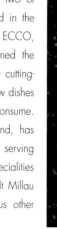

THIS PAGE (FROM TOP): Indulge in style at the Giardino Spa; the hotel's lavish gardens exude a unique Mediterranean charm.

OPPOSITE (FROM TOP): Savour gourmet cuisine at its best; the five-star superior Hotel Giardino is known for its warm hospitality; look forward to innovative dishes at Ristorante ECCO.

ROOMS
72

FOOD
Ristorante Aphrodite: Italian and Mediterranean • Ristorante ECCO: modern molecular

DRINK
bar • pool bar

FEATURES
Giardino Spa • indoor pool • outdoor pool • gym • parking

NEARBY
Ascona • Como • Lake Maggiore • Lugano • Milan • Ticino Valley

CONTACT
Via Segnale 10, CH-6612 Ascona, Switzerland • telephone: +41.91.785 8888 • facsimile: +41.91.785 8899 • email: welcome@giardino.ch • website: www.giardino.ch

Anyone familiar with the Italian lakes will appreciate that no visit is complete without some provision for their physical health and an element of outdoor activity, and in this respect the Hotel Giardino comes up trumps yet again. Not only does it boast two swimming pools, the world-class Giardino Spa and a gym, it sits next door to one of Europe's most beautiful golf courses and is within easy reach of both Lake Maggiore and the famous countryside of the Ticino Valley. With all this to offer, the Hotel Giardino is a hotel of which both the Swiss and the Italians can be justifiably proud.

hotel milano alpen resort, meeting + spa

...combines modernity with tradition...

THIS PAGE: *With a cosy ambience and a splendid view of its Alpine surroundings, the Lounge Bar is ideal for a relaxing drink.*

OPPOSITE (CLOCKWISE FROM TOP LEFT): *The Alpen Suite embodies style, nature and modern comfort; the spa's sleek indoor pool; the Exclusive Room's soft colour tones complement the contemporary interior.*

'In all things of nature there is something of the marvellous,' according to Aristotle. The Hotel Milano Alpen Resort has gone to great lengths to harness its surrounding beauty, presenting a plethora of spa, beauty and adventurous activities from its dramatic Alpine setting.

This luxurious, state-of-the-art hotel and spa resort is nestled in the Val Seriana, beneath the soaring Presolana Mountain. This stunning backdrop serves as a constant yet ever-changing reminder of the beauty and healing power of nature. Whether for relaxation, regeneration or invigoration, this family-owned haven combines modernity with tradition, and cutting-edge Alpen Spa techniques with ancient practices to ensure that each guest's every desire is fulfilled. The hotel is also a technologically advanced conference centre, offering an efficient and individualised service for those seeking the ultimate meeting or incentive tourism venue.

The 67 spacious guestrooms at the Milano boast several different design themes. Guests can choose from the sleek, contemporary interiors of the Junior, Standard, Exclusive Bio Eco or lofty Alpen Suites, with their own Turkish bath and shiatsu shower. For a more cosy and traditional approach, try the warmly decorated Classic or Deluxe Rooms. Executives or couples on their honeymoon might prefer the fabulous, wood-furnished Presidential Suite that offers phenomenal views and a private jacuzzi. While immersed within the wonders of mother nature at the Milano, Internet access and LCD TV in the suites ensure guests remain connected to the outside world.

Adrenaline seekers will embrace the plentiful opportunities of the nearby Alpine environment, explorable with local mountain experts Ernesto and Hugo. Enjoy a structured Nordic trek or mountain bike adventure, surrounded by the pure mountain air and mesmerising beauty of the landscape. In season, activities such as skiing and golf are also available.

With two innovative restaurants—the Caminone and the Enoteca serve the best of regional and international cuisine—and the welcoming Alpen Lounge Bar for private tasting events, the Milano really is an all-encompassing resort with a difference. And the difference lies in its Alpen Spa, the pinnacle of luxurious indulgence in the heart of Italy's Orobic Alps.

Alongside a graceful indoor pool, the spa offers an impressive array of treatments. These range from themed mini-breaks to week-long itineraries for '360-degree well-being'. Select from one of the proposed menus that provide health, relaxation, beauty, nature or adventure focused activities. Alternatively, guests can opt to create a personalised spa experience to suit their preferences.

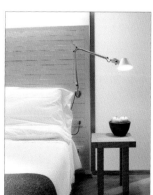

To dip into the menu of the Alpen Spa, there are weekends themed around the natural elements of earth, wind, water and fire. Couples may treat themselves to a specially designed stay for two, or indulge in an Oriental weekend. From lemon balm wraps to stone massage, Pilates to yoga, honey peels to detoxifying Bio Eco massages, the Alpen Spa and certainly the Hotel Milano Alpen Resort as a whole are just waiting to impress.

ROOMS
67

FOOD
Il Caminone: international •
Enoteca: regional and Alpine

DRINK
Alpen Lounge Bar • Enoteca: wine cellar

FEATURES
Health Club Alpen Spa • sauna •
indoor pool • steam room • solarium •
gym • massage and wellness services •
complimentary mountain bikes •
childcare programmes

BUSINESS
conference rooms • training rooms

NEARBY
Presolana Golf Club • Albenza
Golf Club Bergamo • Franciacorta
Golf Club Brescia • ski facilities at
Presolana and Monte Pora

CONTACT
Via Silvio Pellico 3, 24020 Castione
della Presolana, Bratto •
telephone: +39.0346.31 211 •
facsimile: +39.0346.36 236 •
email: info@hotelmilano.com •
website: www.hotelmilano.com

l'albereta

...lacks for absolutely nothing in terms of high-end luxury and world class hospitality.

THIS PAGE (FROM TOP): *The breathtaking deluxe Honey Room with its equally stunning view of the Alps; the Library Bar's relaxing atmosphere is well accompanied by its impressive wine list.*

OPPOSITE (ANTI-CLOCKWISE FROM TOP): *Sample Chef Gualtiero Marchesi's delectable Italian cuisine in his restaurant; relaxing treatments aside, guests can look forward to aquafitness workouts at the spa; L'Albereta's peaceful and countryside setting is the ideal sanctuary for body and soul.*

Italian connoisseurs often rate the quality of a hotel according to its ability to measure up to the five Cs—Cortesia (courtesy), Carattere (quality), Calma (tranquillity), Charme (charm) and lastly, Cucina (cuisine). While some establishments are capable of scoring high marks in one or two of these categories, very few score well in all five, and those that receive top marks in each and every one can probably be counted on the fingers of one hand.

L'Albereta is one such hotel. This former hunting lodge and distinguished member of the illustrious Relais & Chateaux chain is as close to perfection as a country house hotel gets, be it in Italy or anywhere else. Located on a hill among the beautiful vineyards in the renowned wine-making region of Franciacorta, L'Albereta sets the standards by which others should be judged, and it is hardly surprising that it has become something of a respected icon within the fashionable circles of Milanese society since its opening in 1993.

L'Albereta owes much of its success to the fact that it is privately owned and run by the legendary Italian hotelier and wine producer Vittorio Moretti and his daughter Carmen Moretti de Rosa. It was they who had the wisdom and foresight to realise the potential of the property in the first place, and who oversaw its subsequent meticulous conversion and restoration into the glorious, gleaming, many-faceted jewel that it is today.

Apart from the immaculate setting and the personal involvement of the Moretti family, there are several key factors that have contributed to L'Albereta's status as one of Italy's leading hotels, starting with the 57 magnificent rooms and suites, no two of which are alike. All reflect extraordinarily good taste and style—for which the Lombardy region is justly famous—and come fully-equipped with every modern amenity, so that on entering them a guest cannot help but feel an immediate and overwhelming sense of immense privilege.

This sense of privilege extends also to the public areas, including a library, chess room, billiard room and several terraces, but perhaps reaches its apogee in the hotel's elegant restaurant. Here, under the superlative guidance of internationally acclaimed Head Chef Gualtiero Marchesi, classic and nouvelle Italian dishes are served daily to an admiring and distinguished clientele. Even by the exemplary standards of Italian haute cuisine the food is

outstanding. It has been rightly rewarded with no fewer than two highly prized Michelin stars, and the service, as throughout the rest of the hotel, is always of the highest order.

Since 2003, L'Albereta has also been able to boast one of the finest well-being centres in this part of Italy. Following an investment of more than two million euros, the 1,400-sq-m (15,069-sq-ft) Henri Chenot Espace Vitalité offers every conceivable state-of-the-art facility, therapy and treatment, which together with the superb indoor pool and tennis court means that L'Albereta lacks for absolutely nothing in terms of high-end luxury and world-class hospitality.

ROOMS
57

FOOD
Ristorante Gualtiero Marchesi: Italian

DRINK
Library Bar

FEATURES
SPA Espace Vitalité Henri Chenot • indoor pool • tennis court • library • personal trainers • billiard room • chess room • helipad

BUSINESS
meeting rooms • exhibition space

NEARBY
Franciacorta Vineyards • Lake Iseo • Bergamo • Brescia • Milan • Venice • Verona

CONTACT
Via Vittorio Emanuele II 23, 25030 Erbusco, Brescia • telephone: +39.030.776 0550 • facsimile: +39.030.776 0573 • email: info@albereta.it • website: www.albereta.it

palace merano
espace henri chenot

...effortlessly melding classic Italian design with genuine Alpine luxury...

THIS PAGE (FROM TOP): *Junior Suites combine art, style and luxury; enjoy fine dining in the lavish setting of La Table du Palace.*

OPPOSITE (FROM TOP): *Palace Merano's sleek interior; take in the beauty of the Alpine surroundings from the terrace; with its peaceful environs, the pool is an ideal place to relax in.*

The renowned thermal spa town of Merano occupies a lush, flower-strewn setting at the convergence of three dramatic valleys in northern Italy. A hotel like no other, the grand Palace Merano is the only five-star hotel in this breathtaking town, effortlessly melding classic Italian design with genuine Alpine luxury to offer one of the most unique and talked-about spa experiences in Europe.

The Palace boasts 105 impeccably finished rooms, the refined La Table du Palace restaurant and the cosy Jockey Club Bar, named in deference to Merano's celebrated racecourse. Yet it is the Merano's signature spa centre—the world-class Espace Henri Chenot— upon which this superb destination's reputation rests.

The Espace Henri Chenot is the original proponent of 'biontology'. This exclusively developed and now widely recognised philosophy is designed to benefit body, soul and psyche. Encapsulating a world of naturally informed yet scientifically advanced methods, biontology focuses on health, wellness, nutrition and aesthetic medicine, together with an impressive array of hydro-biontology and spa treatments. These complementary approaches combine to help guests attain aesthetic and physical goals, while rediscovering former energy and vitality levels.

This atypical centre offers a plethora of creative spa treatments alongside a dedicated wellness centre, complemented by Palace Merano's 100 per cent natural Sources de Santé beauty products. With 18 private massage rooms, hydrotherapy cabins, indoor and outdoor pools, a Finnish sauna and an invigorating hammam, a week often feels too short a sojourn.

Following a medical and bio-energetic consultation, the health centre helps to tailor-make a programme of energising, regenerating or detoxifying treatments. This will cater to each individual's needs, from weight loss and de-stressing to anti-ageing treatments. Henri Chenot's professional nutritionists will then follow up with a personalised dietary plan, to augment and further the positive progress achieved at the spa and health centre. In addition, Henri Chenot's qualified therapists also offer an extensive range of laser and micro-injection treatments for cosmetic tone-ups.

For those with the luxury of a week or more at Palace Merano, an entirely personalised Henri Chenot programme might include a detoxifying diet, a biotest to check energy levels, regenerating massages, energising treatments, hydrotherapy, mineral-enriched phyto-mud therapy sessions and group activities in the pool or gym. To shake up a sedentary lifestyle and get back in shape, the Chenot's essential individualised programme is an ideal starting point.

Henri Chenot's exclusive approach has been honed to perfection with over 30 years of experience. Its treatments are all the more beneficial for being performed in the pristine Alpine environment of Merano. From serious sports massage to sheer spa indulgence, the Merano Palace-Espace Henri Chenot shines as one of Europe's benchmark luxury spa hotels.

ROOMS
105

FOOD
La Table du Palace: natural cuisine •
La Terrasse Diététique: dietetic

DRINK
Jockey Club Bar

FEATURES
beauty centre • hydrotherapy •
indoor pool • outdoor pool • solarium •
hammam • Finnish sauna • tennis •
fitness centre • bicycle rental •
babysitter on request • carpark •
medical centre

BUSINESS
business centre

NEARBY
Merano 2000 ski resort • golf •
horse riding • horse races •
the Dolomites

CONTACT
Via Cavour 2, 39012 Merano •
telephone: +39.047.327 1000 •
facsimile: +39.047.327 1100 •
email: reservations@palace.it •
website: www.palace.it •
www.henrichenot.com

palazzo arzaga hotel spa + golf resort

...furnished with either Lombardian or Venetian period furniture...

THIS PAGE (FROM TOP): *The stunning frescoes on the walls reflect the rich history of the Palazzo; relax in the cosy bar lounge.*

OPPOSITE (CLOCKWISE FROM TOP): *The 15th-century Palazzo Arzaga; spacious and luxurious suites ensure a comfortable stay; the hotel's classic décor and grand staircase form the epitome of pure opulence.*

The Lakes region of northern Italy has long enjoyed an unrivalled reputation as one of the world's great destinations for honeymooners and holidaymakers alike. The reasons for this are plentiful and well known, and include the area's magnificent scenery, history and culture, an almost Mediterranean climate and world-class shopping, not to mention the exceptional quality of its cuisine and hospitality. Now, however, thanks to the recent opening of the five-star Palazzo Arzaga, two new attractions can be added to this already extensive list—golf courses and a spa complex that rival the best the rest of the Italy has to offer.

Located in the beautiful rolling hills southwest of Lake Garda, this member of The Leading Small Hotels of the World is set within its 144-hectare (356-acre) private estate, so there's plenty of room for its many facilities, including two world-class golf courses. Arzaga I is an 18-hole, par 72, championship course designed by Jack Nicklaus II, whereas Arzaga II is a 9-hole, par 36, inland links course designed by Gary Player. Both are as challenging as they are beautiful and would certainly earn the respect and affection of those who play them.

Somewhat less demanding but equally impressive is the hotel's beauty and well-being complex. The award-winning Spa at Palazzo Arzaga is set in lavish, soothing surroundings and offers a wide assortment of facilities and therapies, all of which are wholly dedicated to mental and physical rejuvenation. Perhaps the highlight here is the thermalised Slim & Tonic

pool. Kept at a constant temperature of between 30°C–32°C (86°F–90°F), and rich in mineral salts, the pool helps to stimulate the metabolism and slimming process while relaxing the mind at the same time.

The hotel itself is no less remarkable. Occupying a trio of stunning mansions, two of which have been designated historic monuments, it boasts many spacious and luxuriously appointed reception areas and 84 superb rooms and suites. All have been furnished with either Lombardian or Venetian period furniture and offer the last word in elegance, comfort and style. Needless to say, amenities such as en suite bathrooms, air conditioning, wi-fi access and LCD satellite TVs come as standard throughout.

The passion for excellence that is reflected in every aspect of the hotel's facilities and services extends also to its restaurants and bars. Of particular note are the formal and refined Il Moretto restaurant which specialises in gourmet Italian cuisine, and the informal Il Grill Restaurant & Coffee Bar at the Clubhouse that offers snacks and luncheons. Then there is the ever popular Le Bar—the perfect place to enjoy a drink, whether in front of the roaring fire or on the terrace while watching one of Lombardy's legendary sunsets.

ROOMS
84

FOOD
Il Moretto: gourmet Italian •
Il Grill at the Clubhouse: Italian

DRINK
Coffee Bar at the Clubhouse •
Le Bar & Lounge

FEATURES
LCD satellite TV • minibar • wi-fi

BUSINESS
conference room • meeting rooms •
banqueting rooms

NEARBY
Lake Garda • Brescia •
Mantua • Verona

CONTACT
Loc. Arzaga 25080, Carzago di
Calvagese della Riviera, Brescia •
telephone: +39.030.680 600 •
facsimile: +39.030.680 270 •
email: arzaga@arzaga.it •
website: www.palazzoarzaga.com

park hyatt milan

The interiors of the hotel are the epitome of refined elegance.

In a city as restless and dynamic as Milan, it pays to be centrally located and stay somewhere that offers a tranquil respite from the bustle in the streets. The Park Hyatt does just this. Right in the heart of the metropolis, this elegant sanctuary is a few steps from the magnificent Duomo, La Scala opera house and the financial district, not to mention the ultra-chic fashion boutiques on Via della Spiga and Via Montenapoleone.

As sophisticated and classy as Milan itself, the Park Hyatt is built around an exquisite 19th-century palazzo and its décor, although contemporary, retains classical elements in tribute to the historic building. The interiors of the hotel are the epitome of refined elegance. The lobby stands beneath a vast dome, through which natural light filters to create a serene, atmospheric setting. Travertine marble walls alongside the pink granite columns, which sustain the cupola, contrast with the rich silks and dark velvets of the sleek, modern furnishings.

The spacious rooms and suites are quietly luxurious and the carefully selected natural materials and fabrics with which they are decorated make them simply irresistible. The deep beige marble of the walls combines with rich, milky bed linens and the subtle orange hues of the lighting to create a warm, welcoming refuge. The perfect surroundings in which to sit back and enjoy a movie on the Bang & Olufsen satellite TV.

Those unfortunate enough to have to work after hours might even relish the experience, for all guestrooms come with high-speed Internet access and a sizeable desk. It is clearly no coincidence that *Travel & Leisure* magazine named the Park Hyatt Milan 'the best business hotel in Italy.' After all, with three boardrooms and conference facilities, equipped with state-of-the-art multimedia technology, business travellers could not ask for more.

If work or shopping has proven arduous, The Spa at the Park Hyatt is sure to proffer the perfect remedy by offering an exclusive space for guests to relax. A full workout at the stunning gym facility could be followed by a Turkish bath or one of a large selection of massages or beauty treatments—sure to revive even the most battle weary.

THIS PAGE (FROM TOP): Park Hyatt Milan's sophistication beckons; the Junior Suite combines elegance with modern comfort.

OPPOSITE (FROM TOP): Enjoy breakfast outdoors, with the city's grandeur sights in full view; La Cupola's glass dome is a real winner in the restaurant's stylishly classical interior; the marble bathroom has a range of luxurious amenities in addition to a deep soaking tub.

ROOMS
117

FOOD
The Park: classical and contemporary Italian • La Cupola: Mediterranean and international

DRINK
The Park Bar

FEATURES
DVDs • satellite TV • spa • hi-speed Internet access • multi-line phones • rain showers

BUSINESS
meeting room • banqueting room • boardrooms • multimedia technology

NEARBY
financial district • La Galleria • La Scala opera house • Piazza del Duomo • Via della Spiga • Via Montenapoleone

CONTACT
Via Tommaso Grossi 1, 20121 Milan • telephone: +39.02.8821 1234 • facsimile: +39.02.8821 1235 • email: milano@hyattintl.com • website: www.milan.park.hyatt.com

Although Milan is famed for its delectable cuisine, guests need look no further afield than The Park for a truly memorable epicurean experience. The sober, stylish design of this establishment presents an ideal backdrop to savour Italian regional dishes, prepared with the freshest seasonal ingredients by Executive Chef Filippo Gozzoli. With delicacies such as Pan Fried Guinea Fowl Breast with Chestnut and Truffle on the menu, and extraordinary wines from boutique vineyards to complement them, guests will be rushing to make another reservation at the Park Hyatt Milan before they leave.

seiser alm urthaler

...experience a new dimension in Alpine luxury...

The family-run Seiser Alm Urthaler hotel has introduced an extraordinary new design concept that offers a positive glimpse into an ecologically sustainable future. A restful and relaxing property with a sunny disposition in the heart of the Alpe di Siusi Natural Park, it boasts an enviable location high above the Italian Dolomites. Located directly on the mountainside, it offers doorstep access to skiing facilities in winter and myriad hiking trails during summer.

It is the first Alpine hotel in Europe to be crafted entirely from wood, made and felled according to the phases of the moon. Only natural substances—such as stone and handmade carpets—were used for its organic construction, a chemical-free process creating a pure, allergen-free environment in the centre of Europe's highest plateau, the pristine Alpe di Siusi.

The buildings of the elegant Urthaler radiate from a modern circular tower, with 51 guestrooms and 3 luxurious suites. The sleek bathrooms utilise steel, glass and natural stone, while bedrooms are permeated by the evocative scent of wood, as befits their Alpine setting. Harmoniously appointed and with interior moods accentuated by the extraordinary lighting concepts of Ingo Maurer, this hotel has a distinct personality of its own.

In addition to its stunning location, the Seiser Alm Urthaler also boasts the exclusive Antermoia Beauty, Sport and Bath Centre, named after a translucent turquoise lake in the Dolomites. With over 700 sq m (7,535 sq ft) of recreation and beauty space, its philosophy is to promote inner and outer harmony and wellness, in a discrete and stylish environment.

THIS PAGE (FROM TOP): *A different experience awaits at this splendid indoor pool; natural elements are stylishly incorporated into the Seiser Alm Urthaler's interior design.*

OPPOSITE (FROM TOP): *Wood is an integral part of the hotel's décor; the Urthaler is surrounded by the enormous beauty of the Alps; warm lighting and handmade woollen carpets provide rooms with a cosy ambience.*

ROOMS
54

FOOD
Dolasilla Restaurant: Mediterranean and South Tyrolean

DRINK
Onyxbar • Ciulé: wine cellar

FEATURES
Alpine Regeneration Garden • sauna • Finnish sauna • indoor pool • outdoor pool • massages • beauty treatments

NEARBY
Alpe di Siusi Natural Park • ski slopes • hiking • Golf Club

CONTACT
Fam. Urthaler, I-39040 Seiser Alm • telephone: +39.0471.727 919 • facsimile: +39.0471.727 820 • email: info@seiseralm.com • website: www.seiseralm.com

Return from an invigorating dip in the remarkable outdoor pool or panoramic indoor pool to select from a tantalising array of massages, beauty baths and treatments. The apple bath and hay bath are but two of the unconventional choices. To attain a more solitary serenity, escape to the Finnish sauna, aromatherapy baths or relaxation room. Afterwards, a meditative stroll in the idyllic Alpine Regeneration Garden will emphasise the sense of peace nurtured by Antermoia's professional staff.

To replenish the physical as well as the spiritual self, tuck into an impressive breakfast buffet or enjoy a five-course gourmet dining experience in the hotel's Dolasilla Restaurant. Wine lovers will marvel over the selection of rare bottles stored in the atmospheric Ciulé wine cellar. To mingle with fellow guests or peruse the local newspapers, visit the Onyxbar. Extending its welcoming ambience and with yielding leather seats and an open fireplace, it is the social hub of the hotel. The Seiser Alm Urthaler completes a trio of unique Alpine retreats run by this forward-thinking family of hoteliers. To experience a new dimension in Alpine luxury, the Urthaler is, in every sense, the natural choice.

the gray milano

...past and present, tradition, fashion and innovation synergise beneath one roof...

THIS PAGE (FROM LEFT): Rooms pack the best of modern comforts, ensuring an enjoyable stay; luxuriate in the lavish bathroom suite after a day out in the city.

OPPOSITE (FROM TOP): Avant-garde décor is very much part of the hotel's contemporary style; the showpiece lobby swing-seat; look forward to the vibrant and cosy atmosphere at The Gray.

The global fashion capital of Milan revels in its reputation for bold innovation and pioneering design. Doing its home city proud is The Gray design hotel, an intriguing building that surprises at every step. One peek at the shocking pink swing-seat that hangs from the lobby ceiling will assure any potential visitor that this hotel is anything but a grey area.

Located on Via San Raffaele between the Duomo and La Scala opera house, The Gray is at the core of this inimitable Italian city. Its cosmopolitan crowd includes businesswomen accustomed to the highest standards of comfort and convenience, and its young culture hounds on the scent of the art or fashion world's next big thing.

At street level, The Gray is characterised by the columns of its Liberty-styled façade, to which a green diorite and crystal-encrusted wing was recently added. Designed by renowned architect Guido Ciompi—creator of Gucci boutique interiors the world over—this visual duality embodies the juxtapositions that permeate the project's ethos. Here, past and present, tradition, fashion and innovation synergise beneath one roof to produce an experience that exceeds the sum of its parts.

The hotel's 21 individualistic suites variously feature stunning four-poster or hanging beds, private gym equipment, plasma TVs, Turkish baths or large hydro-tubs, while luxurious bathroom suites are a permanent fixture in the rooms. The eminently touchable materials decorating the interiors include glossy ebony for the floors, with granite-like travertine from Tivoli—the city after which this rock is named—and natural silks, skins and rich African fabrics for the soft furnishings.

Niches in The Gray's public spaces contain ancient Chinese vases and have on display the evening gowns of fêted international film stars, while the walls are adorned with unique hangings and stuccoes of towering waves supporting huge, glistening shells.

For fine dining, the hotel's jet black, post-modern Le Noir restaurant is the place to be. Lit by dramatic red Chinese silk lamps, its Mediterranean-inspired menu is created by the talented chef Luciano Sarzi Santori. The glittering Rosenthal cutlery is set off by the crisp white linen tablecloths, and the impressive wine list champions classic Italian and organic bottles.

The hotel's GBar is designed to visually shock and surprise, captivating the eye as much as the palate. It boasts soft velvet sofas, conical lamps and tables on illuminated rail. Recline on the red leather upholstery of the oxidised iron bar stools with a refreshing Mojito or personalised cocktail as contrasting natural images are projected against the bar's fabric screens. If guests prefer the open-air ambience of a star-lit Italian evening, enter the Aria lounge, a conceptual space where refined luxury and cutting-edge design meet.

Encapsulating the dynamism of Milan, the hotel is the perfect starting point to explore the city. Take a little time out to enjoy one of Europe's most culturally colourful cities, right from the luxury of Milan's tailor-made design hotel, The Gray.

ROOMS
21

FOOD
Le Noir: Mediterranean and international

DRINK
Aria lounge • Gbar

FEATURES
four-poster or hanging beds • private gym • Turkish bath • jacuzzi • plasma TV • high-speed Internet access

NEARBY
Duomo • La Scala opera house

CONTACT
Via San Raffaele 6, 20121 Milan • telephone: +39.02.720 8951 • facsimile: +39.02.866 526 • email: info.thegray@sinahotels.it • website: www.hotelthegray.com

the straf

...high-tech functionality and minimalism are cleverly blended with creative lighting...

THIS PAGE: Rooms at The Straf mix avant-garde design with the best of modern comfort.

OPPOSITE (CLOCKWISE FROM TOP): The hotel's stylish hall is the epitome of high fashion and dynamism; with sophisticated décor and a superb menu, the Straf bar is a feast for the senses; the bathrooms inspire with their sleek and luxurious interior; experience Milan's vibrant nightlife at the Straf bar.

There is no denying it—Milan is the earth's design capital. Home to a collection of the world's finest manufacturers of fashion, furniture and accessories, not to mention its predominance in international fairs in these areas, its supremacy in all things designer is undisputed. It is of little surprise then that Italy's industrial capital also houses some ultra-chic hotels to cater for the sophisticated clientele of these powerhouses of design, or for travellers looking for something a little more edgy than the average hostelry. The über-trendy Straf Hotel would fall into this category. Located in the very heart of downtown Milan, literally steps from the Duomo, La Scala opera house and the sensational shopping at Via Montenapoleone, The Straf offers a refreshing, somewhat urban, take on luxury.

Interiors are striking in their austerity; high-tech functionality and minimalism are cleverly blended with creative lighting and fascinating textures to achieve a surprisingly warm, serene atmosphere. A constant juxtaposition of rough and smooth; light and dark; industrial and luxurious characterise the hotel, creating the feeling that one is somehow inhabiting a work of art. Floors and walls are exposed concrete and contrast with the soft, sheer velvets of armchairs and sofas, while striking pieces of contemporary art and plaques of quarry-rough slates, burnished brass and hand-aged mirrors bedeck the walls.

Guestrooms are spacious and sleek, maintaining the minimalist line in décor. Bold, oversized paintings on matt black or concrete walls are mixed with milky-white bedding and wispy, translucent curtains. Soundproofing ensures the quietest of nights despite the hotel's location in the city centre, while every amenity from satellite TV channels, movies and music is available in every room to ensure guests' absolute comfort.

Some rooms come with an irresistible well-being corner, complete with a state-of-the-art massage chair, chromatherapy (colour therapy) appliances and aromatherapy products, ideal to wash away the stresses of the day. Those looking to unwind more energetically, however, can opt for a workout at The Straf's first-class gym facility that is open 24 hours a day and offers the latest equipment. Guests could then head to the sumptuous bathroom for a well-deserved bath. Here, burnished brass floors and dark slates and tiles are subtly illuminated to make for a soothing, zen-like environment, while deep tubs ensure complete relaxation.

The hotel offers two equally tempting dining options which include the cool, elegant restaurant serving a tantalising lunch menu, or the bar offering light, à la carte meals throughout the day. The very same Straf bar becomes one of Milan's hot spots during the evening, attracting a hip crowd, drawn the by the in-house DJ, live music and the vibrant atmosphere.

If one wants to soak up the Milanese culture for design, do so from the most vanguard hotel in the city. With its avant-garde layout and exquisite concept, The Straf is sure to surprise and will definitely not disappoint.

ROOMS
64

FOOD
Straf bar: Mediterranean

DRINK
Pina Picantera

FEATURES
music and movies (all rooms) •
Internet • satellite TV • gym •
well-being corner (some rooms) •
relax rooms with massage chair

BUSINESS
conference facilities

NEARBY
town centre • fashion district •
Duomo • Galleria Vittorio Emanuele •
La Scala opera house

CONTACT
Via San Raffaele 3, 20121 Milan •
telephone: +39.02.805 081 •
facsimile: +39.02.8909 5294 •
email: reservations@straf.it •
website: www.straf.it

villa lake como + portofino paradiso

Both provide a quintessential taste of la dolce vita...

Northern Italy is a destination filled with scenic wonders, history, art and culinary pleasures, and among the top places to see in the world are Lake Como and Portofino.

Whichever of these two destination travellers choose—or both—the Villa Book's luxuriously appointed holiday homes are equipped to provide for a dream trip. With the kind of privacy and comfort they offer, Villa Lake Como and Portofino Paradiso are homes away from home. Both provide a quintessential taste of la dolce vita, with panoramic views, beautiful gardens, stylish interiors, swimming pools and outdoor dining facilities—perfect for both idyllic relaxation and entertainment. Discreet service aside, guests will also enjoy the modern conveniences of high-speed Internet access and satellite TV during their stay.

Villa Lake Como, which dates back to the 19th century, sits grandly on Lake Como's picturesque shore. The villa's majestic entrance hall, with its marble fireplace, frescoed ceiling and chandeliers, embodies the splendour of its rich past. For some fresh air and tranquillity, relax on the outdoor terrace that extends from the spacious living and dining areas. For some gourmet Italian dining, Villa Lake Como offers private cooking lessons, where guests can learn the finer points of Italian cooking. Of course, there is always the option of requesting the services of a professional chef.

Not far from the Villa Lake Como is the popular resort town of Bellagio, which houses the lovely villas of the 18th and 19th centuries, in addition to an assortment of trattorias and a Michelin star restaurant. Public and private boat charters are also available for exploring the towns and villages around the lake.

THIS PAGE (FROM TOP): Enjoy the cool breezes from the garden at Villa Lake Como; a scenic view of the holiday retreat, standing peacefully on the edge of the lake.

OPPOSITE (FROM TOP) : The surrounding tranquillity makes outdoor dining a pleasure; Villa Lake Como's cosy interior.

At the other end of the northern Italian region is Portofino Paradiso, a superb property perched on a hill on 5 hectares (12 acres) of land overlooking the famous coastline of Portofino. Arriving at the property is already an experience in itself, which involves taking a lift 76 m (249 ft) up to the entrance gate—but not before passing through a tunnel under the rocks. That's not all. Guests still have to walk along a garden path before finally reaching the front door. Once inside, there is no shortage of stunning ocean views, which can be seen from every window. With spacious and airy living areas, in addition to the personalised yet discreet services of the housekeeper, waiter and chef, Portofino Paradiso makes an excellent oasis. While the property itself enjoys a secluded spot, it is only a few minutes walk from the bustling town centre, featuring a variety of shops and fine restaurants.

The Villa Book's prestigious properties at Lake Como and Portofino are sophisticated and elegant, yet warm and unpretentious. Both provide the best in comfort, luxury and convenience, while managing to capture the essence of Italy, so that all guests will leave with a unique and memorable experience.

Villa Lake Como

ROOMS
7

FOOD
in-house chef on request

DRINK
wine list

FEATURES
pool • fireplace • barbecue • Internet • satellite TV • private cooking lessons • public and private boat charters

NEARBY
trattorias • water sports • Lake Como • Benedictine Abbey • Brown Castle • Bellagio • Lecco • Bergamo • Milan • Lugano • Portofino

Portofino Paradiso

ROOMS
5

FOOD
in-house chef on request

DRINK
pool bar • wine list

FEATURES
pool • satellite TV • Internet • public and private boat charters

NEARBY
Portofino • Benedictine Abbey • Brown Castle • water sports

CONTACT
12 Venetian House, 47 Warrington Crescent, London W9 1EJ • telephone: +44.845.500 2000 • facsimile: +44.845.500 2001 • email: info@thevillabook.com • website: www.thevillabook.com

venice+northeast italy

AUSTRIA

LIECHTENSTEIN

SWITZERLAND

SLOVENIA

Tarvisio

Tolmezzo

Gemona del Friuli •

• Udine

• Palmanova

Trieste •

Gulf of Venice

Garda

Treviso

Vicenza •

Verona

Padua

Venice •

> Bauer Il Palazzo
> Bauer Palladio Hotel + Spa
> Ca Maria Adele
> Ca'Pisani
> Charming House DD.724
> Hotel Gritti Palace
> Hotel Monaco + Grand Canal
> San Clemente Palace Hotel + Resort

CROATIA

Hotel Villa del Quar <
Palazzo Viviani <
Grand Hotel Baglioni <

Piacenza

• Ferrara

Parma

• Modena

Ravenna •

Bologna

N

Rimini •

Gulf of Genoa

SAN MARINO

Legend

═	Highway
▬	Main Road
—	Other Road
✈	Airport
○	Lake
●	2000–3000 m
●	1500–2000 m
●	1000–1500 m
●	500–1000 m
●	200–500 m
●	100–200 m

0 km   25   50   75 km

venice + northeast italy

With the very name Venice come visions of floating palaces on a
blue lagoon. Once at the helm of one of the most powerful republics
ever in the world, Venice is now the world's most spectacular theme
park, renowned for its Carnival and more recently as a modern art hub. The Venetian
Republic reigned supreme over the northeast of Italy until Napoleon crashed the party.
In its heyday it gave birth to some of the country's finest artists and remains one of its
most beautiful regions—Verona, Vicenza and Padua are only a handful of the art cities
here, and those craving peace and quiet will adore the exquisite hill towns of Arqua
Petrarca and Asolo, as well as the Palladian masterpiece Villa Barbaro at Maser.

Friuli Venezia Giulia is somewhat schizophrenic—part Venetian and part Austro-
Hungarian. South of Venice is the wealthy region of Emilia-Romagna where stylish yet
unpretentious Bologna was home to Europe's first university. In almost a straight line
stretching from Piacenza to Rimini, there are the art cities of Parma, Modena, Ferrara
and Ravenna, each one more unique and sophisticated than the next. Rimini brings
light relief; again there's art, but there's also the sea and a serious dose of kitsch too.

venice: trip the light fantastic

The Venetian Lagoon is one of Italy's most beautiful treasures. It has remained almost
untouched since its heyday in the 18th century—there are no cars, just the sound of
footsteps, and the swish of the gondolier's oar or the chug of the vaporetti. Immortalised
in countless paintings, the city once commanded a vast empire: gold cascaded in and
genius spilled out. Between the 9th and 12th centuries Venice was a Maritime
Republic. Its prime position in the Adriatic Sea made the city-state flourish as a gateway
between Europe and the Byzantine and Islamic worlds. Not content just to call the shots
at sea, Venice set its sights on terra firma, ultimately controlling Istria, Dalmatia (now
Croatia) and the Veneto and Friuli Venezia Giulia regions, holding on to her dominion
until the 18th century when Napoleon conquered the city and ended an era.

*PAGE 84: The gateway to La
Serenissima beside the Doge's
Palace—wherever the Venetians
held sway there is a podium
with the lion of St. Mark's.*

*THIS PAGE (FROM TOP): Dining
by the Grand Canal in the
gentle glow of Venetian glass.
Murano is home to Venice's
famous glassblowing industry;
a scene from St. Mark's Square.*

*OPPOSITE: The square from across
the blue lagoon on the island
of San Giorgio Maggiore.*

Venice, known as the City of Light, is divided into six sestieri, the Canareggio, Dorsoduro, San Marco, San Polo, Santa Croce and Castello. The S-shaped Grand Canal is Venice's main thoroughfare. Byron, a famous former resident, who had a club foot, preferred swimming to walking: in Venice he was in his element. The who's who of Venice, the powerful merchant elite, lived on the Grand Canal, and for centuries only their heirs were permitted to live here.

The best way to see the palaces is from the water and no one ever tires of the view. One of the most beautiful is the Ca' d'Oro, meaning the golden house, and now the Galleria Franchetti. Ca' Rezzonico—also open to the public—was home to Robert Browning and studio to artist John Singer Sergeant. Palazzo Grassi (now owned by French businessman François Pinault) hosts a modern art gallery, with impressive exhibitions and a new restaurant-café, the Vecio Fritolin. Nearby is the famous Palazzo Malipiero, former home to an elderly senator who took the young Casanova under his wing. It's here that Casanova honed his art of entertaining the ladies and where he was eventually shown the door after being caught with someone Malipiero had his own eye on. Near the Rialto there's the exquisite Palazzo Contarini del Bovolo with its winding stairway and beautiful view over the rooftops, open to the public.

The beautiful Palazzo Labia is a baroque extravaganza created by a Spanish arriviste family, who scandalously bought the title and the right to live there. Spanning the canal are just three bridges; the Rialto (the oldest and most famous), the Accademia and the Scalzi. A fourth bridge by Spanish architect Calatrava is work in progress. New architecture in Venice always creates waves and most projects never get off the ground. Le Corbusier's hospital was one of these, although a new University of Architecture building is presently being built.

piazza san marco

St. Mark's Square, or Piazza San Marco, looks almost exactly the same as in Canaletto's paintings. Here you'll find the Doge's Palace, St. Mark's Basilica and campanile and the two remaining cafés of Venice's heyday: the Caffè Florian and the Gran Caffè Quadri. By the water's edge are pedestals with the lion of St. Mark and a statue of St. Teodoro of Amasea: these marked the gateway to the Republic. Glowing in golden Byzantine splendour is St. Mark's. As glitteringly beautiful inside as out, the best views are gained if you climb the small stairways in the entrance. These lead to an internal balcony then a small room holding the genuine Roman bronze horses of St. Mark. Beyond is the rooftop, with its beautiful replicas, but irreplaceable panorama.

The Palazzo Ducale was both the Doge's residence and the city's prison. Inside are room after room of paintings and frescoes. Special tours are available showing the Secret Itinerary, Casanova's escape route from the prison in 1755. The romantic-sounding Bridge of Sighs was named so by Byron in the 19th century after he imagined convicts' sighs as they took one last fleeting look at their beautiful city before being sent into the darkness. Legend has it that kissing beneath the bridge on a gondola at sunset will assure eternal love. Plenty of people try.

behind closed doors: a wealth of art

There's no need to go indoors for art in Venice, it's everywhere you look, and most painters came here for the natural light. That said, the city has a treasure trove of art attracting tourists in their hordes. The Accademia, set in the Dorsoduro district, shows some of the city's masterpieces, which give a valuable insight into daily life and fashion in the Republic. Elsewhere are the Scuole, or confraternities, each with its own chapels. The Scuole Grande were linked to monasteries, such as the Dominicans; the Scuole Piccole were linked to trade guilds. Each Scuole vied to outdo the other in terms of prestige and beauty, patronising Venice's top artists. Santa Maria Gloriosa dei Frari has

THIS PAGE (FROM TOP): Carnevale once dominated the Venetian social calendar. Nowadays, the masked ball Mascheranda held in Palazzo Pisani Moretta is one of the main events and attracts the cream of Venetian society; a luxurious gondola for the quintessential Venice experience.

OPPOSITE: The never-ending play of light and water means views never stay the same. St. Mark's Square is frequently flooded in winter when the city, often swathed in mist, holds a particular charm.

work by Titian and Bellini as well as Canova's tomb; the Scuola di San Rocco has some of Tintoretto's finest work. Opera was sung in the Teatro La Fenice, site of several operatic premieres. Ironically, given its name, it has twice burned down and been rebuilt in 1836 and 1996.

While Venice may not seem an obvious mecca for contemporary art, it has attracted innovators in the art world since the dawn of the Republic. The Venice Biennale is now the world's oldest and highest-profile international art jamboree. Started in 1895, it gradually internationalised and since the two world wars, grew ever more innovative. Likened to the Olympics, it is first and foremost a competition for the top prize of the Golden Lion. A small select group or a single artist represents each country (72 of them in total). The choice of entrant for each country is a controversial business but the choice of winner even more so as she or he is catapulted to international stardom in the art world. Ostensibly a non-commercial fair (official sales were stopped in the 1960s), the party atmosphere encourages copious wheeling and dealing and as soon as the Biennale's over, work is snapped up by private collectors, or artists are assured shows the world over. Gustav Klimt, Pablo Picasso and Henry Moore all exhibited here, Moore winning the prize for sculpture in 1948.

Other treasure boxes of modern art are open year-round. The Ca' Pesaro houses the Galleria d'Arte Moderna. Once home to the Pesaro family's art collection, it was progressively sold off as times got tough. In 1898 the palazzo was bequeathed to the city as a museum of modern art. Fine paintings by Morandi, De Chirico and Boccioni as well as Klimt, Kandinsky and Chagall now decorate the walls. Peggy Guggenheim, niece of New York's Solomon Guggenheim and former wife of Max Ernst, established a museum in her former home on the Dorsoduro, housing her very personal collection of modern art.

THIS PAGE: *Becoming increasingly representative, the 2007 Biennale saw the first pavilions from Africa, Mexico, Turkey and India, as well as from the Roma people, with work by 16 artists spanning eight countries.*
OPPOSITE: *Stylish Verona, where designer boutiques line the Via Mazzini, leading from the Arena to Pizza delle Erbe.*

Augmented by work from the Nasher Collection, the impressive array of art includes pieces of Cubism, Surrealism and Abstract Expressionism, as well as Italian Futurism and American Modernism.

Venice was home to an important pioneer of fashion: Andalucian, Mariano Fortuny. He lived in a grand gothic palazzo on the Campo San Beneto, which his widow then converted into a museum featuring a collection of his work, sketches and paintings. Inspired by classical Greece, the couple created the groundbreaking plissé silk dress, the Delphos evening dress, and the Knossos scarf. Famed for liberating women from the corsets of old in fin-de-siècle fashion, and his textile and dyeing innovations, Fortuny inspired countless generations. His fabric factory producing silks and velvets on the Giudecca is still open.

Attached to the Biennale, the world-famous Venice Film Festival is now in its 75th year. Held on the Lido, at the end of August into early September, it attracts a heavenly host of international stars, all competing with new films for the prestigious Golden Lion.

verona: romance and rogues

Long before fair Verona became a place of pilgrimage for sweethearts, it was a Roman city. Catullus hailed from here as did Vetruvius, the father of Renaissance architecture. Pretty Piazza Bra is at the city's cobbled core, its earthquake-battered 1st-century amphitheatre the backdrop for more doomed romances in Verona's annual opera festival, which commenced in 1913. Lovebirds languish around the evocative Piazza delle Erbe and the Piazza dei Signori, with their beautiful Renaissance frescoes, while the striped Palazzo della Ragione, home to the law courts and 12th-century campanile Torre dei Lamberti, perhaps appeal to more judicious types.

Cynics should really steer clear of Juliet's House. The pretty palazzo, scarcely visited inside, dates from the 13th century. Two rooms show sets and costumes from Zefferelli's film of *Romeo and Juliet*. Outside, the courtyard scene kills any romantic notions; graffiti is everywhere. Juliet's statue is pawed by the masses—people touch her breast to bring fortune to their love lives. Her tomb is no better, Romeo gets off lightly in modern-day Verona.

In between bullying and battling, the Scaligeris of Verona had fine buildings raised in their honour, and by supporting Dante they earned a dedication in his *Paradise*. Their family tomb is in Castelvecchio. Inside the Romanesque Duomo is a beautiful Titian; the font in the nearby Baptistery is carved from one giant piece of marble. Further afield, the Basilica di San Zeno is another Romanesque masterpiece, its 12th-century rose window showing the wheel of fortune, 'Poor Man's Bible' bronze doors, and an Andrea Mantegna triptych of 1459. The Galleria d'Arte Moderna, in Palazzo Forti near the gothic Sant'Anastasia, stages regular exhibitions as well as housing a permanent collection. Works include De Pisis, Boccioni and Birolli.

padua's intelligentsia

Padua has long been a place of learning, and was nicknamed la dotta (the learned) in 1221 after its great university was established. Alumni include Dante, Petrarch and Galileo. Italy's oldest astronomical clock—it's still working—can be seen at the photogenic Palazzo dei Signori. At the law courts in the Palazzo della Ragione is a vast medieval hall once frescoed by Giotto. The pietra (stone) del vituperio in the corner is where bankrupts had to sit naked for three sessions before the courts to expiate their sin before being sent into permanent exile. Times were tougher in those days. Galileo taught in the Palazzo del Bo, part of the university. You can still see his wooden pulpit. There's also the world's first ever anatomical theatre, of 1594. Gio Ponti designed the new university arts faculty at the Liviano beside the Palazzo del Capitanio in 1939.

Students were a force to be reckoned with in Padua. Classier than your average student union was their café society of the 1830s, which gathered in the Caffè Pedrocchi. Famous for never closing, it was the site of endless nights of political posturing as well as a secret bordello. Its extension, the Pedrocchino, is famous for clashes with the police in 1848—you can see the bullet holes. It still functions as a café.

Padua is also home to the exquisitely frescoed Scrovegni Chapel by Giotto. Built by a son to pay back wrongdoings of his father (a loan shark who died shrieking for the keys to his safe), the chapel was completed in 1305 and dedicated to Santa Maria della Carità in an attempt to redeem the family name. Usury was a crime under Venetian law and moneylenders were denied Christian burials. Anonymous letterboxes where people were once encouraged to sneak on guilty parties are still common sights. Elsewhere in the town is the heavily gilded Basilica di Sant'Antonio. As church of the patron saint of children, unmarried women, and other things, it attracts pilgrims from all over the world. Donatello made the altar as well as a fine equestrian bronze in the square outside.

Southwest of Padua is the exquisite town of Arqua Petrarca, where Petrarch lived and died. In the visitor's book of his villa are the signatures of Lord Byron and his then lady friend, the Contessa Teresa Giuccioli, who visited in 1818. North of Padua is

THIS PAGE: *Caffè Pedrocchi, Padua's first building to receive gas lighting. A labyrinth of rooms, it also housed an early stock exchange, billiard room and casino attracting Padua's aristocracy and writers such as Stendhal and George Sand.*

OPPOSITE: *Thought to be Italy's largest square, Padua's Prato della Valle plays host to large crowds for the evening ritual of the passeggiata and a huge market every Saturday.*

Asolo, nicknamed the town of a hundred horizons, quite justifiably if you climb up to the Rocca. A walled hill-town, it hosted the enlightened Renaissance court of Queen Catherine, muse to many an artist and writer. The perfect place to be beautifully idle, Robert Browning lived here. Castelfranco Veneto is the hometown of Giorgione, one of the most enigmatic artists of the Renaissance. There's a small museum to him here and one of his tragically few paintings, the *Castelfranco Madonna*, in the town's Duomo.

of grappa + gold

In Bassano del Grappa there are plenty of places to sample the local speciality; the best is Nardini's, an inn unchanged since the 1600s. Elsewhere in the town is the stylish Poli distillery. There's plenty of fine food to soak up the grappa and Bassano is as pretty a place as you'll find. It's also a ceramics centre and nearby Nove has a national pottery school. A little further away is Marostica, where a game of life-size chess is played during September weekends of even years. A tradition since 1454, two would-be duellists were ordered to compete for a lady over a game of chess instead.

THIS PAGE: Bassano is best known for its beautiful green, rapid-flowing river spanned by the famous wooden bridge, the Ponte degli Alpini, designed by Palladio in 1568.

OPPOSITE (FROM TOP): Treviso's Piazza Dei Signori, its cool portico offering shade and a quiet spot for coffee; stepping back in time in the Caffè degli Specchi, Trieste.

Affluent Vicenza is a town famed for two things: Andrea Palladio and gold. Set in a picturesque spot below Monte Berici, there are many Palladian villas to visit as well as some 800 goldsmiths, who come together at the town's renowned jewellery fairs. The facelift Andrea Palladio gave to Piazza dei Signori was his first major work in 1549. The Teatro Olimpico, the oldest operational theatre in the world, however, is his swansong. Sadly, Palladio died before he saw its first performance, *Oedipus Rex* in 1585, from which the stage set by Vincenzo Scamozzi remains. For less highbrow activity, there are tempting boutiques, bars and osterie on every corner.

Despite its canals and fine buildings, an old fishmarket, and the perfect piazza in the town's old heart (the Piazza dei Trecento), Treviso is often overlooked. While the city suffered devastating air raids in the war, much of its medieval and Renaissance architecture lives on. San Nicolò is a gem as is the bombed church of Santa Caterina, with its medieval masterpieces by Tommaso da Modena, a pupil of Giotto. Modern art is on show in the Galleria di Arte Moderna in the Museo Bailo. Treviso is the Italian capital of the small business, and top restaurants abound, as do stylish shops. Benetton started here and still maintains a strong presence.

trieste: sipping coffee with spies

Long part of the Austro-Hapsburg Empire, Trieste is a noble city on the Adriatic with a split personality. Once a main stop on the Orient Express and a free port, its finest sight is outside the city on the Carso, at the Castello del Miramare. Occupied by allied forces after World War II, Trieste rejoined Italy in 1954—Tito of the former Yugoslavia wanted Trieste for himself. Only in 1970 was the border issue finally resolved. A cosmopolitan hotbed of intrigue, Trieste attracted aristocratic bon viveurs, spies and writers. James Joyce lived here after eloping with the unpromisingly named Nora Barnacle.

Piazza Unità d'Italia is the city's hub located right on the seafront; concerts are held in summer, while the Bora wind howls mercilessly in winter. Look for the railings to cling to. Belle Époque cafes are one of the city's prime attractions: the Caffè degli Specchi

THIS PAGE (FROM TOP): *The splendour of the mosaics in Aquileia's Romanesque basilica. Ravenna, further down the coast in Emilia Romagna, has an unsurpassed collection of Byzantine mosaics dating from the same period; the beautiful floor mosaics inside the Basilica of Aquileia.*

OPPOSITE: *Bird's-eye view over medieval Bologna or, for those with a head for heights, from the Torre degli Asinelli.*

especially. Illy is based in Trieste and Italy's coffee tradition started here, after taking Vienna by storm. Cafés to seek out are the Stella Polare, Caffè San Marco and Il Tommaseo. Joyce favoured the Caffè Pirona. There's a whacky museum to the Bora wind, fine exhibitions at the art nouveau Central Fish Market as well as the Museo Revoltella, a Renaissance palazzo with a Carlo Scarpa extension. One of Italy's best modern art collections can be seen here.

Emperor Justinian named Aquileia the greatest city in the west in 6 AD. The northernmost city in the Roman Empire, it once played host to King Herod of Judea and latterly Marco Aurelius. Its beautiful basilica was built in 313 AD, with mosaics covering the entire floor. Geometric shapes and symbols from the animal kingdom predominate—early Christians were persecuted, so imagery often had specific coded meaning. The battle between the cockerel and the tortoise, for example, reflects that between enlightenment and darkness. More familiar are the good shepherd and Jonah and the whale. When the town was totally trashed by Attila the Hun in 432, most of the settlers fled to the lagoons, leading to the rise of Venice. Aquileia rose again, however, reaching its second peak in the 11th century before its port silted up and it was abandoned. A fine archaeological museum shows Roman mosaics, stone carvings and sculpture, as well as gemstones and glassware.

Palmanova, north of Aquileia, is Renaissance perfection. Built in 1593, the fortress is in the form of a perfect nine-pointed star. There's a central square with the cathedral, and all around in radial symmetry are walls and moats.

Friuli's capital city, Udine, was the last city to be liberated at the end of the war. Its central square, the Venetian-gothic and Renaissance Piazza della Libertà is a magical creation in beautiful pink stone. The art nouveau Caffè Contarena is a good place to stop and take in the surroundings. Near the old market square is the pretty Oratorio della Purità and Duomo with its clock tower containing works by Tiepolo. The Galleria d'Arte Moderna contains works by Gattuso, Severini and De Chirico as well as Dufy, Nicholson, Picasso and Braque.

red + radical to pretty in pink

A more beautiful and less pretentious city would be hard to find in Italy: Bologna is red brick through and through. It has no less than 70 km (43 miles) of porticoed arcades and communal squares, the finest being Piazza Maggiore, with its noble cathedral, and Piazza del Nettuno. A successful city since medieval times and one of Italy's first free communes, Bologna once bristled with fortified towers (there were 180 at the city's peak). Only two remain, the Torre Asinelli, which you can climb, and Torre Garisenda. Both were built in 1199.

Red in more ways than one, Bologna has always been a socialist city. It was fiercely partisan during the war, its rulers have long been enlightened and it is home to Italy's oldest law faculty, where important codes were established to help negotiations between the Pope and the Holy Roman Emperor. Its leftist politics have helped create a forward-thinking, sophisticated city, which has always attracted artists and thinkers.

For art lovers the Pinacoteca Nazionale, on the Via Belle Arti near the university, has a plethora of great work from Giotto to Raphael. Guido Reni and the Carracci brothers, all Bologna-born, are well represented. Elsewhere, the church of Santa Maria della Vita has Nicolo dell'Arca's moving terracotta Lament over the Dead Christ, which recalls Edvard Munch's Scream.

Giorgio Morandi, who lived here most of his life, has a fine museum, showing mostly still life works but also landscapes of his country home at Grizzana. Linked to this are two other modern art venues, the Villa delle Rose, outside the city, which holds temporary exhibitions and has a fine sculpture garden, and the

MAMbo, the Museum of Modern Art Bologna, which opened in April 2006 as part of a mammoth re-modernisation project in the former Renaissance port area. The inaugural exhibition focused on the work of Arte Povera artist Giovanni Anselmo, who contributed a giant compass for the new venue.

Nearby in the complex is the Cineteca del Comune di Bologna, an impressive cinematheque housed in a former slaughterhouse. There's a vast library, graphic arts section and a film and soundtrack archive, with thousands of DVDs which visitors can watch in hi-tech viewing stations. Top film restorers work here; they are currently working on Charlie Chaplin's entire works. Back in the centre, there's the Museo Pelagalli, an award-winning museum devoted to audiovision, focusing on radio, the phonograph and television.

Beyond Bologna, the town of Dozza hosts a regional enoteca, where you can taste 600 regional wines—perhaps not all on the same day. There's also a biennale held in September, called the Muro Dipinto, which sees house walls as blank canvases.

Parma is pink and prosperous—life is sweet in Italy's wealthiest city. Famous for its rose-marble cathedral and baptistery, it's best known for two of Italy's top foods: Parma ham and parmesan. Romanesque splendour inside and out, the baptistery has a

beautiful ribbon frieze of animals and birds, while the cathedral is dominated by its 3D Renaissance painted ceiling vaults featuring floating saints on fluffy clouds. A short stroll away is the beautiful Piazza Garibaldi and the yellow Palazzo del Governatore, complete with its fine clock and sundials. Elegant shops, bars and restaurants are plentiful. Parma is also known for its musical heritage. The Teatro Regio, one of Italy's finest opera houses, attracts a discerning public; Toscanini was born here and Paganini is buried in the town's Villetta cemetery (many thought his genius was the devil's work and he was refused burial elsewhere). And at nearby Busseto visitors can visit the home of the great Giuseppe Verdi.

A jewel of the Renaissance is the Camera di San Paolo by Coreggio, commissioned by an enlightened abbess for her convent near the Cathedral. Her chosen theme was the conquest of moral virtue: she is portrayed in the robes of Diana. All around her is codified imagery, impossible to decipher, but beautiful to look at.

modena: sweet and sour

Hometown of the late Luciano Pavarotti, home to Maserati, Ferrari, balsamic vinegar and the world's second biggest military tattoo, Modena also plays host to several contemporary arts festivals. The town centres around the beautiful Romanesque Duomo di San Geminiano, completed in the 13th century, with its fine reliefs of mythological creatures and allegories. Look out for the fork-tailed siren and the hermaphrodite. Next door is the leaning Torre della Ghirlandina. Ruled over by the D'Este family, who transferred here from Ferrara in the 16th century, the Galleria Estense houses an impressive art collection, with works by Tintoretto, Bernini, Velazquez, Guido Reni and the Carraccis. A decidedly more modern art form can be seen at the Galleria Ferrari, to the south of the city, founded in 1945 and filled with glorious vintage cars and memorabilia. One of metaphysical architect Aldo Rossi's seminal works is also here: the Cemetery of San Cataldo (1971). Conceived as a city of the dead, Rossi designed his extension as the collective memory of its people.

THIS PAGE (FROM TOP): Barrels of balsamic vinegar for decanting; a much loved member of the Modenese community, world-famous tenor Luciano Pavarotti, who died in September 2007.

OPPOSITE: Parma's octagonal baptistery built in 1196 and designed by Benedetto Antelami. A masterpiece of restrained beauty, its impressive size was necessary to house the queues of people attending the baptisms.

high art and high drama

Everyone cycles in Ferrara, a beautiful ochre town with crenellated walls, a moat and castle and a divine cathedral. Casanova and Verdi came here to make mischief with the ladies, and the ruling D'Este family were no better. During their long period of rule, they were known for their enlightened patronage of the arts and their villainous debauchery.

As well as the castle there is the beautiful Palazzo Schifanoia, a summer retreat for the family, featuring beautiful murals depicting scenes of the months. The Renaissance Palazzo dei Diamanti, covered with diamond motifs (the D'Este emblem), now houses an important modern art gallery (previous exhibitions have included Rasuchenberg, Derain, Corot and the Symbolists), as well as two other museums containing both Renaissance art and local work. The Palazzo Massari has three more museums. The Museo Michelangelo Antonioni is a multimedia temple to the late influential director.

beach meets kitsch

Not just a beach resort, Rimini was also the hometown of the late great film-maker Federico Fellini. While countless northern Europeans and Italians spend their summers here, it also has a stylish edge to it with exclusive clubs and restaurants away from the hoi polloi. The quintessential 1960s holiday romances were filmed here, with scenes of saucy Swedish bombshells falling for the unlikely balding Italian with a good sense of humour. Away from the beach, the charming old Roman town has pretty streets with a lively nightlife.

In a place renowned for summer transgressions, the city's cathedral is suitably named after one of history's least godly aristocrats, Sigismondo Malatesta, a tyrant given a canonisation to hell by Pope Pius in 1462. His hunchback son, Giovanni, was awarded a place in Dante's *Inferno* after he killed his wife and younger brother, having discovered them in flagrante. Renaissance pioneer Leon Battista Alberti converted the gothic church for the Malatestas—it's a curious mix of Paganism and Christianity. A short drive inland is San Marino, a cross between Vulgaria and Ruritania. Other medieval villages are close by—San Leo and Montegridolfo are veritable gems.

Other medieval villages are close by—San Leo and Montegridolfo are veritable gems.

bauer il palazzo

When the visionary hotelier Francesca Bortolotto inherited the renowned 18th-century Bauer Hotel on the Grand Canal—just steps away from St. Mark's Square—she decided to create a collection of quintessentially Venetian hotels of unparalleled luxury and elegance. And this is exactly what she did, promptly dividing the original hotel into the historic Bauer Il Palazzo and the more contemporary Bauer Hotel, the building at the back which was created during the 1940s

In addition, Bortolotto used her unerring eye to acquire and renovate several new buildings. At the 16th-century Bauer Casa Nova, guests are able to rent self-catering apartments, while still enjoying the exceptional amenities offered by the neighbouring Bauer Hotels. At the Palazzo Mocenigo, a Gothic palace also close to the city centre, Bortolotto has created a supremely luxurious five-bedroom villa. Last, but certainly not least, comes the gorgeous Bauer Palladio Hotel & Spa located across the Grand Canal on Guidecca Island.

THIS PAGE (FROM TOP): The elegant Royal Suite with its classic Venetian-style furnishings; jacuzzi with a view of the city's architectural splendour.

OPPOSITE (FROM TOP): The foyer's antique furnishings add to Bauer Il Palazzo's opulent charm; with a lavish décor that includes a Murano glass chandelier, the living room embodies sophistication and luxury.

Perhaps the jewel in the crown of this illustrious family is the Bauer Il Palazzo. Ranked by *Travel & Leisure* magazine as the city's best hotel in 2007, the Bauer Il Palazzo is truly palatial in every sense, as the lobby's elaborate marble floors, Murano chandeliers, intricately carved wooden panels and stucco ceilings attest. However, this is only a foretaste of the magical experience to come.

The individually designed rooms and suites feature sumptuous, Venetian tapestry fabrics, with matching wallpaper alongside original artworks and antiques creating an exquisite air that is both intimate and opulent. Given that most of the accommodation comes with a terrace or balcony, guests will never be far from the breathtaking vistas of the city.

While at first glance it may appear that little has changed at the Bauer Il Palazzo since the 1800s, nothing could be further from the truth. Following a 50 million-dollar refurbishment, the hotel now comes with first-class amenities and services including a state-of-the-art gym and

spa. There is also a rooftop jacuzzi that has become a favourite spot to unwind and watch the sun go down over Venice and the lagoon. As if this was not enough, guests with an adventurous spirit can choose to enjoy a round of golf, horse riding or water sports on the nearby resort island of Lido.

Cuisine at the Bauer Il Palazzo is as memorable as the hotel itself. At the award-winning De Pisis, guests have the option of dining in the gracefully appointed interior or on the irresistible terrace, under its signature red awning. Suffice to say that the experience of a four-course meal at the water's edge and overlooking some of the greatest splendours of Venice is simply beyond compare. With all the Bauer Hotels excelling in every aspect of the hospitality they provide, there remains only one problem—prospective guests are literally spoilt for choice.

ROOMS
82

FOOD
Settimo Cielo lounge: breakfast •
De Pisis: Mediterranean and
international

DRINK
B-Bar cocktail lounge • Bar Canale

FEATURES
CD player (some suites) • wi-fi •
satellite TV • wellness centre •
hair & beauty salon • jacuzzi on
rooftop terrace • multilingual staff •
babysitter on request

BUSINESS
business and secretarial
services • banquets

NEARBY
St. Mark's Square • museums •
shopping • Lido Island: water
sports, tennis courts, horse riding,
18-hole golf course

CONTACT
San Marco 1413/d, 30124 Venice •
telephone: +39.041.520 7022 •
facsimile: +39.041.520 7557 •
email: marketing@bauervenezia.com •
website: www.bauerhotels.com

bauer palladio hotel + spa

...elegant and characterised by vast, vaulted ceilings...

THIS PAGE: *The Junior Suite's exquisite tapestries go hand in hand with its rustic décor.*

OPPOSITE (FROM TOP): *Part of Bauer Palladio's appeal lies in its tranquil location; the hotel's picturesque setting on the island of Giudecca; soft colour tones and a warm ambience make the spacious hall the ideal place to relax.*

The recently opened Bauer Palladio Hotel & Spa forms part of the celebrated family of Venetian hotels owned by Francesca Bortolotto. Like its sister hotels, the Bauer Il Palazzo, Bauer Hotel, Palazzo Mocenigo and Bauer Casa Nova, the Bauer Palladio once again reveals Bortolotto's talent for renovating buildings in a manner that revives the atmosphere of the ancient city.

Originally designed as a monastery by the legendary Renaissance architect Andrea Palladio in the 16th century, the Bauer Palladio stands at the water's edge on the quiet island of Giudecca. Slightly off the beaten track, this irresistible hotel offers a secluded alternative to those in the city centre; yet, with its own private launch, guests can be in St. Mark's square in a matter of minutes. The fact that guests can also share the facilities of the other Bauer Hotels increases its attraction.

If much of the success of the Bauer Hotels can be attributed to Bortolotto's ability to create interiors that are both sublime and true to the building's original purpose, then the Palladio's public areas are a supreme case in point. Sober yet elegant and characterised by vast, vaulted

ceilings shrouding heavy, wooden furnishings and rich oriental rugs, they truly capture the essence of the historic edifice. Equally impressive are the light, spacious bedrooms that offer breathtaking lagoon, garden or city views. Beautifully decorated with tapestries, hand-painted wall designs and original antiques, they provide the perfect sanctuary after a hectic day spent jostling in the city's crowded streets. And what better way to revive than to soak in a deep, Italian marble bathtub, soothed by the aromas of boutique toiletries, in anticipation of an evening out.

Unusually for a Venetian hotel, the Palladio has an extensive, impeccably landscaped garden. In fine weather, guests can sit out here under stylish sunshades and enjoy a delectable breakfast before setting out to discover the treasures of the world's most romantic city.

Last but not least comes the newly-opened Palladio's Spa. In a city as busy as Venice, guests will relish the opportunity to unwind in what will be a world-class facility in every sense. In a masterfully adapted area of the ancient building, an impressive array of body treatments, relaxing massages and beauty therapies will be available, each one using the exclusive, herbal-based Care Suite products of Daniela Steiner.

The Bauer Palladio Hotel & Spa and the rest of the Bortolotto hotels are rapidly becoming legends in their own right and for good reason. Housed in such magnificent buildings, complete with ideal locations and offering outstanding service, guests will want to experience each and every one of them.

ROOMS
50

FOOD
Garden Restaurant: Mediterranean

DRINK
Garden Bar

FEATURES
Daniela Steiner SPA • wi-fi • B-Mare solar boat rides to and from other Bauer Hotels • multilingual staff • satellite TV • babysitter on request

NEARBY
Venice city centre • shopping district • St. Mark's Square • Lido Island: water sports, tennis courts, horse riding, 18-hole golf course

CONTACT
Giudecca 33, 30133 Venice • telephone: +39.041.520 7022 • facsimile: +39.041.520 7557 • email:marketing@bauervenezia.com • website: www.bauerhotels.com

ca maria adele

Smart, sexy, sophisticated and incredibly romantic...

THIS PAGE: *The Lounge Living Room captivates with an exotic décor, including Moresque furnishings and a welcoming fireplace.*

OPPOSITE (ANTI-CLOCKWISE FROM TOP): *Ca Maria Adele's appeal lies in its opulent Venetian style; with a stunning chandelier and rich tapestries, the Doge's Room is the epitome of luxury; relax and enjoy a drink in the warm ambience of the Moroccan-inspired Terrace.*

If there is a single overriding factor that draws travellers to the wonderful city of Venice, it is the incredible sense of romance the city engenders. Whether one seeks to ignite the flames of a newly formed relationship, or to rekindle those of a more established one, there can be few better places to visit than this, arguably the most romantic city on earth. For this reason it's crucial to choose a hotel in keeping with the rest of the city—a hotel that doesn't clash with the romantic environment but rather adds to the experience of being there. Attributes such as intimacy assume a new and vital importance not normally required of hotels in other destinations; so too do attributes like comfort and the highest standards of personalised service. Not taking them into account means there's a fair chance that the holiday will fail to live up to expectations.

Only a handful of Venice's hotels meet all of these criteria, and the Ca Maria Adele is one of them. Once a historic 16th-century palazzo, it has recently been completely remodelled to combine the most attractive elements of traditional Venetian hospitality with the more practical

amenities of the finest modern hotel. The result succeeds where many others have failed, creating a miniature wonderland of unadulterated romance. This can't be more evident than in Ca Maria Adele's inspiring façade and its equally stunning interior.

Located in one of the city's most prestigious neighbourhoods, overlooking the main canal and the glorious church of Santa Maria della Salute, the Ca Maria Adele occupies a position second to none. Almost all of the main tourist attractions are within easy walking distance, and a private landing stage means that those lying further afield can be easily reached by gondola or speedboat. And if the setting is exceptional, then so too is the décor, where typical Venetian fixtures, Murano chandeliers and lavish damask tapestries blend effortlessly with more exotic furnishings such as wooden furniture from Africa, Oriental silks and Moorish lamps.

The sense of opulence and the passion for detail also extend to the 12 individually styled rooms and two suites, one of which even comes with its own jacuzzi. Five of these have been artfully decorated to reflect themes from Venetian history, so that the Doge's Room is draped in

deep red brocades while the Oriental Room is inspired by the travels of Marco Polo. Many enjoy sublime views of the surrounding city and all come with en suite bathrooms, plasma TV sets, CD and DVD players, and wi-fi connection.

Smart, sexy, sophisticated and incredibly romantic, the Ca Maria Adele is everything that a five-star Venetian hotel should be, and the fact that it doesn't have a restaurant of its own is probably a blessing in disguise, for it means that guests will, from time to time, have the perfect excuse to leave the luxury of their surroundings and explore the intriguing city itself.

ROOMS
12

FOOD
breakfast: American à la carte

DRINK
Terrace

FEATURES
plasma TV • CD and DVD players • wi-fi • soundproof rooms • terrace • safe • Lounge Living Room

NEARBY
Santa Maria della Salute Church • Guggenheim Collection • Accademia Gallery • St. Mark's Square • Doge's Palace

CONTACT
Rio Terà dei Catecumeni 111, 30123 Dorsoduro Venice • telephone: +39.041.520 3078 • facsimile: +39.041.528 9013 • email: info@camariaadele.it • website: www.camariaadele.it

ca'pisani

...experience Venice with a modern twist...

THIS PAGE: Decorated with Art Deco furnishings, the spacious guestrooms provide comfort with creative style.

OPPOSITE (ANTI-COCKWISE FROM TOP): Ca'Pisani's eclectic décor is evident in its reception, which combines exquisite furniture with contemporary design; guestrooms are equipped with the latest technology for an even more comfortable stay; the hotel's avant-garde interior.

There is no denying the fact that most hotels in Venice opt for reviving the historic atmosphere of the gothic palaces that house them. Baroque interiors laden with chandeliers, tapestry wallpaper and rich brocaded drapes predominate, leaving no alternatives for those looking for accommodation that is a little more upbeat, a little more sleek and altogether less traditional. No alternatives, that is, until Ca'Pisani opened its doors as the first design hotel in Venice.

Slightly removed from the hustle and bustle of the downtown area, yet well located for two vaporetto stops and within 15 minutes walking distance of St. Mark's Square, this extraordinary hotel is housed in a 16th-century palazzo. The virtually untouched antique façade belies the seductively eclectic interior, which mixes the minimalist influences of 1920s futurist graphic artists with the cool sophistication of original Art Deco furniture. And true to its claim to being a design hotel, there is not one single detail or accessory in Ca'Pisani that was not painstakingly crafted for its aesthetic impact.

Guestrooms are sleek and luxurious in every sense, while maintaining a slightly offbeat and innovative quality. Divine original beds from the 1930s and 1940s bedecked in real linen sheets undoubtedly form the centrepiece of each of the spacious rooms and are perfectly complemented by polished wooden floors strewn with retro zebra-skin rugs. Quirky metallic desks are offset by snug leather armchairs, while subtle lighting and beamed ceilings or exposed rafters make rooms cosy and inviting.

To ensure that guests really do relax on returning from a day's sightseeing, rooms are kitted out with state-of-the-art technology that allows guests to control the stereo system as well as adjust the window blinds from the comfort of their beds. As for the bathrooms, the multi-jet showers, huge jacuzzi tubs alone make a stay at Ca'Pisani worthwhile. During the summer months, sun lovers can enjoy the rooftop solarium terrace with its stunning views over Venice, while visitors in the cold winter season will welcome the prospect of a steaming Turkish bath in the evening.

Just as Ca'Pisani offers a refreshing alternative to the rest of Venice's hotels, so does its small and highly stylised restaurant. Oozing character, La Rivista is a popular haunt for hip Venetians who frequent it as much for its outstanding cuisine as for its exceptional design. Descending a dazzling futurist-inspired staircase, guests will find themselves amid an eclectic ensemble of valuable 1930s artwork, alongside metallic hat racks and red leather sofas. Yet it is perhaps the original 1940s bar that was salvaged from a demolition that will really catch the eye. The restaurant offers creative seasonal menus, together with a big selection of wines—also by the glass—and Italian cheeses.

To experience Venice with a modern twist, in a hotel where customer satisfaction has been perfected, and with a secluded location away from the frenetic pace of the city centre, Ca'Pisani is too good to miss.

ROOMS
29

FOOD
La Rivista: Venetian with modern twist

DRINK
La Rivista • wine list

FEATURES
wireless Internet access • satellite TV • jacuzzi • Turkish bath • rooftop solarium

NEARBY
city centre • vaporetto stop • Accademia bridge • Peggy Guggenheim Collection

CONTACT
Dorsoduro 979/a, 30123 Venice • telephone: +39.041.240 1411 • facsimile: +39.041.277 1061 • email: info@capisanihotel.it • website: www.capisanihotel.it

charming house dd.724

...avant-garde, cutting-edge and contemporary...

Terms such as 'avant-garde', 'cutting-edge' and 'contemporary' do not immediately spring to mind when one thinks of Venice and all things Venetian. The city is more famous for the past than the present or the future—not least due to the way that time seems to have stopped there, leaving it immune and untouched by the changes experienced by the rest of the world. All that is set to change, however, with the recent opening of an avant-garde, cutting-edge and contemporary little bed and breakfast called Charming House DD.724.

Located at the end of a private cul-de-sac in Dorsoduro, the most prestigious and peaceful part of the city, Charming House DD.724 is the brainchild of owner Chiara Bocchini and designer Mauro Mazzolini. By drawing on their considerable skills, they have been able to completely rethink all of the traditional stereotypes usually associated with the City of Light to create a dramatic and modernistic enclave within it. Here clean lines, neutral tones and recessed lighting have replaced Murano chandeliers, red brocades and scalloped curtains. Modern art by renowned Italian artist Raimondo Galeano—all of it original—decorates the walls instead of Baroque tapestries. Bespoke armchairs upholstered in Frigerio fabrics substitute for the heavy wooden furniture seen in other establishments.

If all of this stripped-down minimalism makes the Charming House DD.724 sound somewhat stark and unwelcoming, nothing could be further from the truth. The hotel more than lives up to its name—it really is charming—and the perfect antidote to the sensual overload that can easily arise after a day spent in the hustle and bustle of this vibrant city. Furthermore, the hotel's small size means there is a sense of that intimacy missing from most other hotels,

enabling the staff to get to know their guests personally, and provide assistance and advice accordingly. Though similar in style, all of the four rooms and three suites have their own unique appeal. One features a small fireplace; another a canopy bed; another exposed beams; and each one has a differing view over the surrounding city. But all have one thing in common—a warm and luxurious feel augmented by a rich array of hi-tech amenities that include high-speed Internet access and the very latest LCD TVs.

The en suite bathrooms, sumptuously equipped with every possible accessory, are another highlight, as is the intimate breakfast area where delicious dishes are individually prepared for each and every guest. Add to this the superb location, just yards from the Accademia and the Peggy Guggenheim Collection and it's not difficult to understand why locals are so excited about the Charming House DD.724.

ROOMS
7

FOOD
breakfast: Italian

DRINK
Lounge Bar

FEATURES
plasma TV • wi-fi • air conditioning

NEARBY
Accademia • Punta della Dogana • Ponte dei Pugni • Palazzo Ducale • Santa Maria della Salute • Peggy Guggenheim Collection • Piazza San Marco

CONTACT
Dorsoduro 724, 30123 Venice • telephone: +39.041.277 0262 • facsimile: +39.041.296 0633 • email: info@dd724.it • website: www.dd724.it

grand hotel baglioni

...elegant columns and a sweeping marble staircase add to the feeling of palatial splendour.

THIS PAGE (FROM TOP): **Furnished with exquisite French antiques and delicate drapery, the Presidential Suite exudes a stylish and opulent charm; unique and intricate ornaments are plentiful in guestrooms.**

OPPOSITE (CLOCKWISE FROM TOP): **Italian cuisine at I Carracci; the lobby's pristine white walls make for a grand entrance; the breathtaking ceiling casts a brilliant aura over I Carracci.**

There are many reasons for visiting the historic city of Bologna in the north of Italy aside from its convenient location between Milan, Florence and Venice. Bologna is home to one of Europe's oldest universities, founded in the 12th century, and houses a myriad of medieval palaces and magnificent churches amid porticoed streets and quaint squares. In addition, the countryside surrounding this bewitching town produces some of Italy's finest wine, balsamic vinegar and white truffles.

The ideal vantage point from which to appreciate Bologna's ancient treasures is the Grand Hotel Baglioni. Located in the heart of the city, this glorious hotel was built in the 18th century as a bishop's seminary and first received paying guests in 1911. After several refurbishments, the latest in the spring of 2007, the Grand Hotel became the luxury retreat that it is today. For nearly a century now, the hotel has kept up with its tradition of providing the best for guests—impeccable service, comfortable stay and warm hospitality.

A magnificent lobby sets the stage for the sublime interiors, where high ceilings, adorned with Murano chandeliers, frame elaborate black and white marble floors. Authentic gilt furniture, elegant columns and a sweeping marble staircase add to the feeling of palatial splendour. Every part of the hotel has a distinctive charm. Its lavish rooms, for example, are reached through expansive corridors lined with draped windows and period works of art. And with soaring ceilings and baroque fireplaces, the rooms themselves are a symphony of comfort and grandeur. Decorated in rich brocades and tapestry wallpapers, exquisitely combined with regal semi-canopied beds and antique furnishings, the hotel is truly the stuff of fairytales.

Car enthusiasts will love the opportunity to visit the Ferrari, Maserati and Lamborghini galleries, which are all located nearby. The culturally inclined will enjoy an afternoon stroll around the picturesque Piazza Maggiore and the church of San Petronio, as well as the two colossal 12th-century towers of Asinelli e Garisenda which define the city's unique skyline. On returning to the Grand Hotel, guests might take a long soak in the jacuzzi, followed by a dazzling dinner at its I Carracci Restaurant. This restaurant is legendary in Bologna and really has to be seen to be believed. With its vast, vaulted ceiling displaying original 15th-century frescoes by the apprentices of the Carracci School, combined with classically elegant table settings, there is no finer place to dine in the city. Bologna is famous for its flavoursome cuisine,

and traditional dishes from the region are prepared by Chef Pasquale Falanga. A well-stocked wine cellar that includes the finest Italian labels provides the perfect accompaniment to any mouth-watering feast.

As part of the illustrious chain of Baglioni Hotels across Europe, the Grand Hotel Baglioni is frequented by dignitaries and celebrities for the simple reason that this hotel is as good as it gets. Hence it comes as no surprise that the hotel has scooped up a slew of awards from the renowned *Condé Nast Traveller* magazine, including a coveted place on its prestigious Top 100 list.

ROOMS
109

FOOD
I Carracci Restaurant: Italian

DRINK
Caffè Baglioni • wine cellar

FEATURES
wireless Internet access • jacuzzi • satellite TV • spa and fitness centre • butler on request • babysitter on request • personal shopper on request

BUSINESS
business centre • conference rooms

NEARBY
Due Torri • Piazza Maggiore • Ferrari gallery • Maserati gallery • Lamborghini gallery • Ducati gallery

CONTACT
Via Indipendenza 8, 40121 Bologna • telephone: +39.051.225 445 • facsimile: +39.051.234 840 • email: reservations.ghbbologna@ baglionihotels.com • website: www.baglionihotels.com

hotel gritti palace

...the very quintessence of classical Venetian luxury...

Opulent yet intimate, Hotel Gritti Palace sweeps the board when it comes to delivering star-quality Venetian style. The 16th-century residence of Doge Andrea Gritti, duke of Venice, this sumptuous Starwood property has represented the very quintessence of classical Venetian luxury for decades in this most magical of destinations.

According to travel experts Frommer, 'everyone who is anyone has stayed here over the centuries', the guest list including illustrious names such as Greta Garbo, Winston Churchill and Ernest Hemingway. Noted for its attentive service and superb location, the hotel was recently rated one of Europe's Top 50 Hotels by *Travel and Leisure* Magazine, and was placed in *Condé Nast Traveller*'s 'Top 75 Resorts in Europe' and its Gold List Reserve.

Venice is a vibrant, open-air museum, and this legendary palazzo is a microcosm of this. It boasts antique-laden lounges and suites, impressive artwork, intricately woven rugs and a hand-painted grand piano. Its 91 rooms feature gilt-trimmed mirrors and inlaid antique furnishings, with dressers painted in the 18th-century Venetian style. For a genuine glimpse into Venice's grand past, the tall windows are adorned with tented curtains and the veiled nooks contain authentic box-sprung beds. Modern conveniences have not been overlooked, with high-speed Internet access and a vast movie selection available in each air-conditioned room.

With a privileged setting overlooking the Grand Canal, the hotel's premier suites boast ancient stone balconies and high ceilings from which impressive chandeliers hang. Cutting-edge Bang & Olufsen personal entertainment systems are juxtaposed against a backdrop of elaborate mirrors and precious 17th- and 18th-century furnishings. Another welcome innovation is the hotel's trademark Luxury Bed, designed to ensure a perfect night's sleep.

The Hemingway Suite is the hotel's pièce de résistance. With floor-to-ceiling windows overlooking the Grand Canal, it blends creature comforts with lavish décor to offer over 80 sq m (86 sq ft) of exclusive Venetian luxury, decorated in the stunning colours of ivory and green.

THIS PAGE (FROM TOP): Enjoy a meal on the terrace that overlooks the magnificent Grand Canal; the showpiece Hemingway Suite embodies the lavish style of Hotel Gritti Palace.

OPPOSITE (FROM TOP): Elegance and luxury aside, guestrooms are also known for providing the best of modern comforts; the hotel's opulent charm has attracted many famous personalities over the years.

The Club del Doge is the hotel's elegant marble and wood-beamed restaurant, designed to cater for up to 60 guests with mouth-watering displays of Mediterranean and Venetian cuisine. In summer, diners spill out onto the Bellavista terrace to observe and enjoy the everyday life of this fascinating island. With paintings on the ceiling, atmospheric wall lamps and soothing piano music, it is easy to see why the Club del Doge is a focal point for international high society. The view is nothing short of a Canaletto landscape brought to life.

The hotel's bar is named after the 18th-century painter whose work adorns its walls—Pietro Longhi. Murano glass appliqués and a carved marble bar are in keeping with the refined atmosphere. Intimate, friendly and elegant, Bar Longhi is the ultimate place to recover from an exhilarating boat trip around the city's intricate canals. There is also an exclusive boat service to sister hotels The Westin Excelsior, Venice Lido Resort, and the Hotel Des Bains, Venice Lido Resort, for access to a private beach, pools and tennis courts. When in Venice, for physical, as well as cultural stimulation, look no further than the Hotel Gritti Palace.

ROOMS
91

FOOD
Club del Doge: Venetian and Mediterranean

DRINK
Bar Longhi

FEATURES
in-room movie library • high-speed Internet access • Luxury Bed • electronic safe • laundry and pressing service • in-room massage • theatre ticket reservations

BUSINESS
meeting rooms

NEARBY
Marco Polo International Airport

CONTACT
Campo Santa Maria del Giglio, 2467 Venice •
telephone: +39.041.794 611•
facsimile: +39.041.520 0942 • email: grittipalace@luxurycollection.com • website: www.luxurycollection.com/grittipalace

hotel monaco + grand canal

...a refreshing blend of old world charm with an ultra-modern atmosphere.

Touted as the most romantic city in the world, Venice has the added virtue of being unique in just about every other way imaginable. Boasting canals instead of streets, and vaporettos—water buses or water taxis—instead of the usual road transport, perhaps its greatest charm lies in its outward appearance that has remained unchanged for centuries. Each of its magnificent buildings is steeped in a world of history, and the Hotel Monaco & Grand Canal, whose origins date back more than 300 years, is no exception.

Before assuming its current identity as a luxury boutique hotel, the original Gothic palace which occupied the premises was, for 130 years, the city's most notorious gaming house frequented by none other than Casanova himself. Later transformed into a Rococo theatre, the Hotel Monaco still retains vestiges of its grandiose past which makes for stunning interiors.

The foyer is a breathtaking 17th-century salon complete with intricately crafted mouldings, elaborate Ionic columns and a second-floor balustrade, all under an exquisite hand-painted ceiling. In fitting contrast, following a substantial renovation in 2003, some elements of the hotel are cutting-edge contemporary, creating a refreshing blend of old world charm with an ultra-modern atmosphere.

Rooms are slightly more sober than the foyer, but no less impressive. With panoramic views over the Grand Canal to the island of San Giorgio and the quintessentially Venetian landmark, the Church of Santa Maria della Salute, guests will be bowled over. Classically elegant furnishings, in warm beiges and rich creams, combine with antiques and Murano glass details to create a charming retreat.

Those looking for something a little more intimate might consider the Palazzo del Selvadego. A short distance from the hotel, this stylish, 34-room annex has a modern design with a cosy Italian country feel, which is reflected in the beamed ceilings, four-poster

THIS PAGE (FROM TOP): Facing gondolas and the magnificent dome of the church of Santa Maria della Salute, a different dining experience awaits guests on the chandelier-lit terrace of the Grand Canal Restaurant; the hotel's stylish interior.

OPPOSITE (FROM TOP): The Ridotto Ballroom is ideal for a gala dinner or any special event; the Ridotto exudes exquisite style; the hotel's charming façade.

ROOMS
134

FOOD
Grand Canal Restaurant: Venetian

DRINK
Bar Hotel Monaco & Grand Canal

FEATURES
restaurant on terrace with
waterfront views

BUSINESS
conference room • meeting rooms

NEARBY
Venice city centre • St. Mark's Square

CONTACT
San Marco 1332, 30124 Venice •
telephone: +39.041.520 0211 •
facsimile: +39.041.520 0501 •
email: mailbox@hotelmonaco.it •
website: www.hotelmonaco.it

beds and polished wooden floors. Like the Hotel Monaco itself, the Palazzo del Selvadego is a stone's throw from the glorious Piazza San Marco—or St. Mark's Square—and some of the city centre's must-see boutiques.

Probably one of the finest and most memorable places in the world to dine in is on a terrace overlooking the Grand Canal. The Grand Canal Restaurant at the Hotel Monaco will certainly live up to anyone's expectations of what a spectacular dinner in Venice should be.

Situated right on the water's edge, before the gondola moorings, this elegant, open-air restaurant commands some of the best views in the city. Such an excellent ambience is complemented by impeccable service, and matched only by its superb cuisine. Its Venetian menu will impress even the most demanding culinary aficionado with its offerings of local specialities that comprise only the freshest seafood and vegetables. Relish the Salmon and Sword Fish Tartare with Lemon and Basil, followed by homemade Pumpkin Gnocchi with Sage and Smoked Country Cheese. End the memorable evening sipping a Bellini cocktail at the chic Bar Hotel Monaco & Grand Canal, and wish for a longer stay.

hotel villa del quar

Furnished throughout with antiques, neoclassical furniture and original works of art...

When Relais & Chateaux first pioneered the idea of the privately owned, luxury hotel concept some forty years ago, they can hardly have imagined the success that it was to become. Today, the brand represents almost 500 such places on all of the five major continents. Despite this dramatic rate of expansion, however, there have always been certain hotels that stand out from the crowd, and the Hotel Villa del Quar—the beautiful creation of the Montresor-Acampora family—is one of them.

Occupying an artfully reconstructed 16th-century Venetian villa that was recently declared a National Monument by the Italian government, the hotel sits within the magnificent rolling countryside of Valpolicella—an area famous for the wine of the same name—a couple of miles north of the romantic city of Verona and close to the renowned tourist attraction of Lake Garda, as well as other gorgeous towns like Vicenza and Mantua. But as every aficionado of Relais & Chateaux knows, a beautiful building and magnificent setting are not enough to justify inclusion in their portfolio. Only those hotels that offer the highest standards of hospitality, cuisine and services are accepted, and in this regard the Villa del Quar leaves nothing to be desired.

Two words immediately spring to mind on arrival at this quintessentially Italian villa resort —elegance and excellence. These two elements seem to permeate every aspect of the Villa del Quar experience, right up to and including the very air that one breathes. Whether guests are lounging in the library or enjoying a relaxing swim in the outdoor pool, they can't help but feel the all-too-rare sense of exalted satisfaction at having chosen the perfect holiday or business destination.

Furnished throughout with antiques, neoclassical furniture and original works of art that reflect the golds, blues, reds and greens typical of the Venetian tradition, the interior spaces are stately yet comfortable at the same time. In a similar fashion, the 18 spacious rooms and 10 suites all exude a beguiling charm that combines the latest in modern amenities with all the warmth and stylish luxury for which Italy is famous.

THIS PAGE (FROM TOP): Decorated with a Murano chandelier and exquisite paintings, guests can dine in style at the Eurosia; its rustic décor complements the villa's countryside feel perfectly.

OPPOSITE (FROM TOP): Antique furnishings provide guestrooms with an old world charm; natural beauty, peace and tranquillity surround the villa; enjoy fresh air and a relaxing swim in the hotel's outdoor pool.

ROOMS
28

FOOD
Ristorante Arquade •
Gazebo Restaurant

DRINK
Cantina Bar • Tea room • wine cellar

FEATURES
outdoor pool • massage room •
gym • sauna • jogging track •
vineyards • heliport

BUSINESS
meeting room

NEARBY
Verona • Lake Garda •
Mantua • Vicenza

CONTACT
Via Quar 12, 37020
Pedemonte, Verona •
telephone: +39.045.680 0681 •
facsimile: +39.045.680 604 •
email: info@hotelvilladelquar.it •
website: www.hotelvilladelquar.it

And if the accommodation is special, then so too is the dining experience. Only a handful of Relais & Chateaux hotels are ever admitted to the very select circle of Relais Gourmands each year, and the Villa del Quar's restaurant, Arquade, has been a distinguished member of that exclusive club since 2005. Arranged in two beautiful rooms—the Tresor and the Eurosia—it is complemented by one of Italy's most comprehensive wine cellars. The Arquade has also earned two Michelin stars and Three Forks in the Gambero Rosso Guide. For all these reasons it is little wonder that the Villa del Quar continues to stand out from the crowd.

palazzo viviani

...following a twisting road, occasionally up through the cloud-line...

THIS PAGE (FROM TOP): Guestrooms are furnished with exqusite frescoes, highlighting personal style and characteristics; warm colour tones and a fireplace enhance the cosy ambience of the living room.

OPPOSITE (FROM TOP): Guests can look forward to a different vacation in the medieval surroundings of the Palazzo; take a walk in the clouds up to the Castello di Montegridolfo; four-poster beds add a touch of rustic charm and luxury.

For a travel sensation as close to experiencing medieval Italy as possible without having to hurtle back through time, explore Castello di Montegridolfo's Palazzo Viviani. This incredible stone citadel dates back to 1337 and is so intriguing, it should be made a required destination on any serious Italian itinerary.

This enchanting walled village perches precipitously on top of a steep hill in the lush Valconca Valley, high in the green and rolling landscape above the Adriatic. Fellini's hometown of Rimini and the picturesque seaside resort of Cattolica are both within easy reach, ideal for any day-trip plans. Based in Montegridolfo's Borgo Antico (ancient village), the stunning Palazzo Viviani hotel is owned by fêted fashion designer Alberta Ferretti, recent star of *Condé Nast Traveller*'s Italian Fashion Hotels feature. Ferretti's sensitive restoration of Montegridolfo's magnificent stone Palazzo into a luxury boutique hotel demonstrates her eye for aesthetics that has turned her creations into absolute essentials for the well-heeled fashionista.

This well-hidden enclave can be found by following a twisting road, occasionally up through the cloud-line, into Montegridolfo itself via the tall, narrow arch of the town's clock tower. Once within, the panoramic vistas all around are of beautifully manicured gardens and a wider landscape liberally sprinkled with old towers, ancient churches and historical sites.

Palazzo Viviani is located in the centre of this unique medieval village. The main building features eight Renaissance-style suites, each featuring original frescoes and fireplaces. These spacious suites and luxurious lounges are furnished with antiques, dynamic colours, richly coloured drapes and thick, woven rugs. To emphasise their individuality, each suite has earned its own evocative name, from the Balcony Suite to the Fresco and Canopy Suites. There are a further seven double rooms in the romantic Casa del Pittore (Painter's House), housed near the inviting pool within the palace grounds. These rooms have vibrant names that match their personalities as well, translating as the Violet, Rose, Poppy and the Fleur de Lys bedrooms. The newer Borgo Nuovo area is the location of the hotel's comfortable, larger apartments, which were designed to combine sheer comfort with maximum privacy.

Gastronomic opportunity and fine wine pleasure await around every corner in Montegridolfo, where guests get to taste the best of traditional fare in equally rustic surroundings. Ristoro di Palazzo Viviani offers haute cuisine in the fascinating environs of the old wine cellars, while Osteria dell'Accademia serves local dishes on a terrace that overlooks

the sea. For deliciously authentic pizzas and pastas, Grotta dei Gridolfi—judging by the aromas emanating from its wood ovens—is the place which to be; it also offers outdoor dining in the Piazzetta during summer.

Creating the impression of being a tiny village unto itself, Palazzo Viviani and its grounds are an idyllic holiday or wedding venue, with enough bars and cafés in the buzzing piazza to keep guests entertained for days. Though perhaps initially difficult to find, Palazzo Viviani at Castello di Montegridolfo is notoriously difficult to leave.

ROOMS
46

FOOD
Ristoro di Palazzo: seasonal haute cuisine • Osteria dell'Accademia: traditional • Grotta dei Gridolfi: Italian

DRINK
bar

FEATURES
pool • safe • mountain bike rental • car rental • wedding services • doctor on call • excursions and tours

BUSINESS
audio-visual • fax and computing facilities • Borgo Nuovo Meeting Centre

NEARBY
Rimini • Pesaro • Forlì • Ancona

CONTACT
Via Roma 38, 47837 Montegridolfo, Emilia Romagna •
telephone: +39.0541.855 350 •
facsimile: +39.0541.855 340 •
email:montegridolfo@mobygest.it •
website: www.mobygest.it •
www.hotelphilosophy.net

san clemente palace hotel + resort

...reflecting a diverse but quintessentially Venetian selection of styles...

THIS PAGE (FROM TOP): The hotel's opulent charm is evident in the lobby's exquisite décor; antique furnishings in the Executive Suite remind guests of a bygone era; Gli Specchi offers American dynamism in a Venetian setting.
OPPOSITE (FROM TOP): The hotel's impressive 17th-century façade; the hotel's grand staircase maintains this luxurious feel; the Ca' dei Frati restaurant has a superb menu to go with its splendid view of San Marco.

Goethe once famously said that 'Venice can only be compared to itself'. He had a point. There are some things in life that are so unique and special that they have no natural competition. The wonderful city of Venice certainly qualifies, and so too does the city's San Clemente Palace Hotel and Resort, on the beautiful and historic island of the same name.

San Clemente's origins date from the early 12th century when it had a reputation as a place for the 'recovery of the soul and spirit' for those preparing to make their way to the Holy Land. Today, almost 1,000 years later, it has retained and even enhanced this reputation, allowing visitors to relax and recuperate in the most consummate of styles and in an environment as distinct as it is magical.

The reason for its enduring appeal is due in part to the island's superb location. With exquisite views over the Lido, Giudecca and the city of Venice itself, it is both close enough to the city to be easily accessible, yet distant enough to enjoy the seclusion of a private retreat. Originally a magnificent 17th-century monastery, the San Clemente Palace Hotel and Resort recently underwent a massive renovation that skilfully blended the old world atmosphere of its ancient heritage with all the facilities and amenities of a 21st-century luxury hotel.

Then there's the space that this distinguished member of The Leading Hotels of the World enjoys. The island is large enough to benefit from its own 2-hectare (5-acre) centuries-old park but still has room for two tennis courts, a swimming pool, a three-hole executive golf course, and a Beauty & Wellness Centre offering a wide variety of treatments and therapies, and facilities including a steam room, sauna and gym.

If these qualities help the hotel distinguish itself from its Venetian counterparts, then the sheer scale of the place yields another advantage. With no fewer than 200 spacious and elegantly furnished rooms, reflecting a diverse but quintessentially Venetian selection of styles, the hotel can accommodate up to 400 guests at any time. Together with almost 557 sq m (6,000 sq ft) of meeting space, it is perhaps the only logical choice for anyone organising a conference, banquet or meeting in the city.

Though close to Venice and all of its culinary attractions, the hotel also has a selection of its own outstanding restaurants, including the formal Ca' dei Frati, the more casual and very Venetian Le Maschere and last but not least, the outdoor La Laguna and Bar. Add to this the American-style bar of Gli Specchi and the highest standards of professional service, even the many attractions of Venice start to pale by comparison.

ROOMS
200

FOOD
Ca' dei Frati: gourmet Mediterranean • Le Maschere: Venetian • La Laguna: Mediterranean buffet

DRINK
Gli Specchi • Le Conchiglie • La Laguna and Bar

FEATURES
park • pool • tennis courts • three-hole executive golf course • Beauty & Wellness Club

BUSINESS
conference facilities • business centre • secretarial and translation services

NEARBY
Palazzo Ducale • Piazza San Marco • Piazzetta dei Leone • Rialto Bridge

CONTACT
Isola di San Clemente 1, San Marco, 30214 Venice • telephone: +39.041.244 5001 • facsimile: +39.0.41.244 5800 • email: sanclemente@thi.it • website: www.sanclemente.thi.it

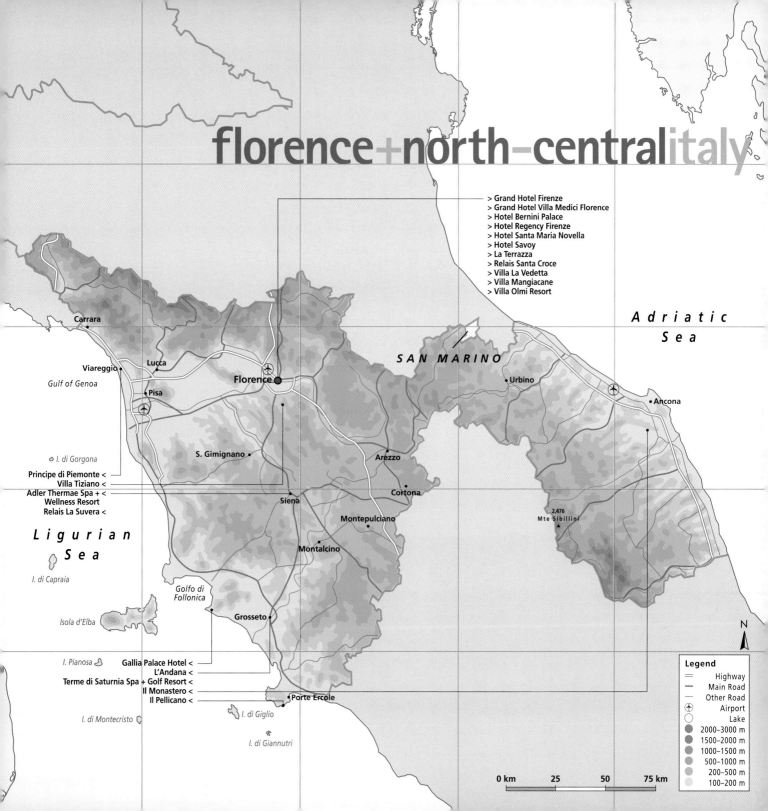

florence+north-centralitaly

> Grand Hotel Firenze
> Grand Hotel Villa Medici Florence
> Hotel Bernini Palace
> Hotel Regency Firenze
> Hotel Santa Maria Novella
> Hotel Savoy
> La Terrazza
> Relais Santa Croce
> Villa La Vedetta
> Villa Mangiacane
> Villa Olmi Resort

Adriatic Sea

SAN MARINO

• Urbino

• Ancona

Carrara

Lucca

Viareggio

Gulf of Genoa

Pisa

Florence

⊚ I. di Gorgona

S. Gimignano

Arezzo

Cortona

Principe di Piemonte <
Villa Tiziano <

Adler Thermae Spa + <
Wellness Resort
Relais La Suvera <

Siena

Montepulciano

2,476
Mte Sibillini

Ligurian Sea

I. di Capraia

Montalcino

Isola d'Elba

Golfo di Follonica

I. Pianosa

Gallia Palace Hotel <
L'Andana <
Terme di Saturnia Spa + Golf Resort <
Il Monastero <
Il Pellicano <

Grosseto

• Porte Ercole

I. di Montecristo

I. di Giglio

I. di Giannutri

N

Legend

═	Highway
──	Main Road
─	Other Road
⊕	Airport
○	Lake
⬤	2000–3000 m
⬤	1500–2000 m
⬤	1000–1500 m
⬤	500–1000 m
⬤	200–500 m
⬤	100–200 m

0 km   25   50   75 km

florence, tuscany + le marche

The birthplace of the Renaissance, Florence offers all that Italy is famed for. For as well as some of the country's best architecture and art, Florence has some of its finest shopping and dining. All around the town are exquisite refuges from the crowds, and the view from the Boboli Gardens is one that will never leave you. Beyond, the treasures of Siena, Lucca and Pisa await, as well as the fine wines and hilltop towns of Montepulciano, Montalcino and San Gimignano. By the coast there's the marble centre of Carrara; the art nouveau cheer of Viareggio, and the exclusive resorts of Elba and the Argentario. Across from Tuscany on the Adriatic coast is Le Marche. Not so well-manicured, people come for the poppy-strewn pastures of the Monte Sibillini or exquisite clifftop walks of the Conero. The gorgeous town of Urbino, home to Raphael, was a major hub during the Renaissance too, leaving behind a wealth of art to savour within its ochre walls.

florence: renaissance brilliance + fabulous shoes

Florence is an exquisite time warp and, as with the rest of Tuscany, modern architecture is rarer than a badly-dressed Florentine. The birthplace of the Renaissance no less, it could be argued that the city has rested on its laurels ever since. But what it may lack in drive and forward-thinking, Florence more than compensates for in beauty, style and sheer charisma. But it's no secret. And unfortunately, given its small, if perfectly formed proportions, it may seem that the whole world has descended on the city. Luckily, enclaves of tranquillity do exist.

Florence became a self-governing commune in 1115. As one of the leading Guelph (pro-pope) cities, she had no shortage of enemies. The start of medieval Florence's rise to ascendancy is one of battles and power struggles, mostly with Pisa, Siena and Pistoia. The Florentines themselves divided between the Blacks and the Whites (two opposing Guelph factions) and, with the addition of a class struggle, the city was a constant battleground—one big bloodbath after another.

PAGE 124: *The Loggia dei Lanzi, an open-air sculpture gallery in the heart of Florence.*

THIS PAGE (FROM TOP): *Loyalist parish flags unfurl in Siena before the hotly contended Palio; a lookout over Florence.*

OPPOSITE: *The Medici stronghold of the Palazzo Vecchio.*

Despite all the turmoil, the city became rich through its wool trade and banking: the gold florin, Europe's first common currency, originated from Florence. With the defeat of Pisa, Florence finally had a seaport and the city-state just got wealthier. The Medici went from being the most successful merchants and bankers, to top dogs in the world of politics. Both Cosimo de'Medici and his grandson Lorenzo were key to Florence's Renaissance—an era marked not just by military might, propaganda and nepotism but also by innovations in the worlds of art, science and humanism. Some of the world's finest ever artists based themselves in Florence, along with the great minds of Galileo, Dante and Machiavelli. Florence's Golden Age was a combination of supreme confidence, wealth and home-grown genius—a serendipity lasting 200 years.

Florence's prime sites are on Piazza del Duomo and Piazza della Signoria, connected by the pedestrian thoroughfare of Via dei Calzaiuoli. The Loggia dei Lanzi on Piazza della Signoria is a sculpture gallery with Cellini's Perseus, Giambologna's

Rape of the Sabines and a bronze of Cosimo de'Medici as well as a copy of Michelangelo's David (the original is in the Accademia). Close by is the Piazza della Repubblica. These squares are the centres of life and good places to sit and observe life. One of the most historic cafés in the city is here—the Giubbe Rosse.

Trying to see too much art is most visitors' downfall in Florence: Stendhal Syndrome, an illness caused by excessive beauty in art, is a real risk for a small minority. The best advice is to take it slow and include lots of shopping. Of the list of must-sees are Florence's chief landmark, the cathedral, featuring Brunelleschi's extraordinarily innovative and impressive dome of cantilevered brickwork. Next door is Giotto's campanile and the Baptistery, a masterpiece of late medievalism. The Palazzo Vecchio on the Piazza Signoria, the Medici's first home and government building, is next door to the Uffizi, once a vast secretariat, now a famous gallery housing the Medici family's private art collection. The bar here has a terrace overlooking the Piazza della Signoria, a view worth queuing for on its own. The Ponte Vecchio is Renaissance Florence's only surviving bridge—the others were blown up by retreating Germans in the war. Underneath is the Corridoio Vassariano, which connects the Uffizi and Palazzo Vecchio with the Palazzo Pitti, the Medici's residence across the Arno, and recently reopened to privileged visitors.

Inside the enormous Pitti Palace are eight museums, including a gallery of modern art. Behind the palace are the Boboli Gardens, offering some respite. The Oltrarno district is much quieter and mellow, and worth coming for is the Santa Maria del Carmine, which houses the Brancaccio Chapel, whose frescoes inspired Leonardo.

Florence's myriad of churches have a gallery of masterpieces: frescoes by Fra Angelico are the highlight of San Marco; Gaddi frescoes, Della Robbia terracotta roundels and a Cimabue crufix in Santa Croce; and a Giotto crucifix and Ghirlandaio frescoes in Santa Maria Novella. To see Donatello and Michelangelo sculptures, head for the Bargello, while more Michelangelo masterpieces are in the Accademia or the Medici Chapels. For fabulous design from more recent times, the world's finest shrine to shoes is at the Museo Salvatore Ferragamo, in the basement of the historic headquarters

in Palazzo Spini Feroni. And there is a handful of fine modern buildings such as the Rationalist station of Santa Maria Novella built in 1933 by local architect, Michelucci. Made in the same stone as the nearby Santa Maria Novella it is full of pioneering design. Nearby is the Palazzina Reale, built for the Royal Family on a visit to Florence in the 1930s—the Pitti Palace was already a museum by then. The stadium Artemio Franchi, home to the legendary football team ACF Fiorentina, is also of great interest. Built in 1931 by Pier Luigi Nervi, it was way ahead of its time when inaugurated. The stadium forms a giant D-shape, recalling the initial letter of Dux or Mussolini, whose influence in 1930s architecture was enormous.

siena: from sublime to saddle sore

Siena gave its name to a colour and the same burnt sienna tones imbue much of the medieval architecture of this spellbinding town. It's also home to one of Italy's finest cathedrals and, in a land of cathedrals, that's a compliment indeed. On the highest part of the city, its beautiful black and white striated marble façade is covered with statuary. The golden Venetian mosaics were an afterthought in the 19th century. Inside, the vaulting is painted a celestial blue and dotted with golden stars. But, it is the floorshow—an acre of inlaid marble pictures—that catches most people's eyes. The stained glass is equally dazzling. Pinturicchio frescoes line the adjacent library, the Biblioteca Piccolomini, while in the Baptistery there's work by Donatello. Opposite, the stylishly converted Complesso Museale Santa Maria della Scala holds frequent exhibitions, mostly modern. In 2007 these included Chagall, Mirò and Emilio Pucci.

In Siena's Piazza del Campo, where the annual and bloodthirsty Palio is held, visitors can get a unique perspective by climbing the Gothic Torre del Mangia, the second highest tower ever built in Italy at 102 m (334 ft). Competing in the Palio are 10 of the 17 contrade or parishes. Much is made of this bareback race—the dirty play, the violent rivalries, the loser's mortification (second place is named the loser, not the other eight places), and the winner's euphoria. It's all over in a minute and the

THIS PAGE: Picturesque farmland around Siena. From poppy-filled pastures and wheat fields to lush vineyards and stark limestone desert, Tuscany's scenery is unforgettable.

OPPOSITE: The raw excitement of Siena's Palio, held each summer on the cobblestoned ellipsis of the beautiful Piazza del Campo.

...burnt sienna tones imbue much of the medieval architecture of this spellbinding town.

winning side receives a silk banner, or palio, as prize and gets to lord it over the other parishes for the rest of the year. Despite the high drama of the Palio, Siena is generally a smart if sleepy little town with fine boutiques, restaurants and enoteche (wine cellars) as well as views to die for.

puccini's lucca

Lucca's Roman origins are given away by its grid-like layout, even though its famous walls and fortifications date from after the violent age of the commune, when the city was a powerful trading post and a big rival of Florence. Nominated for its silk production, and more recently cigars, Lucca remains one of the region's most stylish towns. It is also the birthplace of Giacomo Puccini.

The Cathedral, San Martino, is in the Pisan style, its façade entirely decorated with Romanesque colonnades and statues. The San Michele church in Foro is also rich in Romanesque detail such as corkscrew columns, Cosmati lozenges and wild animal frescoes (both real and fantastical). Via Fillungo—a window shopper's paradise—has fine art nouveau wrought ironwork and plenty of bars to mellow in. If you walk along the grassed ramparts you can peek into the Palazzo Pfanner, famed for its formal gardens filled with statues of gods and goddesses. Or you can go in the normal way via Via degli Asili and admire the villa in its entirety.

high and dry with pisa's twin towers

Pisa was once one of Italy's leading powers as a Maritime Republic. Defeated by Genoa in 1286 at the monumental Battle of Meloria, it lost its port in the 15th century when it literally silted up. The birthplace of Galileo, Fibonacci and physicist Enrico Fermi, Pisa has long been an important university town and remains one of Italy's best to this day. En route for the Campo dei Miracoli, home to Pisa's Leaning Tower, is Giorgio Vasari's beautiful Palazzo della Carovana on the Piazza dei

THIS PAGE: *The shopping hot spot of Lucca's Fillungo Street.*
OPPOSITE: *Reflecting on a glorious past at Pisa's Field of Miracles.*

Cavalieri. The Duomo is magnificent, with a four-tiered façade dating from 1064; the Baptistery was designed a century later by Nicola and Giovanni Pisano. The famous Leaning Tower is soon to have a twin. A new tower of exactly the same height 57 m (187 ft), made of glass and steel, is due for completion in 2008. Designed by Dante Oscar Benini to house offices and apartments, the new tower will create an optical illusion, with lighting to give the impression that it too tilts. Around it will be two lower buildings recalling the Baptistery and Duomo of the original. Facing each other across the Pisa skyline, the intention is to unite the historic Tower with its futuristic Doppelganger.

Near Pisa at Gombo, Romantics can make a pilgrimage to where Shelley's body was washed ashore in 1882 after drowning at sea. His body was cremated on the beach in accordance with his wishes, while Byron, Leigh Hunt and Trelawney looked on.

tuscan idyll

A jewel of a town, Cortona provided the backdrop to the film *Under a Tuscan Sky*. The archetypal idyll, it has a fortress at the top of the town with views over Lake Trasimeno in Umbria and a network of meandering old medieval streets leading to olive groves and vineyards. Art aficionados will enjoy the Museo Diocesano with work by Fra Angelico and Luca Signorelli and the church of San Francesco, where there's an Annunciation by Pietro da Cortona as well as Signorelli's tomb.

Fans of the film *Life is Beautiful* by Roberto Benigni will recognise the little streets of Arezzo as soon as they arrive. The little medieval town is renowned throughout Italy for its monthly antique market, held in the Piazza Grande. Just outside the town is the birthplace of Michelangelo; the town changed its name to Caprese Michelangelo—just Caprese didn't cut it with the tourists. Back in Arezzo there are excellent trattorie and

THIS PAGE: Savour quintessential Tuscany at Montechiello.

OPPOSITE: Twilight over San Gimignano, and its medieval Manhattan cityscape.

shopping opportunities, especially for antiques. Its cathedral has beautiful terracottas and stained glass by 16th-century French master, Guillaume de Marcillat. But it's the church of San Francesco that holds the finest treasure: a complete fresco cycle by Piero della Francesca telling the Legend of the True Cross.

Wine is the biggest draw to Montepulciano. Its vino nobile can be sampled in town but it's nearby Montalcino's top wine, Brunello, that has the edge. The homonymous town is exquisitely pretty; its Enoteca La Fortezza inside a 14th-century Medici fortress is one of the best places to taste the wine. San Gimignano is almost the only town in Italy to have kept its medieval Manhattan aspect. Built by rival noble families, only one of the remaining 12 towers here can still be visited. Of the art on offer in the Museo Civico, Memmo di Filippucci's Wedding Scene frescoes are a highlight. An intimate glimpse into newly weds' lives in the 14th century, it looks like the bride has a bit of a headache.

finding your marbles

Carrara is famous for its marble and throughout history Carrara marble has been sought—the Romans for their masterpieces, Michelangelo and Henry Moore to name a few. London's Marble Arch is Carrara marble, as is the foyer of Chicago's Town Hall. Even today there are almost 100 quarries in use and an annual exhibition attracts architects and artists from around the world. There's also a sculpture academy and dozens of ateliers where you can watch masters at work. Michelangelo opened up his own quarry in rival town Pietrasanta, which is now home to a thriving artists' community. Fernando Botero has a workshop here, as do artists in residence, Kan Yasuda and Igor Mitoraj. Mountainous Lunigiana was once home to a prehistoric people wiped out by the Romans. Dozens of marble stelae (of 2000–1000 BC), many of which look extraordinarily contemporary, have been found in the area, and some are now on show in the Castell del Piagnaro in Pontremoli.

puccini by the lake

The seaside town of Viareggio is well known for its Carnival, art nouveau hotels and pavilions. The Gran Caffè Margherita, by Stilo Liberty architect, Galileo Chini, is one of the town's finest cafés. Popular with Puccini, he spent 30 years at nearby Torre del Lago—a festival is held every summer at his former house on the shores of Massaciuccoli Lake. In 1966 the festival moved to reclaimed land, where the present theatre was built, and today an impressive new theatre is under construction, due to be inaugurated in 2008. Since 2000 the Puccini Festival organisers have collaborated with international artists from Pietrasanta in an exciting project called Sculpting the Opera. Since its inception Ken Yasuda and Arnaldo Pomodoro have created sets for *Madama Butterfly*, Igor Mitoraj for *Manon Lescaut* and *Tosca*, Jean Michel Folon for *La Bohème*, Pietro Cascalla for *Turandot* and Nall for *La Fanciulla del West* and *La Rondine*. The theatre also performs new works. In 2006 Japanese composer Shigeaki Saegusa and librettist Masahiko Shimada had their European premiere of their work *Junior Butterfly* here.

THIS PAGE: Carnival fun at Viareggio, an annual event that started way back in 1873.

OPPOSITE: Urbino's perfect Palazzo Ducale, once the grand residence of Urbino's rulers.

islands of exclusivity

Elba and Giglio, two of Italy's most beautiful islands, are besieged by Florentines in high season. Elba once made its living from mining—iron pyrites, magnetite and hematite—and there are still traces of this around the island as well as untouched beaches with crystalline seas and excellent diving. Napoleon spent just under a year here in exile before he escaped to his Waterloo. Giglio lies opposite the Monte Argentario peninsula, an island itself until the 1700s. Now a lagoon, it is both nature reserve and chi-chi resort. The Terme di Saturnia attracts people all year round. Porto Ercole and Porto Santo Stefano are the two main towns, both bustling ports with a lively passeggiata and low-key glamour. Porto Ercole is where Caravaggio died in 1610; his tomb is believed to be at Sant'Erasmo. Fine beaches here include the dunes at La Feniglia where flamingos breed in wintertime.

natural + renaissance perfection

A tiny region, renowned for its green flower-strewn pastures, secluded beaches, snow-capped mountains and Renaissance art towns, Le Marche was colonised by exiles from the Magna Graecia. Under Federico da Montefeltro, the Duke of Urbino, the region reached its zenith.

Pesaro, once an important Byzantine port, is now a charming resort town with a 3-km (2-mile) beach. Famous in the Renaissance for its ceramics, it is now best known as the birthplace of opera maestro Gioacchino Rossini in 1792. There's a museum and theatre named after him, as well as a festival in August. There's some fine Stilo Liberty architecture along the seafront, such as the Villino Ruggeri designed by Giovanni Brega in 1907.

Urbino, the home of the powerful Duke of Urbino, is not the easiest place to get to. Once there, however, visitors succumb to the ample charms of this redbrick, walled town. The Palazzo Ducale exhibits all the perfection of the

Renaissance; it is also the birthplace of Raphael. Federico da Montefeltro, one-time Duke and occupant of the Palace, was a great patron of the arts and is famous for his library—the second in stature to that of the Vatican. Frederico and his equally enlightened son Guidobaldo, were the inspiration behind Baldassare Castiglione's four-book *Il Cortegiano* (The Book of the Courtier), which for centuries set standards of what characterised the ideal gentleman. In book three he describes the perfect lady. Inside the Palace is the Galleria Nazionale delle Marche: there's just one painting by Rapahel but many other masterpieces on display, including Piero della Francesca's *The Flagellation*. Elsewhere in Urbino, the new university building by Team X architect Giancarlo De Carlo, completed in 1980, is well worth a look. Other work by him is dotted around the campus.

Ancona, Le Marche's capital, saw its peak under the Greeks when it was settled by exiles from Siracusa in 5 BC. As the region's chief port it became wealthy and powerful. The Pinacoteca Comunale Podesti e Galleria d'Arte Moderna houses works by Titian, Guercino, Gentileschi, local 18th-century painter Podesti and a good collection of local contemporary art. Ancona's chief attraction, the limestone coastline of the Conero, lies to the south. Portonovo is a beautiful place for a swim and a bite to eat while the towns of Sirolo and Numana are fairly busy resorts. The best beaches, such as the Sassi Bianchi and Due Sorelle, are only accessible by boat. Of Le Marche's other charms, the 13th-century fortress at San Leo is worth seeking out. Hanging over a precipice, it was praised by Machiavelli and used as a model by Dante for his *Purgatory*.

The breathtaking Monte Sibillini is shared by Umbria and Le Marche: stay at pretty Arquato del Tronto to explore the area. To the south, Ascoli Piceno stands out, with its beautiful Piazza del Popolo, and a fine modern art gallery, the Civica Galeria d'Arte Contemporanea, in the 16th-century Palazzo Malaspina.

Finally, no visitor to Le Marche should miss the pilgrimage town of Loreto, where Mary of Nazareth's house, which was brought from Palestine in 1291 after the Crusades—not carried by a host of angels, as many believe—is said to stand. It's kitsch but Loreto is a pretty town in its own right and particularly moving during pilgrimage times.

...praised by Machiavelli and used as a model by Dante for his Purgatory.

adler thermae spa + wellness resort

...a paradise for relaxation and holistic wellness.

THIS PAGE (FROM TOP): Brightly lit and with a feature pool at the entrance, the buildings shine like a jewel in the night; an open-air thermal pool.

OPPOSITE (FROM TOP): Enjoy Adler Spa's relaxing massages; the renowned healing waters of Bagno Vignoni; the resort offers a range of spa and beauty treatments.

One of the lesser known facts about Tuscany is that beneath its verdant hills and poppy-filled meadows, boiling, thermal waters flow, whose curative powers were enjoyed by the Etruscans and Romans alike in time immemorial. Just some walking distance away from these waters, nestled within one of the most breathtaking countrysides in Tuscany, is the picturesque town of Bagno Vignoni, which boasts a surreal aqua piazza of billowing steam.

With the recent opening of the Adler Thermae Spa and Wellness Resort—which combines the ancient tradition of thermal baths with stunning, modern luxury—a new era has dawned in Bagno Vignoni. At this hotel, the Sanoner family, who have been owners of the Adler Spa Resort in the Dolomites since 1810, has succeeded in creating a paradise for relaxation and holistic wellness.

Although constructed only recently, the Adler Thermae Spa has been carefully designed to blend in with its sublime rural setting. Its contemporary, elegant interiors exude warmth through earthen tones and the use of natural materials such as terracotta tiles, travertine marble and wooden finishings. Bright, spacious rooms with terraces or balconies overlooking the glorious landscape of the Val d'Orcia district are tastefully appointed with all the necessary amenities to ensure absolute comfort.

Water is seemingly ubiquitous here and its recreational and therapeutic qualities are exploited in just about every way imaginable. Lake-sized outdoor thermal and freshwater pools, a 'wild river flume' and a children's fun pool provide but a few of the outdoor water-based activities. Indoors, guests will find a myriad of options for relaxation, including a herbal caldarium, an Etruscan brine steam bath, an olive wood sauna and a subterranean brine bath.

For those seeking the ultimate pampering, the Adler Spa offers a wide array of treatments, and it is no surprise that guests would return for more. The spa covers everything from baths and wraps to massages and physiotherapy, all manner of beauty treatments, and Ayurveda and Oriental applications, to name but a few. There really is no chance of anyone leaving this hotel with any sign of stress.

In order to ensure that all aspects of guests' health are taken into consideration, a doctor with Adler Thermae Spa is available to determine each guest's personal nutritional and physical needs. Exercise enthusiasts will also love the weekly fitness programmes such as yoga, stretching, outdoor trekking, biking and running activities.

Dining is taken very seriously here and healthy menus have never tasted better. The delectable lunch buffet features seasonal produce cleverly crafted into succulent dishes that include Tuscan specialities and antipasti, while romantic evening dinners under the stars are too good to miss. Those with a sweet tooth will welcome the delicious cakes and desserts that are served every afternoon.

Once fully refreshed after an indulgent day at the Adler Thermae Spa, guests can sit on the hotel's panoramic terrace and sip on a premium, locally produced Barrolo wine and contemplate the next day's pleasures.

ROOMS
90

FOOD
Adler: Italian with Tuscan specialities

DRINK
Adler Cocktail Bar

FEATURES
satellite TV • Internet • gym • training circuit • fitness programme • freshwater pool • indoor thermal pool • outdoor thermal pool • children's pool • water flume • kids' club • babysitter on request • doctor's consultation on request

NEARBY
Bagno Vignoni • Pienza • Siena • Montepulciano • Montalcino

CONTACT
1-53027 Bagno Vignoni, Tuscany • telephone: +39.0577.889 000 • facsimile: +39.0577.889 999 • email: toscana@adler-resorts.com • website: www.adler-resorts.com

gallia palace hotel

...masterpiece in modernist architecture with ample spaces and panoramic windows.

THIS PAGE (CLOCKWISE FROM TOP LEFT):
The Gallia Palace Hotel is known for its warm hospitality; suites are spacious and filled with refreshing sea breezes; enjoy Mediterranean fare by the beach at La Pagoda.

OPPOSITE (CLOCKWISE FROM TOP):
Modernity amid rustic charm; horseriding lessons are conducted by qualified coaches; with pedalos, sailboats and canoes easily available, guests can try their hand at a few sea sports at the Gallia Beach Club.

When planning a trip to Tuscany, most people focus on the obvious: a few days in Florence and a visit to Siena and some of the picturesque hill towns surrounding it. Not many take into consideration, however, the glorious Alta Maremma coastline, where rolling, green hills with flowering meadows and elegant pines drop down to pristine, white sandy beaches and the crystal clear azure of the Mediterranean. At only an hour's drive from Siena, it really is surprisingly easy to fit a little sea and sun into any Tuscan holiday. The Maremma coastline is a paradise for outdoor pursuits and is home to numerous medieval towns and Etruscan sites, as well as quaint fishing villages, offering something for all tastes. The focal point of activity in this seaside adventure playground has, since the early 1960s, been the Gallia Palace Hotel.

This gorgeous hotel stands on a magnificent property extending as far as the eye can see, where expansive manicured lawns and colourful Mediterranean gardens, interspersed with majestic trees, captivate guests from the moment of their arrival. Its picture-perfect, private beach is a few minutes walk away on a quiet bay, with only the odd sailboat interrupting the sublime sea view; the ideal place to while away an afternoon, sipping on a cool cocktail and soaking up the Tuscan sun.

For those with a little more energy, conditions along the 7-km (4-mile) beach could not be better for water skiing, sailing and canoeing. And with tennis courts and a swimming pool on the property, not to mention the riding school next door and three golf courses in the vicinity, the Gallia Palace hotel offers no end of possibilities. What's more, guests exhausted from an action-packed day can unwind and relax at the hotel's first-class spa and beauty centre.

The hotel's original buildings are a masterpiece in modernist architecture with ample spaces and panoramic windows. The recently refurbished rooms are luxuriously appointed with a country feel. With light, polished wooden floors and elegant light wood furnishings, they make for a cool retreat from the searing sun. Marble bathrooms reflect the fresh colours of the region in their exquisite tiling, while the boutique toiletries capture its fragrant aromas.

Guests are spoilt for choice when it comes to dining at the Gallia Palace. Those enjoying a lazy day on the beach can savour fresh salads, barbecued seafood and other delicacies at the Pagoda restaurant, while up at the hotel, the elegant La Terrazza offers delectable breakfasts and evening meals al fresco, overlooking the spectacular garden.

There are far too many good reasons to stay at the Gallia Palace Hotel. Take a detour off the beaten track, it is well worth it.

ROOMS
83

FOOD
La Pagoda: Mediterranean •
La Terrazza: Italian

DRINK
Bar & Piano bar

FEATURES
satellite TV • tennis courts • pool •
stationary bicycle • views over bay

NEARBY
Etruscan ruins • Follonica and Toscana courses • Hot springs at Terme di Saturnia • Maremma National Park • Massa Marittima • Punta Ala • Punta Ala yacht club • riding school

CONTACT
58040 Punta Ala, Tuscany •
telephone: +39.056.492 2022 •
facsimile: +39.056.492 0229 •
email: info@galliapalace.it •
website: www.galliapalace.it

grand hotel firenze

...tantamount to stepping back in time to the glory days of the Italian Renaissance.

THIS PAGE (FROM TOP): The Grand Deluxe Florentine's spectacular interior is enhanced by stunning frescoes and lavish tapestries; the Royal Terrace gives a bird's eye view of the Arno River.

OPPOSITE (FROM TOP): Enjoy a drink after a sumptuous Italian meal at InCanto; the ballroom is one impressive setting for any occasion; the luxurious Winter Garden is the perfect venue to hold prestigious events in Florence.

For some people, wandering the streets of Florence for days, marvelling at its limitless reserves of architectural and artistic treasures and breathing the air imbued with centuries of unparalleled cultural achievement is simply not enough. These are the people for whom one visit to Florence could never suffice, and for whom to be able to experience a taste of the city as it was during its golden age would be the realisation of a dream. For these—and other visitors to Florence seeking luxury accommodation of a kind rarely seen—the Grand Hotel is the place to stay.

Located in the heart of the great city, on the banks of the Arno River, this sumptuous 19th-century palazzo, forming part of the Starwood Luxury Collection, has been receiving discerning guests for over 100 years. Indelibly linked to the Renaissance, the building that originally occupied the property 400 years ago was designed by none other than the great Brunelleschi himself, and today's charming neoclassical façade pays tribute to this.

Oozing opulence, with arched colonnades and luxurious, classical furnishings, the magnificent lobby is a spectacle in itself. Its elaborate marble floor design is echoed in the painted glass roof which gives the immense space a cathedral-like grandeur.

Entering the palatial rooms at the Grand Hotel is almost tantamount to stepping back in time to the glory days of the Italian Renaissance. A truly staggering attention to detail makes the interiors utterly authentic in every conceivable way. From the intricately painted coffered roofs, to the wrought iron chairs and chandeliers, and the walls bedecked with exquisite period frescoes, the hotel's décor is one visual feast. The rich velvets and brocades in regal golds, teals and deep reds that adorn armchairs, sofas and the majestic canopied beds will envelop guests in what will be an unforgettable experience.

Needless to say, the timeless charms of these remarkable rooms are complemented with all manner of technology firmly rooted in the 21st century. And with bathrooms as lavishly appointed as the guestrooms, even the most precious of Florence's splendours won't draw guests away from the Grand Hotel all that easily.

Restaurant InCanto at the Grand Hotel, apart from its excellent service, adds a contemporary twist to the classical interior—an open kitchen and stylish, modern leather chairs all combine to create an amenable ambience for diners to relish exceptional Italian cuisine. Over 200 wine labels are carried by the restaurant, which also offers guests the chance to savour them in the atmospheric private wine cellar, InCantinetta.

ROOMS
107

FOOD
Restaurant InCanto: Italian

DRINK
InCanto Bar • InCantinetta: wine cellar • Winter Garden lounge area

FEATURES
DVD and CD player • Bang & Olufsen Beocenter (suites only) • wi-fi (public areas) • high-speed Internet access

BUSINESS
business centre • banqueting rooms • conference rooms

NEARBY
Ponte Vecchio • Uffizi Gallery • town centre

CONTACT
Piazza Ognissanti 1, 50123 Florence • telephone: +39.055.27 161 • facsimile: +39.055.217 400 • email: grandflorence@luxurycollection.com • website: www.luxurycollection.com/grandflorence

grand hotel villa medici florence

...furnishings are draped in regal red and gold silk.

THIS PAGE: The Medici's classic yet stylish décor is a fitting tribute to its illustrious past.

OPPOSITE (FROM TOP): The Penthouse Suite's luxurious jacuzzi; antique furnishings give rooms an exquisite touch; take a swim amid the lush greenery of the garden.

The Medici name is synonymous with power and influence in Florence. Throughout the 13th–17th centuries, art, culture and humanism flourished in Florence under its governance, and the family is credited with the birth of the Italian Renaissance. The five-star Grand Hotel Villa Medici bears its historic name with pride. The central location of this former monastery and sumptuously restored 18th-century palace means the renowned Ponte Vecchio, the Duomo and Florence's prestigious boutiques are all within close proximity.

This elegant property retains many original features such as domed ceilings, proscenium archways and smooth marble columns. The furnishings are draped in regal red and gold silk. Beneath this traditional veneer, the Medici is an ultra-advanced model of efficiency. Classic style meets contemporary technology throughout, its lavish suites featuring multimedia TV, high-speed Internet access and personal voicemail facilities.

The hotel's 100 rooms and suites are of two types. Some follow contemporary design lines, while the majority abound with ornate period pieces, precious silk wall coverings and glamorous velvet curtains and, in some rooms, a romantic roof terrace. The palatial bathrooms are carved from genuine Carrara marble, and boast thoughtful luxuries such as plush bathrobes, slippers and fine toiletries. Many also have deep spa baths.

Ascend to the upper floors of the hotel to discover the premium Penthouse Suites, for spectacular views or a refreshing dip in a private jacuzzi. Covering over 100 sq m (1,080 sq ft), the Royal Suite is the hotel's pièce de résistance, its Royal Hall listed as a cultural treasure. Featuring a private plunge pool and with space large enough to house a private banquet, this is the most sought-after address in downtown Florence.

As Florentine twilight falls, the hotel's Lorenzo de' Medici Restaurant and Conservatory comes into its own. Within its informal yet refined ambience, exquisite cuisine and superb service are the order of the day. Chef Giuseppe del Vecchio's diverse menu fuses traditional flavours with global inspiration. His signature dishes include Tuscan Tomato Soup with Fresh Basil, Calamari Mille Foil and Lucchese Steak. A recent addition, the splendid Conservatory is a cosy corner overlooking the walled garden and pool in which guests may choose to dine.

When culture-fatigue sets in, simply absorb the generous Tuscan sunlight from the inviting open-air pool, amid the hotel's own private walled garden—the only one of its kind in the city centre. Or for more applied physical activity, adrenaline junkies will welcome the well-equipped SINA Fitness Centre, which boasts a state-of-the-art gym and an invigorating Turkish bath that guests can enjoy before disappearing into the hazy mists of the sauna.

For an early evening pick-me-up, visit the contemporary Jockey Bar, which is renowned for its Negroni cocktail—an intriguing blend of Campari, red vermouth and gin created in the 1920s by the Florentine Viscount himself. This exclusive meeting point in the heart of the city is a wonderful point of departure for the first of many memorable Tuscan evenings.

ROOMS
100

FOOD
Lorenzo de' Medici: Tuscan

DRINK
Jockey Bar

FEATURES
satellite TV • Internet • wi-fi •
minibar • safe • in-room massage •
fitness club • banqueting rooms

NEARBY
horseback riding • tennis • golf •
bicycle rental • Ponte Vecchio •
Duomo • Santa Maria Novella Church

CONTACT
Via Il Prato 42, 50123 Florence •
telephone: +39.055.277 171 •
facsimile: +39.055.238 1336 •
email: villa.medici@sinahotels.it •
website: www.villamedicihotel.com

hotel bernini palace

As precious as the city it stands in, the hotel is a masterpiece in elegance and sophistication.

Despite housing the world's finest collection of Renaissance art and architecture scattered through dozens of churches, palaces and museums, most of Florence's landmarks are in a surprisingly compact area. Spanning both sides of the Arno River and bridged by the legendary Ponte Vecchio, the historic centre is eminently manageable on foot, making an incredibly centrally located hotel the key to a successful visit. And if that hotel also happens to be housed in a luxuriously appointed 15th-century palazzo, and the recipient of numerous awards from prestigious travel magazines, then so much the better. Forming part of the celebrated family of Baglioni Hotels, the Hotel Bernini Palace is ideally located in the heart of Florence's historic centre, next to Piazza della Signoria and just two blocks from the sublime treasures of the Uffizi Gallery. Fashion enthusiasts will be pleased to know that the city's most exclusive shopping district, the Via Tornabuoni, is only a short walk away.

Built according to the classic Florentine architectural style, the ancient palazzo is presumed to have been originally owned by descendants of the Peruzzi family, the most powerful financiers in Florence at that time. History surrounds the building. During the late 1800s, it housed the parliament of the fledgling Kingdom of Italy, of which Florence was the capital. Today, guests can have breakfast in what used to be the vast parliament salon, beneath a breathtaking, authentic frescoed ceiling.

As precious as the city it stands in, the hotel is a masterpiece in elegance and sophistication. The recently renovated lobby and bar areas reflect classical Italian style with an exotic North African twist, in recognition of the spice merchants who frequented the city during its golden age. Warm taupe walls contrast with imperial yellow brocades and deep purple velvets of the upholstery, while

shimmering golden urns reflect the subtle lighting to create a truly seductive atmosphere. It is in this unique lounge and bar that guests can sip on a delectable cocktail, or, given its versatile design, order from a tantalising menu boasting national and international specialities.

Exquisitely decorated in pastel colours, with panelled walls, heavy drapes and original antiques, the spacious rooms offer a classic style. For those looking for a genuinely Renaissance experience, the recently renovated guestrooms on the Tuscan Floor are the place to be. Here, terracotta tiled floors in orange hues blend with sumptuous four-poster beds to create a cosy

retreat with a historic feel. Bedecked in rich fabrics in earthen tones, complemented by wooden furnishings and beautifully designed illumination, these alluring hideaways exude warmth and reassurance. Despite such old world quality, guests can rest assured that all rooms in the hotel are equipped with state-of-the-art amenities, providing the best in modern comfort.

With interiors as captivating as the stunning city itself, in addition to the flawless service typical of the Baglioni hotels, the Bernini Palace should be one of the first stops for visitors to Florence.

ROOMS
74

FOOD
Brunello Lounge Bar & Restaurant:
Italian and international

DRINK
Brunello Lounge Bar

FEATURES
high-speed Internet access •
satellite TV • babysitter on request •
shuttle service on request •
personal shopper on request •

BUSINESS
business centre • conference room

NEARBY
Duomo • Piazza della Repubblica •
Piazza della Signoria • Uffizi Gallery •
Via Tornabuoni

CONTACT
Piazza San Firenze 29,
50122 Florence •
telephone: +39.055.288 621 •
facsimile: +39.055.268 272 •
email: reservations.berninifirenze@
baglionihotels.com •
website: www.baglionihotels.com

hotel regency firenze

...refined elegance and the highest standards of hospitality...

When it comes to architecture, history, cuisine and culture, there are few places in the world as blessed as Florence. But if the city is famous for one thing in particular, then it is perhaps its association with art and artists—Leonardo da Vinci and Michelangelo are just two of the notable residents. Bearing this in mind when visiting the city, it should come as no surprise that guests would look forward to staying in a hotel that is itself a living work of art. Such is the charm and attraction of the Hotel Regency, a long-time member of The Leading Hotels of the World. Centrally located on the Piazza D'Azeglio, the magnificent 19th-century villa in which the hotel is housed, once served as a retreat for the government's high officials and ministers of state. While more than a century has passed since those days, little seems to have changed in this.

Today, these ancient walls are still able, quite effortlessly, to summon the gentle demeanour and chivalrous spirit of an era when refined elegance and the highest standards of hospitality were the norm. The Hotel Regency is anything but a museum piece, however. While great care has been taken to retain the character of the past, equal attention has also been paid to creating an environment that is as warm and welcoming as it is modern and luxurious. The 30 rooms and five suites, for example, while sumptuously furnished with soft Tuscan tones, tapestries and Renaissance artworks, all enjoy the kind of modern amenities expected of the finest boutique hotel. Features such as walk-in closets, en suite bathrooms and satellite TV sets naturally come as standard.

Exquisite accommodation is equalled by superb levels of personal service, resulting in an atmosphere that is a serene blend of luxury, intimacy and comfort. This even extends to the public areas, including a private garden that provides an oasis of tranquillity and calm all too rare in the city.

Of course, no hotel of this stature would be complete without a world-class dining experience to match, and the Hotel Regency is no exception. Its restaurant, the award-winning Relais Le Jardin, offers guests the choice of eating in the unique Zodiaco Room that features a grand boiserie. Attracting connoisseurs from far and wide who congregate daily to sample the delicious offerings of Head Chef Rino Pennuci, Relais Le Jardin certainly lives up to its reputation. Like the bar, the restaurant also overlooks and extends to the beautiful private garden.

Under Pennuci's expert guidance, a skilled team of professionals harnesses the passions and flavours for which Tuscany is famous to create culinary masterpieces exceptional even by Florentine standards. Dazzling the eye as much as the palate, dishes here include homemade Italian pastas and regional delicacies, complemented by the excellent range of wines. This is gourmet dining at its very finest, and another of the many reasons why the Hotel Regency is the obvious choice for the discerning traveller wishing to visit the city.

ROOMS
35

FOOD
Relais Le Jardin: Italian

DRINK
Bar Lounge • wine cellar

FEATURES
private garden • multilingual staff • satellite TV • walk-in closets

BUSINESS
wi-fi Internet access

NEARBY
Piazza del Duomo • Ponte Vecchio • Uffizi Gallery • Verdi Theatre • San Marco Museum

CONTACT
Piazza M. D'Azeglio 3, 50121 Florence •
telephone: +39.055.245 247 •
facsimile: +39.055.234 6735 •
email: info@regency-hotel.com •
website: www.regency-hotel.com

hotel santa maria novella

...an atmosphere that is utterly enchanting and full of pleasant surprises.

There's a well-known saying that money can't buy happiness, but those who have been lucky enough to stay at the Hotel Santa Maria Novella in Florence might beg to differ. There's something very special about this wonderful little hotel, something almost magical that many other hotels aspire to but fail to achieve.

No one factor can single-handedly account for this magic, but it can be explained in part by the hotel's address. Located on the piazza of the same name, it is surrounded by a number of the city's foremost cultural and historical landmarks, including the church of Santa Maria Novella. Other attractions such as the Duomo, Ponte Vecchio, Galleria dell'Accademia and the Uffizi Gallery are all within easy walking distance, while some of Italy's finest shopping is to be found just around the corner on Via Tornabuoni, making it the perfect base from which to explore the city's many attractions.

Another factor is surely the building that houses the hotel—actually five separate buildings, all of which interconnect seamlessly to create one stunning whole. Once the hangout of artists and writers from around the world, the hotel has been thoughtfully and painstakingly restored in recent years, with no expense spared and no detail overlooked. Through the inspired use of colour schemes, distinctive potpourris, original artwork and decorations related to the nearby church, this restoration has cleverly succeeded in creating an atmosphere that is utterly enchanting and full of pleasant surprises, so that no matter how often one stays at the hotel, each visit feels like the first.

THIS PAGE (FROM TOP): The entrance, striking in its simplicity; the hotel's neoclassical style is evident in its interior design.

OPPOSITE (FROM TOP): The private terrace of the Suite Bellavista provides a splendid view; a tastefully decorated suite that could easily have been found in a friend's home; enjoy an expresso in the cosy ambience of the hotel.

ROOMS
48

FOOD
Italian light dishes

DRINK
bar

FEATURES
satellite TV • gym • sauna

NEARBY
Basilica Santa Maria Novella • Duomo • Ponte Vecchio • Uffizi Gallery • Galleria dell'Accademia • Via Tornabuoni

CONTACT
Piazza Santa Maria Novella 1, 50123 Florence • telephone: +39.055.271 840 • facsimile: +39.055.2718 4199 • email: info@hotelsantamarianovella.it • website: www.hotelsantamarianovella.it

There are 48 rooms and suites, each individually designed and furnished to create an enjoyable environment that combines stylish comfort with consummate luxury. Many of them have spectacular views of the surrounding city, and all come fully-equipped with satellite TVs, en suite bathrooms and the sort of amenities that one can expect of one of Florence's chicest boutique hotels. Of particular note is the Suite Bellavista on the top floor that has its own 70-sq-m (753-sq-ft) private terrace and comes with breathtaking views of the Duomo and the Campanile di Giotto.

In addition, the hotel has an elegant and fashionable bar, a sauna and gymnasium. It also offers guests some of the best breakfasts to be had in the city, and all of these contribute to the magic of the Hotel Santa Maria Novella. But perhaps what really makes this place stand out from the competition is the quiet and courteous efficiency of the friendly staff, and the sense that one isn't staying in a hotel at all, but sharing a private house with old friends instead. Here, happiness is all but ensured.

hotel savoy

...interiors, while extremely elegant, have a refreshingly contemporary edge.

As cultural cities go, Florence is in a league of its own. With every square inch of the city occupied by magnificent architectural treasures and museums with unparalleled collections of Renaissance art, one would almost need a lifetime to see them all. For those with slightly less time at their disposal and a desire to immerse themselves in the artistic spirit of Florence, the stunning Hotel Savoy is the perfect place to stay.

Ideally located on the quiet Piazza della Repubblica in the heart of the ancient city, the Savoy is so close to Brunelleschi's Duomo and Giotto's bell tower that guests can almost reach out and touch them. Although the Savoy has a long history on the premises, a complete renovation by the Rocco Forte Hotel Collection in 2000 transformed it into one of the city's finest luxury hotels. Enveloped in the antique buildings of the city centre, the Savoy's interiors, while extremely elegant, have a refreshingly contemporary edge. Sleek and modern furnishings combine well with light, parquet floors, while the occasional antique sculpture juxtaposes whimsical works of modern art, splashing colour across the walls. The overall effect of this tastefully eclectic approach to design is truly dazzling.

Maintaining a modern feel, the expansive bedrooms, which are decorated in rich creams and milky whites and bathed in warm sunlight, offer a cosy retreat at the same time. Double-glazed windows ensure a peaceful night's sleep, while data ports, dual-line phones and wireless Internet access provide the ideal

accoutrements for business travellers. After an exhausting day battling the crowds in some of the world's most spectacular museums, enjoy a soak in a deep, marble tub in a sumptuous bathroom that features exquisite Venetian mosaics and boutique toiletries, and unwind.

Fitness enthusiasts will enjoy the rare opportunity to continue sightseeing even while working out at the state-of-the-art gym facility at the Hotel Savoy. Providing the latest equipment, the gym also offers panoramic views over the cathedral and the Uffizi Gallery. With such a beautiful backdrop, it comes as no surprise that guests are more than happy to run that extra mile.

From the time of its creation in the late 1800s, the Savoy has employed some of Florence's most celebrated chefs, a tradition that is upheld to this day. L'Incontro Restaurant and Bar serves an irresistible menu featuring fine Tuscan cuisine, prepared with the freshest ingredients sourced at the city's markets, and varied according to produce in season. With impeccable service, excellent food and ambience, and a setting that overlooks the piazza, it is no wonder L'Incontro remains one of the most popular restaurants in town. Add to this some premium local wines, even the most discerning connoisseur of Italian cuisine could be not be disappointed.

When the Savoy Hotel first opened back in the 19th century, it was hailed as the most modern, luxurious hotel of its time. Today, Rocco Forte's Savoy Hotel has seen history repeat itself.

ROOMS
102

FOOD
L'Incontro Bar and Restaurant: Italian

DRINK
wine list

FEATURES
wireless Internet access • satellite TV • dual-line phones • banqueting facilities • gym • massages available on request •

BUSINESS
business centre • conference facilities

NEARBY
Duomo • Piazza de la Repubblica • historic palazzos

CONTACT
Piazza della Repubblica 7, 50123 Florence •
telephone: +39.055.273 5831 •
facsimile: +39.055.273 5888 •
email: reservations.savoy@ roccofortecollection.com •
website: www.roccofortecollection.com

il monastero

...personifies style, elegance, warmth and history all under one roof.

The region of Marche is a hidden gem situated in the northwestern fringes of Italy, between the Appenine Mountains and Adriatic Coast. The Villa Book's Il Monastero, near the small town of Apecchio and set amid 5 hectares (12 acres) of land, was once a Benedictine monastery. Recently restored to its current luxurious form, this holiday home for up to 12 guests encompasses the best of old and new, from the original stone walls, marble floors and antiques to modern amenities such as Internet access and a home entertainment system.

Caringly restored by the local craftsmen, the structure, comprising 450 sq m (4,843 sq ft) of living space, has become a classy and elegant home with an authentic medieval feel. Visitors can relax in one of three living rooms, each with its own fireplace; the grand salon is also an ideal area for entertaining up to 25 guests. The five bedrooms are just as impressive, each furnished with antiques and a modern en suite marble bathroom. The central heating ensures cosy warmth during the cold winters while the thick ancient stone walls keep the house cool during the hot summers. The large kitchen boasts the latest professional range of equipment and appliances for the cooking enthusiast, though a chef is always available on request if one just wants to sit back, relax and indulge in delectable Italian fare.

There is a barbeque and wood-fired oven in the outdoor dining area, complete with swimming pool (heated on request), where stunning views and fresh air can be enjoyed. Children are also well catered for with a paddling pool and a wide selection of books, toys and DVDs for their entertainment. Those with a passion for the outdoors will find that the fabulous garden is a true oasis, with vines, fruits and herbs planted during the building's monastic period still thriving.

Nearby are mountain bike and hiking trails, as well as skiing on Monte Nerone during the winter. Il Monastero is also a good base from which to explore the medieval towns of Assisi, Urbino, Gubbio and San Marino. Annual events to look forward to include the Rossini Opera Festival in Pesaro, the open-air festival in Macerata and the truffle season.

Situated in a region that is fast becoming a destination of choice for the discerning traveller, the distinctive holiday home of Il Monastero personifies style, elegance, warmth and history all under one roof.

THIS PAGE (FROM TOP): **Take in the mountain views from your seat beside the pool;** a retreat that ensures privacy.
OPPOSITE (CLOCKWISE FROM TOP): A simple, formal bedroom; Il Monastero's living room, decorated with Italian flair; exposed walls add to the feel of the villa's medieval past.

ROOMS
5

FOOD
in-house chef on request

DRINK
wine list

FEATURES
grand salon • pool • paddling pool •
fruit and herb garden • satellite TV •
home entertainment system •
babysitter on request

NEARBY
mountain bike and hiking trails •
skiing • Apecchio • Palazzo Ubaldini •
Galleria Nazionale delle Marche •
Assisi • Perugia • San Marino •
Urbino • Gubbio • Pesaro • Macerata

CONTACT
12 Venetian House, 47 Warrington
Crescent, London W9 1EJ •
telephone: +44.845.500 2000 •
facsimile: +44.845.500 2001 •
email: info@thevillabook.com •
website: www.thevillabook.com

il pellicano

...offers absolute privacy and tranquillity.

In a romantic gesture to celebrate their first meeting at Pelican Point, California, in 1965, British airman Micheal Graham and American socialite Patsy Daszel set out to look for a secluded location for a Tuscan retreat. They found it on a breathtaking stretch of rugged cliffs overlooking the crystal clear emerald waters of the Argentario coast, and it was there that they built their idyllic hideaway, Il Pellicano. Forty years later, Il Pellicano has become one of the most exclusive retreats in Italy and, according to *Condé Nast Traveller*, 'one of the top hotels in the world'—it is easy to see why.

Nestled amid aromatic, ancient olive trees, exotic palms and twisting cypresses, with panoramic views over a private rocky cove to the sea and archipelago beyond, this boutique hotel is the perfect romantic getaway. Comprising a series of sumptuous villas surrounded by exuberant Mediterranean gardens, Il Pellicano offers absolute privacy and tranquillity. And with 105 staff serving 49 rooms, guests can expect faultless service.

The interiors of the hotel are elegant, yet unpretentious, retaining the intimate feel of the original residence. Polished tiled floors, beamed ceilings and comfortable linen sofas alongside black and white photographs dating back to the Graham-Daszel era create a refined atmosphere in the lobby and bar area.

After a sun-drenched afternoon down by the cove, dipping in the heated saltwater pool, or playing a round of golf at the nearby course, the charming, airy rooms and suites make for perfect, cool retreats. Luxurious in an understated way and all uniquely decorated, they reflect the warm hues of the Mediterranean, and with all rooms featuring furnished terraces, the glorious view can be enjoyed from daybreak to sundown.

Guests looking for a thorough workout will not be disappointed by the first-class gym, while those needing a little more help to unwind will be enraptured by the personalised treatments at the Beauty & Spa. Although sufficiently off the beaten track to ensure a relaxing stay, Il Pellicano is

THIS PAGE (FROM LEFT): *The heated saltwater pool with the full view of the sea in the background; enjoy Tuscan cuisine and a stunning sea view at all'Aperto.*
OPPOSITE (FROM TOP): *Rooms provide the best of modern comfort; the bright and spacious hall; Il Pellicano and the unspoilt greenery that surrounds it.*

ROOMS
49

FOOD
Il Pellicano: international •
all'Aperto: Tuscan

DRINK
Il Puttino Baccante: wine cellar •
The Bar

FEATURES
satellite TV • tennis court • spa •
gym • heated saltwater pool •
private motor boat • water skiing •
cooking courses (April to October) •
Internet (main building) • boutique

BUSINESS
meeting room

NEARBY
golf • horse riding • climbing •
hiking • mountain biking • fishing •
Orbetello lagoon • WWF nature
reserve • Giannutri island •
Giglio island • Porto Ercole •
Porto Santo Stefano • Orbetello

CONTACT
Sbarcatello 1, 58018 Porto
Ercole, Tuscany •
telephone: +39.056.485 8111 •
facsimile: +39.056.483 3418 •
email: info@pellicanohotel.com •
website: www.pellicanohotel.com

surrounded by numerous places of interest in the beautiful Maremma countryside. Quaint medieval villages abound, not to mention the neighbouring 17th-century Spanish fortress and the enchanting seaside towns of Porto Ercole and Porto San Stefano.

As for the restaurants, they certainly don't pale in comparison. The Michelin-starred Il Pellicano is perhaps the jewel in the crown of this exquisite hotel, dazzling guests with local and international cuisine of a quality rarely seen. More informal but equally tantalising is the La Terrazza restaurant, serving fresh, barbecued seafood and prime cuts alongside succulent pastas and salads. Wine aficionados, on the other hand, will be left speechless by the more than 1,000 labels available from the Il Puttino Baccante cellar and will enjoy the daily presentations by the hotel sommelier on the best national wines and their production.

For Michael Graham and Patsy Daszel, there was never a doubt that the romantic retreat of Il Pellicano symbolised the depth of their devotion to each other. For the rest of us, it is, quite simply, paradise on earth.

l'andana

...combination of refined luxury, glamour and elegance that satisfies and soothes the senses...

THIS PAGE: Indulge in exquisite spa treatments that utilise the natural goodness of ingredients from the Maremma region.

OPPOSITE (FROM TOP): Bask in the glorious surrounds of L'Andana; be it the guestroom, spa or otherwise, every part of the hotel exudes the same kind of sophistication and rustic charm.

Among the gourmets, the connoisseurs and the cognoscenti, there is little debate about who is the greatest chef in the world. That man is French-born Alain Ducasse, a modern-day version of King Midas who turns everything he touches into culinary gold. In a career that has spanned 25 years, he has become the first hotel chef in history to be awarded three Michelin stars; the first 'six-star' chef; and the only chef ever to earn three stars for three different restaurants in three different countries. Despite his unparalleled success, there has always been a gaping omission in his considerable portfolio of achievements—namely that he's never had the opportunity to marry his incredible talent with Italy and the country's great culinary tradition. All that changed in 2004 when he opened L'Andana spa and hotel in association with the legendary Italian hotelier and wine producer Vittorio Moretti and his family, owners of L'Albereta in Lombardy.

Once the stately hunting lodge of Leopold II, Duke of Tuscany, L'Andana is a 500-hectare (1,236-acre) property perfectly situated just 8 km (5 miles) from the increasingly fashionable Maremma Coast in the Tenuta La Badiola of Tuscany—a stunning landscape of olive groves, woodland and vineyards, and one of Italy's most charming and least discovered regions.

And if the location is perfect, then so too is the hotel itself. In fact, as is to be expected of any project involving Alain Ducasse and the Moretti family, it is spectacular. Together they have created a living work of art that throws out many of the old conventions associated with the Tuscan villa experience and replaces

them with a combination of refined luxury, glamour and elegance that satisfies and soothes the senses as much as it does the soul.

There are 33 exquisitely decorated rooms and suites, all of which have been individually styled and furnished by one of Italy's leading architects in a stunning combination of old and new that is at once timeless and classic, yet sophisticated and ultra-modern. Most include a fireplace and breathtaking views of the surrounding countryside, and all equipped with en suite bathrooms. The kind of cutting-edge technology that is expected of the very finest hotels—flat-screen TV sets and CD-DVD players for example—come as standard here.

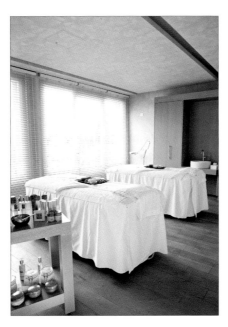

Impressive as the accommodation is, however, L'Andana's founders would never be satisfied until they had a complete package of facilities to offer their guests, and in this regard they have triumphed. Not only does the hotel boast a world-class, ESPA health and well-being centre with a vast array of treatments, therapies, massages and wraps, it also houses Alain Ducasse's only dedicated foray into the Italian culinary world—the Trattoria Toscana—where the flavours and techniques of Tuscan cuisine achieve a state of such perfection that it can only be a matter of time before he acquires a few more Michelin stars to add to his already substantial constellation.

ROOMS
33

FOOD
Trattoria Toscana: Italian

DRINK
bar • wine cellar

FEATURES
ESPA spa • heated pools • heliport • tennis court • nine-hole golf course • wine tasting courses • cookery courses • consecrated church

BUSINESS
banquet facilities • meeting facilities

NEARBY
Grosseto • Marina de Grosseto • Castiglion de la Pescaia • Maremma Nature Reserve • Diaccia Botrona Wetland Reserve • Orbetello Nature Reserve

CONTACT
58043 Castiglione della, Pescaia, Grosseto
telephone: +39.0564.944 800 •
facsimile: +39.0564.944 577 •
email: info@andana.it •
website: www.andana.it

principe di piemonte

...unrivalled quality of accommodation and hospitality...

The small city of Viareggio in the province of Lucca derives its name from the Latin term via regis or 'king's road', which is the name of the highway that runs through it. Constructed during the Middle Ages, this road once served as the main communication link between Rome and the north of Italy and the city saw its fair share of royalty, aristocrats and other dignitaries breaking their journey there. This, coupled with the endless miles of white sandy beaches that Viareggio enjoys, meant that it gradually became one of the country's foremost seaside resorts, developing a reputation for its friendly people and the unrivalled quality of accommodation and hospitality it had to offer.

These are traditions that continue into the modern age, and any king or queen who happens to pass through the city today would almost certainly choose to stay at the Grand Hotel Principe di Piemonte. Built in the early 20th century and located right on the seafront, the Principe di Piemonte is grand in both name and nature—an old-style hotel that has recently been completely renovated so that it now combines the splendour and character of the past with the amenities and comforts of the present.

It's a combination that works on every level, both literally and figuratively. For one of its many attractive features is that each of the five floors has been decorated and furnished according to a different style from history, making a stay here comparable to taking a voyage through the ages. The ground floor, for example, has been designated the 'international' floor. Inspired by the French style of the 18th century, the décor employs the same subtle and delicate tones of the Paris of 300 years ago to create a gentle and enchanting ambience of opulence and elegance.

For those who prefer a slightly more flamboyant touch, the second floor has an Art Deco theme. Reflecting the more modern heritage of the 'roaring twenties', the emphasis here is on dark woods, silken fabrics, ornate mirrors and period furniture from that time. The third floor,

THIS PAGE (FROM TOP): Guestrooms on the colonial floor have lavish, traditional bathtubs; enter a realm of sheer style; exquisite and classic décor furnishes Principe di Piemonte with a luxurious atmosphere.

OPPOSITE: Rich tapestries give Art Deco rooms an air of opulence, reminiscent of the golden age that was the Belle Époque.

on the other hand, reflects the style and décor of the colonial era. Here disparate elements from the Far East, Africa and the Indian subcontinent have been skilfully drawn together, bringing to mind the age of exploration and discovery.

In stark contrast, the Empire style of Napoleon Bonaparte is the theme employed on the fourth floor, where the environment created is all about luxury and indulgence. In keeping with the great general's dreams of grandeur, the fixtures and fittings here are cleverly used to create a sense of the majestic and the imperial, with lacquered furniture, striped fabrics and light-coloured woods combining to complete the picture.

Finally, the fifth and top floor brings the many cycles of history to a close with a thoroughly modern and up-to-date version of 21st-century design. Sharp, clinical lines are favoured and, when combined with state-of-the-art lighting, neutral tones and essential forms, create a minimalist paradise of exceptional luxury and comfort. The fifth floor is also the home of an extensive roof terrace that, apart from offering breathtaking views over the sea and the nearby Apuane Mountains, hosts most of the hotel's entertainment and leisure facilities, including a roof garden, jacuzzi and solarium. Of particular interest is a beautifully shaped sunken pool that must rank as one of the most sublime in all of Italy.

THIS PAGE: Take a swim in the pool that overlooks the stunning horizon where sea meets sky.

OPPOSITE (FROM TOP): Enjoy a relaxing afternoon tea; while rejuvenating mind and body at the Wellness Centre; an extravagant interior complete with a canopy bed gives rooms a palatial feel.

This, though, is just a sample of what Principe di Piemonte has to offer. Located next to the pool, for example, is the Panoramic Restaurant Bar. It serves a wide variety of lunchtime dishes and poolside snacks, as well as cold beers, wines and cocktails, making it the perfect place to enjoy an early evening drink or nightcap. And the hotel is also home to one of Viareggio's finest restaurants, Il Piccolo Principe, which offers diners a selection of Italian and international cuisine all prepared by a skilled and dedicated team of experienced chefs. The pleasure of dining here is enhanced by the presence of an extensive cellar comprising some 400 Tuscan and Italian wines, and it goes without saying that the service in both of these restaurants—as throughout the rest of the hotel—is of the very highest calibre.

Last but not least, the hotel recently opened its own Wellness Centre, an extensive and beautifully laid out spa and gym complex where a guest's fitness and health are given top priority by a team of qualified assistants. Among the wide array of services available are various face and body treatments, a sauna, every conceivable type of massage and therapies that offer a holistic approach to the complete rejuvenation of body and soul.

ROOMS
106

FOOD
Il Piccolo Principe: gourmet •
Panoramic Restaurant Bar: grill

DRINK
rooftop bar • wine cellar

FEATURES
rooftop • jacuzzi • solarium •
wellness centre • TV room •
valet parking

NEARBY
La Spezia • Lucca • Massa • Pisa

CONTACT
Piazza G. Puccini 1,
55049 Viareggio, Lucca •
telephone: +39.0584.40 11 •
facsimile: +39.0584.401 803 •
email: info@principedipiemonte.com •
website: www.principedipiemonte.com

relais la suvera

...encapsulates and embodies the very essence of the Italian hotel experience.

THIS PAGE (FROM TOP): The spacious grounds of Relais La Suvera; the terrace is perfect for taking in the country views. OPPOSITE: Have a drink while basking under the Italian sun.

The world-renowned composer Giuseppe Verdi once said, 'You may have the universe if I may have Italy'. He had a point. Italy, after all, has just about everything a person could ever wish for. Its wines and cuisine are among the most admired and respected in the world; its history and its culture have no peer; its landscapes rank as some of the most beautiful the earth has to offer. Add to this fascinating cities, a superb Mediterranean climate, some of the world's best shopping, and friendly people with an unsurpassed tradition of hospitality, and it soon becomes apparent that few places can rival this destination.

But there is one other factor that is often overlooked in Italy's appeal—the sheer uncompromising excellence of many of its hotels. And while it is extremely difficult to single out any one Italian hotel as superior to all the others, there is one establishment that not only matches the best of the rest in terms of the quality and excellence, but also somehow encapsulates and embodies the very essence of the Italian hotel experience. The property in question is none other than the Relais La Suvera in the Chianti region of Tuscany.

This member of the Small Luxury Hotels of the World group is a family-owned and run deluxe hotel that excels in every aspect of hospitality. The geographical setting, the quality of the food and drink on offer, the levels of service, the all-round excellence of its accommodation and the magnificence of the buildings—in all these the hotel reigns supreme. Furthermore, everything is accomplished with seemingly effortless grace and never-ending attention to detail that only the world's finest hoteliers are able to achieve, and the result is that guests are likely to rate their stay here as one of the best.

There are many ingredients that go into making the Relais La Suvera the establishment it is. Some of the credit must go to the hotel's location which, simply put, would be hard to improve on. 29 km (18 miles) to the west is the city of Siena, without doubt one of the country's most enchanting cities, with its majestic architecture and world-famous Palio; while 56 km (35 miles) to the northeast is Florence, one of the world's great cultural capitals. Closer still are the famous hilltop towns of Monteriggioni, San Gimignano and Volterra, with their charming medieval towers, churches and piazzas, as well as some of the finest vineyards and wine cellars in the country. Not surprisingly, all of these contribute to making this area one of Italy's foremost holiday destinations.

The Relais La Suvera's impressive 1000-year-old complex also has a role to play. Gloriously set on a hilltop overlooking a classic Tuscan landscape of tranquil vineyards and the picturesque hamlet of Pievescola, it was originally built in the High Middle Ages for the legendary Queen of Montemaggio. The building subsequently served as the papal villa of Pope Julius II, as well as a home to numerous counts, princes and dukes. Indeed, the current owners, the Marquis Giuseppe Ricci Paracciana and his wife Princess Eleonora Massimo—who bought the property as a country estate in the 1960s—are themselves both descended from long lines of Italian nobility.

The hotel's illustrious history is evident everywhere, from the antique fixtures and furnishings in the interior to the cloistered walkways and original terracotta-tiled roofs. In fact, the Relais La Suvera is so steeped in history that it is one of the few in the world to have its own UNESCO-recognised museum. Comprising a fascinating collection of documents, furnishings and artwork derived from the Ricci and Massimo families, this museum brings to life the artistic and cultural associations the property and its owners have with the region and the papacy itself.

But a superb geographical location, wonderful architecture and an extraordinary history are just a few of the many factors that have gone into making the Relais La Suvera the destination that it is today. Magnificent as these features are, it is the quality of the facilities and services on offer that give the place that special 'something', without which no truly great hotel would be complete.

The accommodation, for one, leaves absolutely nothing to be desired. The Relais La Suvera boasts 19 rooms and 13 suites, all exquisitely decorated with priceless antiques, furniture, pictures and other historical pieces, so that any one room or suite deserves to be regarded as a work of art in its own right.

Each has been named after the aristocratic ancestors of the owners and is individually styled according to a different theme. There is an Arabic room, a Napoleonic one and another that reflects the art and influences of the Renaissance period, to name but a few. When combined with more modern amenities such as air conditioning, satellite TV and spacious bathrooms equipped with a range of olive-based toiletries, the results are as romantic and sumptuous as they are breathtaking and unique.

Other aspects of the Relais La Suvera are no less impressive, and particular praise must be reserved for its main dining facility, the Oliviera Restaurant, set in the charming surroundings of an arcaded 18th-century olive mill complete with its own shaded terrace. Here, carefully

THIS PAGE (CLOCKWISE FROM TOP): **One of the exotically decorated rooms available at the hotel;** antiques form part of the furnishings everywhere; the mural enhances the old world feel of the room.
OPPOSITE (FROM TOP): **The library is ideal for a quiet read;** soft drapes and lighting make for a comfortable stay.

THIS PAGE (FROM TOP): Gold-framed mirrors and gold taps in the bathrooms are fit for a king; the exposed ceiling reminds one of the building's history.

OPPOSITE (ANTI-CLOCKWISE FROM TOP): Paintings of previous owners; royal blue is predominant in the Suite Duca di Genova; white and gold prevail in the colour scheme of this room.

selected Tuscan and Italian dishes are served by the experienced team of dedicated chefs under the stewardship of Head Chef Gigliola Papa, who uses only the freshest locally-sourced ingredients. The menu changes daily and an extensive wine list representing a vast array of local, national and international wines and champagnes—including some from the hotel's own organic vineyards—is available to complement every dish.

No less enchanting is the Bar dei Limoni where, under the shade of linden trees and near the swimming pool, diners can enjoy lighter meals in a more casual environment, to suit the natural setting. Italian and international dishes are prevalent here, and in the evening there is no better place for guests to enjoy a pre-dinner cocktail, or a nightcap, perhaps with a cigar from the extensive selection on offer.

As if all this wasn't enough to satisfy even the most demanding guest, the Relais La Suvera's most recent addition is the new Wellness Centre. Skilfully integrated into one of the oldest buildings on the property, it comes complete with a steam bath, a small fitness centre and a relaxation area where herbal teas are served. Various massage therapies are also available for guests to choose from, including those based on Swedish, aromatherapy and reflexology techniques, as well as various beauty treatments. Arrangements for activities such as tennis, mountain biking, horse riding and golf can also be made. These, together with an open-air swimming pool heated to a constant 28–30 °C (82–86 °F), all but ensure everyone's mental and physical well-being during their stay.

Finally, the Relais La Suvera also has its own beautiful church—which dates back to the 16th century—and extensive landscaped gardens, making it the perfect place to hold weddings and other exclusive social events, not to mention honeymoons. With all of this to offer, and to paraphrase Verdi, 'You may have the all of the hotels in Italy if I may have the Relais La Suvera'.

ROOMS
32

FOOD
Oliviera Restaurant: Italian

DRINK
Bar dei Limoni

FEATURES
pool • Wellnesss Centre • museum • library • church • gardens • park

NEARBY
Siena • San Gimignano • Volterra • Monteriggioni • San Galgano

CONTACT
53030 Pievescola, Siena • telephone: +39.577.960 300 • facsimile: +39.577.960 220 • email: reservations@lasuvera.it • website: www.lasuvera.it

relais santa croce

...ultimate model in quality and comfort...

THIS PAGE (FROM TOP): The hotel lounge has all the hallmarks of architectural splendour; rooms offer the latest amenities, ensuring a comfortable stay; bathrooms are equally luxurious.

OPPOSITE (ANTI-CLOCKWISE FROM TOP): The origins of the Relais can be traced back to the 13th century; the Duomo is just walking distance away from the hotel; relax in the cosy atmosphere by the open fireplace.

Known as one of the most beautiful cities in the world, Florence is renowned for its famous monuments and prestigious shopping streets. With history, style and elegance fused into an intriguing mix, an unforgettable stay in the city awaits.

Typical of such sophistication is none other than the Relais Santa Croce, a luxurious palace with a cosy atmosphere that exudes a stylish charm at the same time. Soft lighting and a warm welcome from the friendly staff will make guests feel at ease immediately, not unlike being in the familiar environs of their own homes.

At this hotel, each room possesses a different character, just as every guest seems to be treated as unique. Yet, every room is a little oasis in itself, with exclusive Tuscan handcrafted furnishings placed side by side with the most modern technology. A small classic-style bureau, soft leather chair, plasma TV, and Internet access come as standard throughout. In addition, all

rooms are brightly lit with predominantly soft colour tones. No details have been spared in creating an atmosphere of combined luxury and elegance, and where aesthetics blend seamlessly with the best of modern comfort. Every room provides a generous amount of personal space, offering privacy and making it an ideal place to retire to each day.

Havens of pampering and indulgence, the bathrooms are crafted with fine marble in shades of chocolate and cream. Private jacuzzis sit upon stone made from the hotel's original floor, and guests can choose to take a bath in the huge jacuzzi while listening to music at the same time.

The Relais Santa Croce's two great Royal Suites—the 140-sq-m (1,507-sq-ft) Da Verrazzano Suite and the 85-sq-m (915-sq-ft) Dei Pepi Suite—are in a class of its own. Both contain high vaulted ceilings with original 19th-century frescoes and precious antique furniture. With other modern furnishings, they make a stay in either of these suites a fascinating experience. Other amenities in the suites include plasma TV, high-speed Internet access, shower with Turkish bath and sauna, air conditioning and a personal safety deposit box, not to mention a luxurious king-sized bed.

In a place where elegance is a way of life, guests will appreciate the stylish yet serene ambience that surrounds the hotel. And in its constant search for perfection, the Relais Santa Croce has created a home away from home, offering warm hospitality and impeccable

service. Here guests will find the best of Florence, where the finest arts and the great Italian lifestyle reside.

Located in a splendid part of the city, this five-star entity of sophistication nestles snugly amid the artisanal shop fronts and prestigious boutiques of Florence, making it an easy place to find but hard to leave. With mesmerising views over the Florentine skyline and the Duomo, the Relais Santa Croce represents the ultimate model in quality and comfort right in the heart of this romantic, culture-rich corner of Italy.

ROOMS
24

FOOD
Guelfi e Ghibellini Restaurant: Tuscan

DRINK
bar

FEATURES
satellite TV • safe • jacuzzi • butler service (Royal Suites) • limousine

BUSINESS
conference facilities

NEARBY
Duomo • Piazza Santa Croce

CONTACT
Via Ghibellina 87, 50122 Florence • telephone: +39.055.234 2230 • facsimile: +39.055.234 1195 • email: info@relaisantacroce.com • website: www.relaisantacroce.com

terme di saturnia spa + golf resort

A member of The Leading Hotels of the World and Leading Spas...

THIS PAGE: From golf to soothing therapies, providing total well-being is Saturnia's main goal.

OPPOSITE (CLOCKWISE FROM TOP LEFT): Each of Saturnia's treatments is known for its calming effects; the resort combines stylish design with superb spa programmes; take a relaxing dip in the pool.

Almost equidistant from Rome and Florence is the mythical Tuscan Maremma. The award-winning Terme di Saturnia Spa & Golf Resort is at the heart of this magical spot where, according to legend, the god Saturn's thunderbolt once struck Earth to punish men for their war mongering. This caused pacifying waters to pour from a volcanic crater, where the beneficial properties of the waters helped placate those who arrived to enjoy its healing properties.

This world-famous spa is located on the edge of this thermal phenomenon, taking full advantage of its copious advantages, namely mineral-rich waters at 37 °C (99 °F) flowing at 800 l (176 gal) per second. A member of The Leading Hotels of the World and Leading Spas, it has won several accolades, having been frequently voted in *Condé Nast Traveller* magazine as Italy's Best Spa, *Travel and Leisure's* Finest European Spa and one of *Condé Nast Traveller's* UK Best Medical & Thermal Spas in the World.

Revolving around the concept of well-being through psychological equilibrium, the spa offers a vast number of hydrotherapy, beauty, stress-management, diet and fitness treatments. Escape from the hectic whirlpool of everyday life and journey through the sensual strata to

achieve a state of blissful serenity, cocooned in the silken spa waters. With the latest techniques and expertise, Saturnia's knowledgeable staff will be glad to organise a personalised treatment programme. This experience is enhanced with the exclusive Terme di Saturnia skincare range, developed to harness the unique mineral properties of the hot springs.

In addition to the four naturally replenished pools, jacuzzis and waterfalls, the Thermal Park is home to the contemporary Art Gallery, the welcoming Spa Cafe and the open-air Juice Bar, which serves appetising smoothies, vegetable-based cocktails and lighter bites during the day. With an impressive Roman Bath and a variety of sauna and steam baths, one relaxing visit to Terme di Saturnia barely seems sufficient.

The resort's luxurious provision for guests includes 135 harmoniously appointed rooms, three suites and two Grand Suites. Using a holistic design approach, all elements from the lighting effects, flooring materials and selected fabrics add to the feeling of well-being and rejuvenation.

This multi-award-winning complex houses the elegant Aqualuce Restaurant and the traditional Trattoria All'Acquacotta as well. Both provide a fine introduction to local and national specialities, as well as globally-inspired cuisine. The Spa Boutique Terme di Saturnia

also caters for all health and beauty purchases, complemented by the elegant store Cruciani with its precious cashmere and a brand-new Atelier Aldo Coppola by Terme di Saturnia.

To heighten its magnetism on the global stage, the Terme di Saturnia will be opening a world-class, 18-hole golf course in the spring of 2008. With the Maremma's mild climate and stunning natural setting, this could be the ideal destination for 'golf widows' and 'spa widowers' who still love to travel together.

ROOMS
140

FOOD
Trattoria All'Acquacotta: traditional Tuscan • Aqualuce Restaurant: Italian and international • Spa Cafe

DRINK
American Bar • Juice Bar

FEATURES
wellness and fitness centre • natural hot springs • massage • sauna • steam bath • Roman Bath • personalised spa programmes • 18-hole golf course • tennis court • Spa Boutique Terme di Saturnia • Atelier Aldo Coppola by Terme di Saturnia • Cruciani Cachemire Knitwear

NEARBY
horse riding • trekking • mountain biking

CONTACT
58014 Saturnia, Grosseto • telephone: +39.0564.600 111 • facsimile: +39.0564.601 266 • email: info@termedisaturnia.it • website: www.termedisaturnia.it

villa la vedetta

...the panoramic views it affords are among the best the city has to offer...

The charms and attractions of Florence are as numerous as they are varied and as impressive as they are well known. When it comes to cuisine, architecture, history, culture and romance, this Tuscan city has it all, placing it firmly in the top rank of the world's great tourist destinations. So it's only fitting that it has a top-ranking hotel to match, and it comes in the form of the five-star, super-deluxe Villa La Vedetta.

Originally a magnificent neo-Renaissance villa, this exquisite jewel of a property recently reopened as a hotel, thoughtfully combining the palatial elements of old world sophistication and grandeur with modern facilities and five-star levels of quality and service.

Enjoying one of the finest positions in the city, the Villa La Vedetta is situated on a slight hill close to the centre of Florence and just a short walk from the Ponte Vecchio. As a consequence, the panoramic views it affords are among the best the city has to offer, encompassing all of the major architectural highlights on one side and the gentle Fiesole hills on the other.

The superlatives don't stop here, however. The Villa La Vedetta excels in every aspect. The 18 spacious rooms, for example, have all been individually styled to create the kind of warm and seductive environment that once experienced is never forgotten. Original antique furniture and state-of-the-art fittings are prominent throughout, and other luxurious features include walnut herringbone parquet floors, walk-in closets, four-poster beds and en suite, marble-clad bathrooms, complete with jacuzzi bathtubs.

Similarly, the public areas leave nothing to be desired. In fact, right from the moment guests enter the tree-lined drive to be greeted by the warm and welcoming staff, they will become aware of having walked into a rarefied atmosphere where no expense has been

THIS PAGE (FROM TOP): Behind the hotel's charming façade lies a wide range of modern facilities; guests can relax and enjoy the splendid view of the Duomo from the terrace.

OPPOSITE (FROM TOP): Rich furnishings aside, suites offer a breathtaking view of the city; indulge in gourmet cuisine in the stylish interior of Onice.

spared. Perfection is the norm here, and all this before the guests have even had a chance to savour the impressive entrance hall of this romantic villa, its sumptuous lounges and the inviting pool terrace.

Perhaps the most impressive feature of the hotel, however, is its gourmet restaurant, Onice. Under the expert guidance of the head chef, Massimiliano Blasone, this elegantly furnished, barrel-vaulted dining room has quickly acquired a formidable reputation for excellence. A true master of his craft, Blasone fuses the regional cuisine of Tuscany with international, refined and unusual ingredients and techniques, and his creations can justifiably be considered as works of art in their own right. Onice has a separate, über-stylish lounge bar, and the Aurora Garden Restaurant and Pool Bar provide alternative drinking and dining options of the highest quality.

There have always been plenty of great reasons for visiting this world-class city and now, thanks to some brilliant design work, considerable investment and a dedication to the very highest standards, there is another one to add to the illustrious list—Villa La Vedetta.

villa mangiacane

...filled with traditional Tuscan art, history and ambience.

Villa Mangiacane radiates the exclusive air of a luxurious private residence, nestled comfortably in 300 hectares (741 acres) of forest and olive groves. It is just 12 km (7 miles) from Florence, across the vine-strewn symmetry of the Chianti Classico region. For a peaceful retreat within easy reach of the cultural capital of Florence, Villa Mangiacane is the choice.

Its incomparable setting is close enough for its skyline to include the silhouettes of the Duomo and Giotto's bell tower. Yet this elegant villa with its luxurious furnishings and sumptuous interior design is far removed enough to generate feelings of total escape from the tourist bustle of this ancient Italian city. Built as a noble mansion home and renovated to reflect this personal atmosphere, the majestic Villa Mangiacane is filled with traditional Tuscan art, history and ambience. Commissioned by Cardinal Francesco Machiavelli, Michelangelo himself is rumoured to have lent inspiration to its original design.

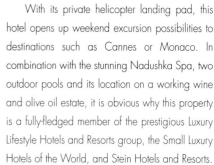

With its private helicopter landing pad, this hotel opens up weekend excursion possibilities to destinations such as Cannes or Monaco. In combination with the stunning Nadushka Spa, two outdoor pools and its location on a working wine and olive oil estate, it is obvious why this property is a fully-fledged member of the prestigious Luxury Lifestyle Hotels and Resorts group, the Small Luxury Hotels of the World, and Stein Hotels and Resorts.

Guest accommodation here is made up of 26 personalised rooms, from the Classic and Superior to Terrace Suites. The vast Royal Suite comprises over 180 sq m (1,938 sq ft) of sheer opulence. Each has a luxurious marble bathroom and, from the private balconies, commit to memory the quintessentially Tuscan images of vineyard or the beguiling rooftops of Florence.

Villa Mangiacane is run by art lover and self-confessed Tuscanophile, Glynn Cohen, who embraces the Italian tradition of sponsoring artistic

works. His unique Sculpture Garden features eye-catching local creations, Lithuanian Cubism and impressive works from artists in Zimbabwe.

The relaxing and rejuvenating Nadushka Spa is nestled in the hotel's 16th-century cellars. It boasts a stunning marble-carved indoor pool, sauna, steam room, jacuzzi and gym. With an aromatic selection of Officina de'Tornabuoni beauty products on hand, this is a sheltered sanctuary in which stress simply dissolves.

Tuscany is renowned for its contribution to European cuisine, and the hotel's chef is poised to

tempt the taste buds of his guests with a plethora of local specialities. His constantly evolving menu delivers its fresh, seasonal cuisine surrounded by the spectacular views from its romantic terraces. For authenticity, try the estate's own terroir-driven and complex Chianti Classico, from estate vineyards blessed with the warmth of the world-famous Tuscan sun.

ROOMS
26

FOOD
Italian

DRINK
lounge bar • private vineyard

FEATURES
Nadushka Spa • outdoor pools • indoor pool • satellite TV • minibar • Internet • safe • sculpture garden • sauna • steam bath • gym • jacuzzi • wedding and banqueting facilities

BUSINESS
conference room

NEARBY
central Florence • Siena

CONTACT
Via Faltigniano 4, 50026 San Casciano, Florence • telephone: +39.055.829 0123 • facsimile: +39.055.829 0358 • email: mangiacane@steinhotels.com • website: www.villamangiacane.com

villa olmi resort

...interiors are enriched with original frescoes, antique furnishings...

THIS PAGE (FROM TOP): Villa Olmi's rooms are spacious and furnished with intricate details; the exquisite décor is reminiscent of the resort's 18th-century past.

OPPOSITE (ANTI-CLOCKWISE FROM TOP): Guests will welcome the serenity from the surrounding greenery; a relaxing and stylish stay in a five-star residence beckons; marble bathrooms add to the luxurious feel of the villa.

The white-washed splendour of the five-star Villa Olmi is apparent even from its sweeping pathway. This age-old Florentine country estate comprises 6 hectares (15 acres) of stately elegance that have been restored to their 18th-century sophistication. For escapism and privacy just 15 minutes from the cultural core of downtown Florence, this villa is a prime contender. Member of the Small Luxury Hotels of the World, Villa Olmi is both exclusive and easy to reach, located in Bagno a Ripoli en route to Chianti country and southern Tuscany.

Today, this luxurious farmhouse hamlet consists of three painstakingly restored residences, or clusters of spacious suites and apartments. The oldest is La Villa, whose 12 charming suites are a fine example of rural-patrician architecture. The stylish interiors are enriched with original frescoes, antique furnishings and elegant Murano glass chandeliers, in addition to technological wizardry such as wireless Internet and plasma TV. Indulgent Egyptian cotton robes await in the cool marble bathrooms, complete with luxurious toiletries and seductive scents for the jacuzzi.

At the heart of Villa Olmi is La Fattoria, home to 38 faithfully refurbished rooms and mini-suites, of which 4 are hosted by Limonaia House. Several of these rooms at La Fattoria come with private garden access, and their interior design is textbook Tuscany, with floors of terracotta from Impruneta, walls of limestone plaster and exposed wooden beams on the ceilings. With simple and elegant furniture, the cosy ambience is enhanced with pure linen bed clothing and authentic antiques. The cloistered pool is located here as well, its loungers overlooking the renaissance-styled vegetable garden or hortus conclusus.

The hotel's wine bar, meeting rooms and gourmet restaurant can also be found at La Fattoria. To experiment with Tuscan cuisine personally, Villa Olmi's private cookery courses are an entertaining diversion. But for guests who just want to enjoy fine cuisine, gourmet food and wine are offered in the inimitable atmosphere of Il Cavaliere, which also has an in-house sommelier on hand to ensure a harmonious meal.

The third of Villa Olmi's exclusive residences is La Colonica, whose classy atmosphere houses two huge multi-roomed apartments. With sturdy chestnut doors and smooth archways overlooking the exquisite garden, these fully-equipped and air-conditioned retreats are ideal for family groups. The wood-burning stove and open kitchen are just perfect for impromptu pizza parties. For a genuine taste of old world Tuscan hospitality mere moments from the heart of Florence, discover the welcoming atmosphere and innovative edge of Villa Olmi.

ROOMS
50

FOOD
Il Cavaliere: Italian

DRINK
wine cellar

FEATURES
Internet • satellite TV • jacuzzi • gym • personal shoppers • art guides • beauty treatments • in-room massage

BUSINESS
conference facilities

NEARBY
Chianti • Palazzo Pitti • Ponte Vecchio • Uffizi Gallery • Via Tornabuoni

CONTACT
Via degli Olmi 4/8, 50012 Bagno a Ripoli, Florence • telephone: +39.055.637 710 • facsimile: +39.055.6377 1600 • email: reservations@villaolmiresort.com • website: www.villaolmiresort.com

villa tiziano + la terrazza

...elegantly furnished to the highest standards...

THIS PAGE (CLOCKWISE FROM TOP LEFT):
*Beautifully furnished rooms
help to evoke an earlier era;
warm colour tones enhance
the charming dining room;
the bathroom is just as luxurious.*

OPPOSITE (FROM TOP): *Enjoy the
views from the gardens;
Tiziano's high ceilings give an
impression of light and space.*

With so many places in the world to choose from, it's never easy to select a holiday destination. Mistakes are inevitably expensive, and while the financial cost can be overcome, the sense of disappointment is much harder to swallow. For this reason, it can be helpful to have a well-established and reliable agency provide a shortlist of those properties best suited to an individual's requirements and, as a consequence, most likely to live up to expectations.

One such agency is The Villa Book, a property rental company run by some of the most experienced people in the sector. In almost 30 years, they have built up a close working relationship with owners and local agents alike, enabling them to cater for each individual's requirements on a bespoke basis. Representing hundreds of properties on three continents, the team at The Villa Book are never short of options, and they are particularly strong when it comes to destinations in Tuscany and two of the finest properties on their books are the Villa Tiziano and La Terrazza.

Located on a hilltop in the beautiful rolling countryside of the Chianti region close to Florence, Villa Tiziano is one of those classic, almost dreamlike villas that only Tuscany can offer. It is magnificently set within formal gardens designed by noted English architect Cecil Ross Pinsent, complete with a spectacular 10-m (33-ft) infinity-edge pool. And if the exterior is grand, then so too is the interior. Enormous rooms have been furnished with period antiques and a warm colour scheme to reflect the aristocratic lifestyle of a bygone age, creating an environment

that is both comfortable and luxurious. Apart from the sumptuously appointed bedrooms, no two of which are alike, the highlight must be the formal dining room large enough to seat up to 24 guests. In addition, a complimentary continental breakfast is served every day except Sunday, and the wide range of amenities includes DVD, VCR and Internet access.

For those seeking a more cosmopolitan and more urban experience, Villa Tiziano's sister property, La Terrazza, offers the perfect solution. This wonderful apartment is conveniently situated close to many of Florence's major attractions, including the Piazza della Signoria, the Pitti Palace, the Duomo and the Uffizi Gallery, all of which are within a few minutes walk.

Entirely renovated in 2005, La Terrazza also benefits from a rooftop location—complete with a 70-sq-m (753-sq-ft) terrace—affording guests the opportunity to savour stunning views over the surrounding city. Like Villa Tiziano, it too has been elegantly furnished to the highest standards, and has all of the amenities expected of such an exclusive retreat, with the added bonus of having one of the world's great cultural capitals on its doorstep.

Villa Tiziano

ROOMS
10

FOOD
in-house chef on request

DRINK
wine list

FEATURES
pool • Internet

NEARBY
San Polo • Florence • Siena

La Terrazza

ROOMS
3

FOOD
in-house chef on request

DRINK
wine list

FEATURES
satellite TV • Internet

NEARBY
Piazza del Duomo • Uffizi Gallery • San Marco Museum • Ponte Vecchio • Galleria dell'Accademia • Pitti Palace • Piazza della Signoria

CONTACT
12 Venetian House, 47 Warrington Crescent, London W9 1EJ • telephone: +44.845.500 2000 • facsimile: +44.845.500 2001 • email: info@thevillabook.com • website: www.thevillabook.com

BENEDICTVS XIV·
PON·MAX
POSITIS SIGNIS ET ANA
GLYPHIS TA
SOLVTVM A·DOM·MDCCLXII
PONT·MAX·OPVS

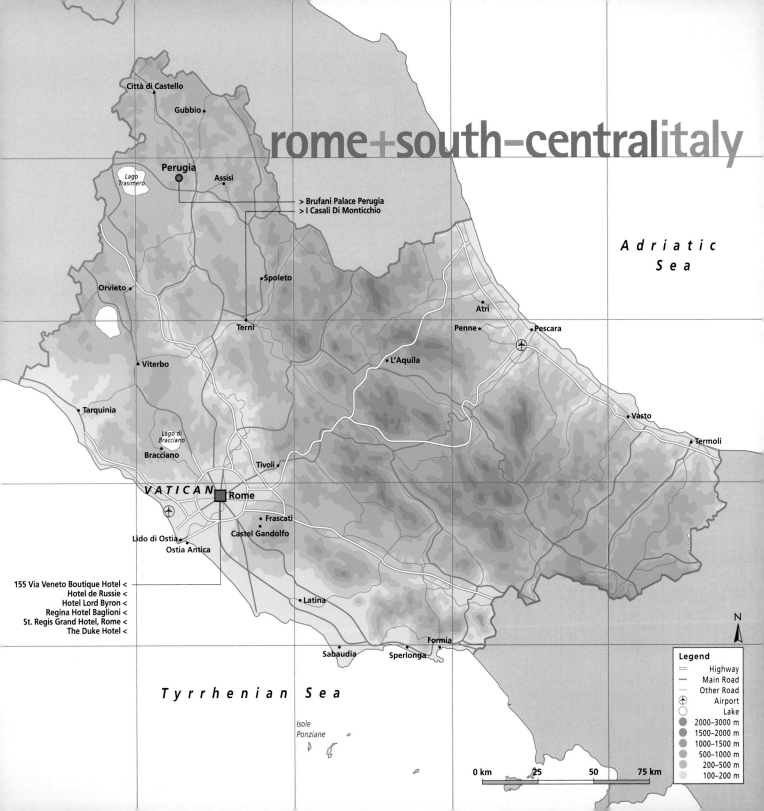

rome+south-centralitaly

Città di Castello

Gubbio

Perugia

Lago Trasimero

Assisi

> Brufani Palace Perugia
> I Casali Di Monticchio

Orvieto

Spoleto

Terni

Viterbo

A d r i a t i c S e a

Atri

Penne   Pescara

L'Aquila

Tarquinia

Lago di Bracciano

Vasto

Bracciano

Termoli

Tivoli

V A T I C A N   Rome

Frascati

Castel Gandolfo

Lido di Ostia

Ostia Antica

155 Via Veneto Boutique Hotel <
Hotel de Russie <
Hotel Lord Byron <
Regina Hotel Baglioni <
St. Regis Grand Hotel, Rome <
The Duke Hotel <

Latina

T y r r h e n i a n   S e a

Formia

Sabaudia   Sperlonga

Isole Ponziane

N

Legend

⚌	Highway
▬	Main Road
▬	Other Road
✈	Airport
◯	Lake
●	2000–3000 m
●	1500–2000 m
●	1000–1500 m
●	500–1000 m
●	200–500 m
●	100–200 m

0 km   25   50   75 km

rome + south-central italy

A legend in its own lifetime, Rome attracts as many tributes as it does visitors each year, and it certainly doesn't disappoint. Home to some of the biggest treasures of the ancient world, such as the Forum, the Colosseum and the Pantheon, the city has always captivated artists, leaving behind an incomparable legacy of monuments, museums, palaces and churches through the ages. From Piazza Navona to the Trevi Fountain, from the world's smallest sovereign state of the Vatican City to the Capitoline Museums, wherever you go there is a historic gem nearby. But Rome could never become just a giant museum, it is a living, breathing capital city. Together with its culture clash of old and new, where ancient history coincides with the future in every square and every street, Rome is prized for its shopping and for its romantic places to stay and dine. There is far too much to see in one visit but don't worry, you'll be back.

Outside Rome, Lazio offers the cool hills of Frascati, Castel Gandolfo or Lake Bracciano, or tanning at the beaches of Sperlonga or Latina. Umbria offers jewels of art, tucked away in medieval hill towns while Assisi tempts with its grand Basilica and idyllic setting. Perugia's National Gallery has the region's best works of art and there is modern art in Città di Castello and Terni. Lovers of the great outdoors will prize the Monte Sibillini, Monte Subasio and blue waters of Lake Trasimeno. Beyond Umbria lie the mountains of Abruzzo and within an hour of L'Aquila, you're at the seaside.

PAGE 184: Quintessential Rome, the Trevi Fountain, made famous in the 1960 classic La Dolce Vita.

THIS PAGE (FROM TOP): Old meeting new at the Museo del Corso, home of major art exhibitions; taking it slow in timeless Trastevere, south of the river.

OPPOSITE: The ancient Colosseum lights up as night falls.

getting your bearings without losing your marbles

Much of Rome's incredible art and architecture is familiar even before you've seen it but, whether it's the first or the 14th visit, just a glimpse of the Colosseum or Piazza Navona sets hearts a-racing. From Roman treasures to baroque splendour, there's more than enough here to keep everyone content. See the marble ruins of the Forum during springtime when wild flowers grow all around, or gaze over the Forum at night from a tiny platform off the Piazza del Campidoglio; walk along the Roman roads towards the

ABOVE: *At the heart of an Empire, the evocative Roman Forum stretches from the Capitoline to the Colosseum. The three pillars of the Temple of Vespasius and Titus rub shoulders with the Arch of Septimius Severus and the Empire's treasury in the Temple of Saturn.*

OPPOSITE: *Leaving the Vatican Museums in style, the former entrance became the exit in 2000, when a state-of-the-art foyer opened to cope with the vast number of visitors.*

Colosseum and sit in the romantic Piazza Navona in the heart of baroque Rome. Alongside the overwhelming choice of things to do, there's the temptation to sit in a square and do nothing but breathe in the beauty of the city. Fortunately the compact nature of the city means that in between sightseeing this is a guilt-free pleasure.

From Piazza Repubblica, near Termini railway station, shopping thoroughfare Via Nazionale leads to Piazza Venezia, the heart of ancient Rome. To the left are the Forum and the Colosseum; to the right are the Capitoline and the Palatine, with the Jewish Ghetto close by. From here the Campo dei Fiori, the Pantheon and Piazza Navona are but a short stroll away. And from Piazza Navona it's no distance to Castel Sant'Angelo and the Vatican City. Veer in the other direction and you come to the Spanish Steps, the Trevi Fountain and Via Veneto. And in between are shops, cafés and restaurants galore. For the finest view over the city, head south to Trastevere and up Via Garibaldi where beneath you will see the seven hills of Rome and the Castelli Romani beyond—all the sites in one sweeping panorama.

sites to set your sights on

The Colosseum, the Roman Empire's greatest amphitheatre, commissioned in 72 AD, was the setting for gladiatorial combat and fights to the death with wild beasts from all across the Empire. It was a bloodthirsty crowd that filled its seats. A short distance away is the Palatine, which housed the luxury residences of the Emperors. The Capitoline Museums, the world's oldest national museums, house some of the finest archaeological finds from the Roman Empire and a vast collection of prestigious paintings. Of all the ancient wonders, the Pantheon is the best preserved. Once a temple to all the gods of Rome, it has long been converted into a Christian church and its monumental dome remains with an oculus opening it to the sky.

Dramatic art and architecture await at the Vatican. Its beautiful 1932 spiralling processional entrance clearly inspired Frank Lloyd Wright's Guggenheim in New York. Less than 1 sq km (⅓ sq mile) away, the Vatican City is home to an overwhelming collection. Michelangelo's Sistine Chapel and the Raphael Rooms are the principal

sights although just about every room contains something awe-inspiring. Recently restored and back on view is the masterpiece, the Laocoon, a 1st-century marble sculpture of a Trojan priest and his sons wrestling two serpents. In St. Peter's Basilica, itself a monument to artistic genius, a climb to the top of the dome rewards visitors with breathtaking views. You can admire Bernini's clever colonnade from above while sipping an espresso. Inside, Bernini's baldachin protects the tomb of St. Peter and Michelangelo's Pietà rests safe behind glass.

oft overlooked treasures

Little gems of art and architecture are hidden around every corner in Rome: Santa Maria del Popolo in the Piazza del Popolo has two exquisite Caravaggios in the Cerasi Chapel; the cloister of San Carlo alle Quattro Fontane by Borromini is a masterpiece of perspective in a tiny space; San Pietro in Vincoli near the Colosseum is home to *Moses*, one of Michelangelo's finest sculptures; while the 13th-century frescoes of angels by Pietro Cavallini in Santa Cecilia in Trastevere is a rhapsody in colour and expression. In Villa Farnesina is Raphael's sublime Triumph of Galatea. The drama of Bernini's 17th-century sculptures in the Galleria Borghese never fails to impress—as Daphne flees Apollo she metamorphoses into a laurel tree, elsewhere David aims his sling at Goliath, grim determination wrought on his beautiful face. Bernini's figures in his public fountains are equally potent.

Just a step away from Termini station is the Museo Nazonale Romano. Inside, the 1st-century frescoes from Livia's Villa showing a four-season garden in bloom are a balm to the soul. The pretty Palazzo Altemps off Piazza Navona has some of the best Roman sculptures while for all things Etruscan, the Villa Giulia is too often ignored. Of all the noble palazzi in the city, one of the homeliest has to be the Galleria Doria Pamphilj. Still lived in by the family, the eldest son narrates the audio guide, telling tales of roller-skating past the ballroom as a child, watched over by the great works of Caravaggio, Velazquez and Titian. Lovers of art nouveau stained glass, meanwhile, will be delighted by the Casina delle Civetta in Villa Torlonia, north of Piazza Fiume—once a private home, it is now a museum.

As a perfect antidote to all that art, shops, eateries and bars proliferate around Piazza Navona, Campo dei Fiori and the Spanish Steps. Small, funky designers occupy the boutiques in the Trastevere area where they sell their clothes and jewellery; there is also a handful of old-fashioned artisans in the area. Via Veneto is no longer where the beautiful people throng, but the Belle Époque hotels remain—the best have stylish cafés and restaurants worthy of the location.

THIS PAGE: From piety to wanton spending, or covetous window shopping, on the Via Condotti.

OPPOSITE: A hush falls as you enter the hallowed interior of St. Peter's, the light trickling through Michelangelo's masterpiece dome.

monumental egos + futuristic fantasies

A crossroad of the past and future is at the Ara Pacis, one of the Roman Empire's most important monuments. The Altar of Peace of 9 BC was created to celebrate the newfound stability established by Augustus' victories across the Empire. Fragmented over time, it took years to reassemble the pieces of the altar, which were found in museums all across the globe. In 2006, Meier's much heralded glass pavilion was opened—protecting the altar from the elements while allowing passers-by to admire its marble splendour. The Capitoline has a museum away from the centre in Garbatella at the Centrale Montemartini. Set inside an old electrical power station, it houses the 'less important' statues from the Capitoline collection in unique juxtaposition. Gleaming steel and copper contrast with the white marble: the industrial revolution meeting the golden age of the artisan head on.

The EUR district, in the south of Rome, is easily reached by metro and shows off some of the city's most interesting modern architecture. The Museo della Civiltà Romana, completed in 1937, was built as a homily to Augustus, the first Emperor of Rome, with whom megalomaniac Mussolini felt a great affinity. A startling mixture of Fascist-classical architecture, the white walls and vast spaces place the massive achievements of the Roman Empire in context with the grandiosity of Mussolini's ambitions.

EUR was planned by Mussolini as a major propaganda exercise—an exhibition to celebrate Fascist Italy in the 1930s. Much of the architecture was designed by the Rationalist Marcello Piacentini, but it was left incomplete with the outbreak of the war. Now home to a thriving business community, its vast park and lake are an oasis in the summer heat with the extraordinary Palazzo della Civiltà di Lavoro at the centre.

More Fascist-era architecture and sculpture can be seen near Ostiense where Nanni Moretti filmed most of *Caro Diario*. In northern Rome is Renzo Piano's new Parco della Musica. Home to the prestigious Santa Cecilia orchestra, its cherry wood interior and cerise upholstery, with perfect acoustics, make it a work of art. Supplementing the outstanding collection of modern art at the Galleria Nazionale d'Arte Moderna, by the Villa Borghese, are several new public galleries. The Museo Carlo Bilotti hosts the

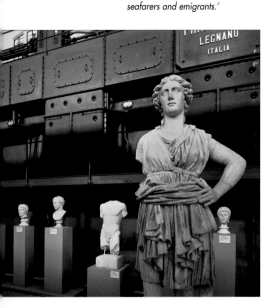

THIS PAGE: Roman versus industrial chic at the museum of Centrale Montemartini.

OPPOSITE: Wistful modernism in Piacentini's Palazzo della Civiltà Italiana. In homage to the legacy of the Italians, the inscription reads 'A people of poets, artists and heroes; saints, philosophers and scientists; seafarers and emigrants.'

private collection of an Italian-American art collector, which includes several works by De Chirico, as well as a family portrait by Andy Warhol. Macro is a new gallery within a converted Peroni brewery. Its collection reflects the Roman art scene since the end of the war. Its sister gallery, Macro Future, recently opened in trendy Testaccio's former slaughterhouse. With a space of over 105,000 sq m (1 million sq ft), there are restaurants, bars and clubs all around the gallery. New buildings are popping up all over Rome. Massimiliano Fuksas' new congress centre, La Nuvola (the Cloud) is in EUR, in the north in Flaminio is Zaha Hadid's new arts centre in a transformed army barracks housing the Museo delle Arti del XXI Secolo or MAXXI, a museum for the 21st century.

escapes from the eternal city

While no one tires of Rome, they may well find it tiring, so it's good to know that just a short trip away there is some respite. One excursion is in the hills of Tivoli, once a summer resort for the ancient Romans. There are three parks to explore. The Roman Villa Gregoriana has its fine grottoes and waterfalls, while Villa Adriana has recreations of the Emperor's favourite buildings in Greece and Egypt amid groves of cypresses and olives. Much was damaged by the Barbarians or carried away to museums far and wide, but it remains a beautiful place to stroll and picnic. The Renaissance extravaganza, Villa d'Este, on the site of a Benedictine monastery, was built for the son of Lucrezia Borgia, Cardinal Ippolito d'Este. The terraced gardens and complex waterworks are masterpieces of garden design by 16th-century architect Pirro Ligurio.

Come summer, the Pope swaps one flock for another and heads up to the cool of Castel Gandolfo, the papal residence overlooking Lake Albano. The town is very pretty with plenty of craft shops, restaurants and bars, but spotting the Pope out and about is highly unlikely. Elsewhere in the Castelli Romani, Frascati is a good retreat from the heat and an obvious place to sample the local tipple. The Museo Tuscolano is well worth seeking out. Set in the beautiful Palazzo Aldobrandini, acclaimed architect Massimiliano Fuksas has created a fine archaeological museum in the former stables.

Lake Bracciano to the north is another popular excursion. Perfect for a swim, it's also where Tom Cruise and Katie Holmes tied the knot at the impressive Renaissance castle, Orsini. Nearby, Etruscan towns Tarquinia and Cerveteri both have museums and burial sites aplenty, and Viterbo has a beautiful medieval centre, ancient thermal pools, and the Villa Lante, which is renowned for its beautiful Renaissance gardens. Bomarzo has an extraordinary garden also by Pirro Ligurio. Filled with surreal sculptures of monsters and fantastical creatures, the Parco dei Mostri was a private folly for the Orsini and beloved by Jean Cocteau and Salvador Dalí.

THIS PAGE (FROM TOP): Cooling off in Villa d'Este, Tivoli. Some scenes of the 1950s classic Three Coins in the Fountain *were filmed here; proud locals in Bracciano joined in the media frenzy of the Tom-Kat celebrity wedding.*

OPPOSITE: Fantastic views over the Campo Imperatore and Gran Sasso combine with an abject sense of isolation and abandonment at Abruzzo's Rocca Calascio, the highest castle along the Apennines.

If time is tight and Pompeii too far, Rome's ancient port of Ostia Antica is impressively preserved and almost as vast. Further south, at Sperlonga, Tiberius's villa complex dating from 2 BC is another attraction. The town's beaches draw the Roman elite, many of who have second homes here or on Ponza, a gem of an island reached by ferry from Formia. Fans of 1930s design will enjoy the resorts of Latina and Sabaudia where there's plenty of Mussolini-era architecture to savour amid the summer sand.

the green lungs of italy

Often overlooked by tourists, the wild terrain of Abruzzo is Italy's green lung—home to the long Apennine mountain range and three national parks. Beautiful little towns await; many bear an air of wistfulness, for Abruzzo and Molise have long fallen by the wayside in history. Witnesses to mass emigration, practically whole villages upped sticks and went to North America in the early 20th century. Abruzzese stock gave us some of America's finest musicians—the quintessential crooners Dean Martin, Perry Como and Mario Lanza as well as composer Henry Mancini and the inimitable Madonna. Molise, devastated by Allied bombs in the war, has a fascinating cultural enclave stemming from 15th-century Dalmatian and Albanian immigration. Though the mainstay here is pastoral farming and crafts, tourism holds the key to the region's future: many houses are being restored and re-inhabited, and rarely by locals.

Prime walking country, the region is as at its best in autumn, when the beech forests are aflame with colour, or in springtime, when wild flowers dapple the emerald green hills. The chances of seeing a golden eagle are not that remote, and if you venture into the upper reaches of the Apennines you enter the hunting ground of the elusive Apennine wolf, Marsican brown bear and Abruzzo lynx. The higher you go the harsher it gets. Fortunately walking is not the only way up. Cable cars dotted around the region take you to some of the summits. The cable car at Fonte Cerreto near Assergi takes you to the legendary Campo Imperatore in the Gran Sasso Park, where Mussolini was rescued from

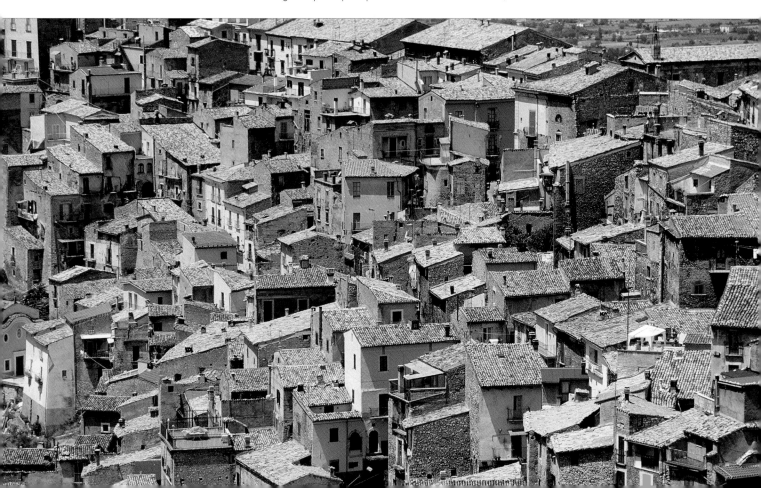

his Allied prison by a daring German paratrooper. Another lift at pretty Scanno takes you to the top of Monte Rotondo. Pescasseroli, the birthplace of philosopher Benedetto Croce, has a cable car to Monte Vitelle, right in the heart of the Parco Nazionale di Abruzzo. Ten km (6 miles) from Ovid's birthplace, Sulmona, is Pacentro—part of the majestic National Park of Majella. L'Aquila, Abruzzo's largest city, was founded by Emperor Frederick II in 1240; its symbol and very name is the eagle. Comprising 99 hamlets, the Fontana delle 99 Cannelle (1272) is another symbol of the city: a fountain with 99 spouts, one for each of the hamlets. A pretty, prosperous university town, the market on Piazza Duomo has been held here every day except Sunday since 1304. An easy drive away is the resort town of Pescara. Though badly bombed in the war, it has a fine 16-km (10-mile) beach. The hill towns of Atri, Penne and Loreto Aprutino, further north, are well worth a diversion. Southward bound is Vasto, the charming hometown of Gabriele Rossetti, the father of Dante Gabriel and Christina Rossetti. Termoli, in Molise, has more beaches, an old harbour and boats to the Tremiti Islands in Puglia.

perugia: medieval art, jazz + chocolate

Perugia's cobbled streets house countless bars and restaurants as well as some serious art. A powerful commune in the Middle Ages, the old town sits pretty on high while the new town, partly by Aldo Rossi, has less obvious charms. Reaching the centro storico is a challenge; cars must park in cavernous car parks below, and escalators take visitors up to the top. Once there, Corso Vannucci leads to the Piazza IV Novembre, where the 13th-century marble masterpiece, the Fontana Maggiore, is found. Opposite is Perugia's magnificent cathedral, which contains a relic believed to be the Virgin Mary's wedding ring: a piece of agate that changes colour. The council buildings in the Palazzo dei Priori are protected by two heavies at the door, a griffin (the emblem of Perugia) and a Guelph lion. The originals are in the adjacent Galleria Nazionale dell'Umbria along with several paintings by Umbrian Renaissance maestro, Perugino. Other highlights include works by Piero della Francesca, Orazio Gentileschi and Pietro da Cortona.

THIS PAGE (FROM TOP): *Waiting for a short back and sides at the local barbers on Corso Cavour in the pretty Umbrian town of Todi; water gushes through the medieval masks of horses, maidens, monks and men at L'Aquila's Fountain of 99 Spouts.*

OPPOSITE: *Located 700 m (2,300 ft) above sea level, picturesque Pacentro has three castles and a beautiful medieval centre, almost entirely intact.*

Perugia has been a university city since 1483. Aside from its vibrant student population, it is home to two major events every year. The first is Umbria Jazz, a music festival held in early July. The 2007 event saw Keith Jarrett, Sonny Rollins, Gilberto Gil and Dionne Warwick. Namesake Perugina is one of Italy's top chocolate confectioners and the makers of Baci, chocolate 'kisses' filled with hazelnut and wrapped in a multilingual love note produced since 1922. Chocoholics will adore the town's second major event, the Eurochocolate Festival. Every year in October, a week of tastings, competitions, cooking classes and banquets are held. There's even a chocolate-themed hotel, with hundreds of chocolate wrappers on show, providing fascinating snapshots into the history of product design.

lake of tranquillity

West of Perugia, in the heart of Umbria, is Italy's fourth largest lake, Lake Trasimeno. Ferries connect the principal towns of Tuoro sul Trasimeno, Passignano sul Trasimeno and Castiglione del Lago. Of the three islands in the centre of the lake, one is inhabited, one is a nature reserve and one was recently up for sale. At Punta Navaccia near Tuoro, the Campo del Sole is a spiral of 27 sculptures in local stone by Italian and foreign artists, a project overseen by Sienese sculptor Mauro Berrettini in the 1980s. The site saw a devastating military ambush in 217 BC, when 15,000 Romans lost their lives fighting Hannibal and his men; the very same day one of Italy's most violent earthquakes racked the country. Beautiful Città della Pieve, to the west, is the birthplace of Pietro Perugino, and a place of pilgrimage for aficionados since so much of his art is on view.

THIS PAGE: Tranquil views amid the lake and the mountains at Tuoro sul Trasimeno.

OPPOSITE: Gubbio's popular Corsa dei Ceri of May 15. A guild race dating from medieval times, three teams carry enormous wooden pillars to the Basilica of St. Ubaldo high over the town. The St. Ubaldo team wins by default but the race for second is toughly fought out.

trading post to tobacco town

Famous for its walled town, fine cathedral and monuments, Città di Castello was a wealthy trading post in the age of the commune, its churches once home to two fine works by Raphael. Alas, *The Crucifixion* is now in the National Gallery in London; *The Marriage of the Virgin* is in Milan's Pinacoteca di Brera. Luckily for those who prefer modern art, the town has a massive collection by local boy Alberto Burri. The Renaissance Palazzo Albizzini has 20 rooms showing his work from 1948 and 1989, while the ex-Seccatoi del Tabacco houses large-scale pieces from 1970–1993. The building itself is interesting: used to dry tobacco leaves for cigar manufacturing until the 1960s, it also acted as a temporary drying store for many priceless books from the National Library which were damaged in the terrible floods that hit Florence in 1966.

Gubbio in northern Umbria is one of the region's most beautiful towns. High on Monte Igino, the buff-toned buildings cascade down the hillside, with the impressive crenellations and tower of the Palazzo del Capitano del Popolo at the top. In the museum are the famous Eugubine Tablets, seven bronze slabs dating from 2 BC that detail rites and sacred sites of the ancient Umbri people. Ceramic shops do big business here and it's worth seeking out the true artisans, who are more tucked away. Nearby Parco del Monte Cucco is also well worth venturing into.

However unspiritual you may feel, Assisi will work its magic. Trapped in time, the rose-coloured stone of the buildings came from nearby Monte Subasio. Particularly beautiful at sunset or sunrise, the views over the surrounding valleys are sublime. Fresco devotees will be in paradise at the Basilica, with Giotti masterpieces to savour. The pretty church of San Damiano, where St. Francis of Assisi composed his *Canticle of the Creatures*, is far simpler. Zeffirelli's film *Brother Sun, Sister Moon* puts you in the mood.

enlightened beauty

Pretty little Trevi hosts the unique Flash Art Museum. The focus is on emerging talent, but the collection boasts work by established Italian names such as Francesco Clemente and Alberto Burri as well as foreign talents Georg Baselitz, Damien Hirst, the Chapmans and Gabriel Orozco. Not far away is the Fonti del Clitunno, its sacred springs having attracted many famous visitors including Virgil and Byron. Much cited in their poetry, the springs remain a beautiful spot to rest.

Terni is interesting for its industrial archaeology. Once the ironworks to the powerful Vatican state and boomtown under Mussolini, there is some fine Fascist architecture. The Grande Pressa, made by an English firm in 1934 and once one of the world's most powerful hydraulic forging presses, has been transformed into a giant sculpture and is on show near the station. Elsewhere, Arnaldo Pomodoro's 30-m (98-ft) obelisk of 27 fused components entitled *Lance of Light* recreates a block of incandescent steel in a homily to Terni's long and noble industry. Nearby, the Cascata delle Marmore is another feat of engineering—a 165-m (541-ft) waterfall—started by the Romans in 271 BC.

The Grand Tourists came to Spoleto to see the grandiose 12th-century Duomo with its exquisite façade of golden and Cosmatesque mosaics. Inside, the Cappella Eroli is frescoed by Pinturicchio. The Galleria Comunale d'Arte Moderna has an impressive collection of contemporary Italian art. But Spoleto is best known for its July arts festival, the Festival dei Due Mondi. Attracting big international names, performances take place all over the town, including in the Roman theatre and amphitheatre.

Orvieto sits high on a tuff platform. Its Duomo's dramatic black and white striated façade with golden mosaics was started in 1290, but it took 300 years to complete. Inside there are alabaster windows and some extraordinary frescoes in the Chapel of Madonna di San Brizio. Predating Michelangelo's Sistine Chapel, Luca Signorelli's *Last Judgment* scenes have an unnerving three-dimensional quality, as well as suitably theatrical content. The town is also famous for its woodwork—somewhat kitsch sculptures, children's toys and furniture redolent of the 1950s—made by the Michelangeli family.

...cited in their poetry, the springs remain a beautiful spot to rest a while.

155 via veneto boutique hotel

...a rarefied atmosphere of romance and exclusivity...

Anybody who plans to visit Rome will soon realise that there is no shortage of hotels to choose from. Even so, very rarely do the establishments live up to their hopes and expectations. This is doubly true for the more discerning traveller looking for a place that combines stylish décor and a central location with the highest levels of service and state-of-the-art facilities.

Perhaps it was for these reasons that legendary Italian hotelier Amedeo Ottaviani—owner of the Hotel Lord Byron Roma and the Hotel Regency Firenze—recently opened the brand-new 155 Via Veneto Boutique Hotel, the newest hotel in the City of Eternal Light. Motivated by a philosophy that emphasises 'irresistible charm, timeless elegance and unparalleled service', it is not difficult to see why the hotel remains one of only a few that meet all of the above criteria.

Located in the very heart of Rome on the fashionable and historic street of the same name, the 155's position could hardly be more advantageous. Many of the city's most famous shops, cultural and culinary attractions are to be found right on the doorstep, and within easy reach is just about every other destination of interest to the visitor. Superb as the location is, however, it is just one of the many factors that go into making this extraordinary establishment the undoubted success it has become in the short time since its opening. From the moment the guest

enters the hotel's 'peristyle' hall, for example, no one can fail to marvel at the opulence and grandeur of the Art Deco interior. Inspired by the sketches of the movement's leading exponent, French designer Jacques-Emile Ruhlmann, the extravagant décor manages to create a rarefied atmosphere of romance and exclusivity that is at once both unmistakably classical and yet utterly modern. The result serves a sumptuous feast for the senses that leaves so many of its rivals looking lacklustre by comparison.

And where there is style, there is also substance. Each of the 120 spacious rooms and suites has been individually styled in the Art Deco tradition, skilfully blended with the latest technology and all of the home comforts to be expected at a modern five-star hotel. The overall effect is one of luxurious intimacy and casual elegance which, when coupled with the devoted team of trained staff, leaves nothing to be desired.

Nor can the facilities be faulted. Whereas most Roman hotels are crowded affairs, the 155 has plenty of room to spare. This has allowed for the added bonus of a fitness centre and spa, and also an open-air rooftop swimming pool. Then there's the library, the ever-popular B'Artdeco Lounge, as well as the intimate and excellent 155 Restaurant, where the fine art of Italian cuisine achieves its ultimate expression at the hands of a dedicated team of Rome's top chefs. With all this and more, the 155 Via Veneto is truly in a class of its own.

ROOMS
120

FOOD
155 Restaurant: Italian

DRINK
B'Artdeco Lounge

FEATURES
spa • fitness centre • library • open-air rooftop pool • interactive satellite LCD TV • multilingual staff • valet parking • complimentary suite minibar

BUSINESS
wi-fi Internet access

NEARBY
Via Veneto • Via Condotti • Spanish Steps • Trevi Fountain

CONTACT
Via Veneto 155, 00187 Rome • telephone: +39.06.322 0404 • facsimile: +39.06.322 0405 • email: info@155viaveneto.com • website: www.155viaveneto.com

brufani palace perugia

...breathtaking views across the Umbrian Valley from its romantic balconies.

Back in the 1800s, the founder of this palatial, five-star hotel was busy assisting wealthy tourists on leisurely stagecoach tours of Umbria. Little did the young but entrepreneurial Giacomo Brufani realise what a tremendous legacy he would leave in the exclusive resort of Perugia, a historic Etruscan town that thrived in an era when Rome was but a village.

A huge success since its grand opening in 1884, the splendid Brufani Palace Hotel is perfectly situated on a hilltop in the heart of Perugia. It boasts breathtaking views across the Umbrian Valley from its romantic balconies. Today, this stylish venue is a member of The Leading Small Hotels of the World group, and an essential pit-stop on any tour of the region.

The Brufani is now managed by the SINA group of luxury properties, whose conscientious revamp of the hotel has enhanced its original charm and historical features. The ceilings retain their original works of art, and the immaculate public spaces showcase authentic stone fireplaces. From the artfully dotted antiques to the eminently touchable rich fabrics that inform the interior design, the Brufani Palace simply breathes elegance.

Guest accommodation takes the form of 94 finely furnished rooms and suites, with views skimming across Perugia's rooftops to the lush valleys beyond. The Brufani Palace's most sought-after suites are its penthouses with their exposed wooden beams. Having said that, all rooms are equipped to the same impressive standards, featuring satellite TV, minibar, computer and hi-speed wireless Internet access.

The highlight of the Brufani Palace is its Fitness Club, where the pool is built beneath the stone arches of the palace's atmospheric medieval vaults, with a transparent glass floor beneath which ancient Etruscan

THIS PAGE (FROM TOP): Guests can relax and relish a quiet read by the great stone fireplace; indulge in regional fare and quality wines at Collins.

OPPOSITE (FROM TOP): The hotel's old world charm is evident from its interior; the Brufani has hosted many distinguished guests in more than 100 years of history; rooms combine traditional décor with the latest amenities.

ruins can be seen. This unforgettable setting also houses a fully-equipped gym, a sauna, steam bath and whirlpool. To complete the quest for total rejuvenation, comfortable chaise longues are also provided for guests to relax.

The culinary experience at the Brufani Palace is exquisite too, with the sun terrace of the Collins Restaurant providing the ultimate dining venue. Its innovative menu is created by Chef Marco Faiella, who has worked alongside illustrious names such as Michael Roux. Savour the Stringozzi with White Pheasant Ragu and Black Norcia Truffle, followed by an irresistible Fondant Chocolate Volcano. Marco's unique interpretations of authentic Umbrian cuisine are complemented by a portfolio of fine Italian wines, of which any oenophile would be proud.

For a refreshing afternoon tea, head to the welcoming ambience of the Collins Bar Open Space. Decorated in classic British 'gentlemen's club' style, its glossy dark wood panelling conceals an entire world of beer, liqueurs and cocktails, expertly prepared to meet each guest's personal requirements. Just the place for a smooth single malt nightcap, in fact, before retiring for a good night's sleep in preparation for another day of Umbrian adventure.

ROOMS
94

FOOD
Collins: Umbrian

DRINK
Collins Bar Open Space

FEATURES
satellite TV • minibar • safety box • Internet • wi-fi • SINA Fitness Club • banqueting rooms • gym • glass-bottomed pool • sauna

NEARBY
Lake Trasimeno • St. Francis • Todi • Gubbio • National Archaeological Museum of Umbria

CONTACT
Piazza Italia 12, 06121 Perugia • telephone: +39.075.573 2541 • facsimile: +39.075.572 0210 • email: brufanipalace@sinahotels.it • website: www.brufanipalace.com

hotel de russie

...the very definition of a luxurious retreat.

Rome has to be one of the most vibrant, enthralling capitals in Europe. With narrow streets bustling with cars and vespas, cafés overflowing onto the pavements, colourful markets in the picturesque squares and a host of ancient, legendary landmarks, there is nothing quite like it. It may come as quite a surprise, then, to find a tranquil oasis in the heart of the city, where an exotic garden creates the stunning backdrop for a truly charming boutique hotel.

The Hotel de Russie must be one of Rome's best kept secrets. Nestled between the Spanish Steps and the Piazza del Popolo, and only short walk from the Vatican City, it was originally built in the early 19th century and was completely revamped in the year 2000 by the Rocco Forte Hotel Collection. The results are quite simply breathtaking.

Built around the original, split-level courtyard that once divided two separate inns, the Hotel de Russie's exterior spaces are as enchanting as its interiors. Its terraced 'secret garden' is being completely restored to its former glory as an exotic, Mediterranean haven, complete with towering palms, ancient yews and aromatic orange trees. To miss a walk by its impeccable lawns and exuberant flowerbeds—splashed with the colours of butterflies from the garden's sanctuary—would be unforgivable.

Needless to say, the hotel's interiors are equally captivating. The bright, airy guestrooms, with courtyard, city or garden views, contain a contemporary, yet classical feel harking back to the sober elegance of the 1940s. Upholstered in rich fabrics in light pastels, with Mapplethorpe photos on the walls—in addition to lavish, marble bathrooms—they are the very definition of a luxurious retreat. For visitors on business, wireless Internet access and dual-line phones make life considerably easier.

In a high-octane city like Rome, an opportunity to unwind and reinvigorate is always welcome and at the De Russie Wellness Zone, the Hotel de Russie has perfected the art of relaxation. This glorious spa provides for complete care of the mind and body, offering a tantalising selection of massages, face and body treatments. Its state-of-the-art gym, complete with a marine hydropool, Finnish sauna and steam baths, only enhance the experience. To ensure a perfectly mellow end to the day, sip on a de Russie Martini at Le Stravinskij Bar.

Great care is taken at the Hotel de Russie to ensure a truly memorable stay and its restaurant, Le Jardin de Russie, is no exception. Serving traditional Italian favourites, prepared with the freshest local ingredients in a refined, cosmopolitan setting, guests will be enraptured. And with al fresco dining at the foot of the magnificent terraced gardens in the summer months, there is arguably no finer place to be in Rome.

ROOMS
122

FOOD
Le Jardin de Russie: Mediterranean

DRINK
Le Stravinskij Bar

FEATURES
wireless Internet access • satellite TV • dual-line phones • spa • gym • art historian-led VIP itineraries

BUSINESS
business centre • conference facilities • banqueting facilities

NEARBY
Vatican City • Piazza del Popolo • Pantheon • Piazza di Espagna • Santa Maria Sopra Minerva • Via Condotti

CONTACT
Via del Babuino 9, 00187 Rome • telephone: +39.06.328 881 • facsimile: +39.06.3288 8888 • email: reservations.derussie@ roccofortecollection.com • website: www.roccofortecollection.com

hotel lord byron

...this hidden gem of a hotel emits an aura of reserved yet stately elegance...

The charms of Rome are many and varied. Some are obvious and known to all, automatically attracting the attention of everybody who visits the city. Others have a more subtle appeal, offering the kind of intimate experience that is of interest only to the more discerning individual. Generally these attractions are less well known and harder to find, but they always repay those who take the time and trouble to seek them out.

The Hotel Lord Byron falls into the latter category. Tucked away among the many embassies of the city's exclusive Parioli district, this hidden gem of a hotel emits an aura of reserved yet stately elegance, and therein lies the magic of its appeal. It succeeds because it offers guests the best of both worlds—a discreet and luxurious hideaway of the highest quality that simultaneously allows easy access to many of the Eternal City's other leading attractions.

Also known as the White House, this long-time member of The Leading Hotels of the World boasts 32 of the loveliest rooms and suites that Rome has to offer. All have been recently restored in the classic Art Deco style, and radiate the warmth, intimacy and class for which Italian hospitality is famous, making them the perfect place to retire to at the end of a long day's shopping and sightseeing.

All guestrooms and suites feature elegant furnishings, not to mention spacious, marble-clad en suite bathrooms, and views over stately villas or the 80 hectares (198 acres) of the nearby Villa Borghese Gardens. Other features such as wi-fi Internet access, satellite colour TV, individual climate control and luxury bathrobes and slippers come as standard.

The hotel is also the proud home of the first-class Sapori del Lord Byron restaurant, one of the city's finest eating establishments, and one that has acquired a worldwide reputation for uncompromising excellence—as reflected daily by its distinguished and cosmopolitan clientele. The menu here features dishes that celebrate the wonders of authentic Italian haute cuisine and can rightly be considered as masterpieces in their own right, all prepared by an expert team of prize-winning chefs using the freshest seasonal ingredients. Its wine cellar is in a class of its own as well. Winner of *Wine Spectator* magazine's Award of Excellence in 2007, it serves a brilliant range of both Italian and international wines. Together with the romantic setting, impeccable service and the assistance of a professional sommelier, the restaurant offers a wonderful combination of style, elegance

and culinary perfection that is quite simply hard to beat. The Il Salotto Lounge & Wine Bar is equally impressive. Decorated with a series of magnificent portraits, it has an intimate setting, providing the ideal environment for a business meeting or just a leisurely chat—before or after that exquisite meal.

ROOMS
32

FOOD
Sapori del Lord Byron: Italian

DRINK
Il Salotto Lounge & Wine Bar

FEATURES
complimentary shuttle service to Via Veneto, Spanish Steps and Piazza del Popolo • multilingual staff • garage • satellite TV

BUSINESS
wi-fi Internet access

NEARBY
Castel San Angelo • Spanish Steps • Stadio Flaminio • Galleria Borghese • Via Veneto • Villa Borghese

CONTACT
Via Giuseppe De Notaris 5, 00197 Rome •
telephone: +39.06.322 0404 •
facsimile: +39.06.322 0405 •
email: info@lordbyronhotel.com •
website: www.lordbyronhotel.com

i casali di monticchio

...an almost dreamlike atmosphere of peace and tranquillity...

THIS PAGE (FROM TOP): Traditional pieces of furniture enhance the antique feel of the place; earthy tones of the room provide warmth and historical flavour.

OPPOSITE (FROM TOP): Old-fashioned lamps on the old manor walls; breathtaking views of the countryside make a stay at I Casali Di Monticchio an experience to remember.

There are dozens of reasons why people regularly visit and revisit Umbria, 'the green heart of Italy'. For some, it's the spectacular scenery and the sublime Mediterranean climate. For others, it's the rich, multi-layered history and seductive charms of its many unspoilt towns and villages. Then there's the unparalleled tradition of cuisine and warm hospitality, together with the long list of sporting activities on offer. Whatever the reason, one thing is certain—there are few places on earth that combine so many wonderful attractions as this natural and cultural paradise; few places that can compete with it in providing the perfect all-round holiday experience. But all of this leaves one unanswered question—where to stay?

By and large, there are two main options. The first is the traditional self-catering Umbrian villa, which has the advantages of privacy, independence and value for money. All too often, however, these come at the expense of the services and creature comforts expected of a truly relaxing holiday. The second option is a hotel. Though these offer more in the way of hospitality, they can be slightly suffocating and restrictive, not to mention impersonal and unnecessarily expensive.

For these reasons the recent opening of I Casali Di Monticchio is to be greatly welcomed. Although it is strictly speaking a hotel—and a member of the esteemed Small Luxury Hotels of the World, no less—almost all of the accommodation comes in the form of self-contained apartments with their own kitchens, living rooms and private gardens. This means that guests get to combine the best of both worlds: the freedom and independence of a villa holiday with the more indulgent services and benefits only offered by the very best hotels.

Originally built in the 1200s, I Casali Di Monticchio is a former 'borgo', or manor house, that has been restored in the traditional style with no expense spared and no detail overlooked. Together with its magnificent setting on a slight hill within its own 81-hectare (200-acre) estate, with classic views to be enjoyed wherever one casts one's eye, all this translates into an almost dreamlike atmosphere of peace and tranquillity that few locations can rival.

The accommodation is equally impressive. There are 12 rooms in all, each one individually furnished and thoughtfully styled with soothing colours and the finest fabrics to create enchanting havens that are steeped in the romance and antiquity of the buildings they occupy. Furthermore, while they all share such luxuries as en suite bathrooms and the modern conveniences of the most luxurious five-star hotels, no two layouts are alike. This means that guests have a wide combination of sleeping arrangements to choose from, making it easy to find the one that best suits their needs, whether it's a honeymoon couple looking for a romantic hideaway or a family looking for something on a grander scale.

THIS PAGE: The spacious, rustic-looking suite lulls guests into a relaxed evening of good Italian wine and conversation.

OPPOSITE (CLOCKWISE FROM TOP): Fine dining at the restaurant; the outdoor swimming pool; each bathroom is equipped with modern facilities; the simple, yet luxurious furnishings provide comfort.

Le Colombelle, for example, is a Junior Suite decorated with the colour theme of 'ciliegio e lavanda' (cherry and lavender) that comes with a large double bed. The furniture here is a mixture of antique and Provenza, and it has its own cooking facilities and a private garden where outdoor meals can be enjoyed in the evening while watching the sun set.

I Papaveri, by contrast, offers apartment-style accommodation. It consists of a bedroom suite with a four-poster bed, and has a separate bedroom with twin double beds and its own bathroom. Here the rooms have been decorated in the colours of 'ecru e rosso mattone' (ecru and brick red), and the furniture is composed of antiques with several more modern, Tuscan-

style elements. I Papaveri also comes with its own private living room with a fireplace, a kitchen, and a garden complete with a seating area and panoramic views that encompass the surrounding hills and even the cathedral of Orvieto, some 20 km (12½ miles) to the south.

When it comes to fine dining, the genius of I Casali Di Monticchio comes into its own with its elegant restaurant. Beautifully situated in the former stable block, the restaurant specialises in delicious Umbrian delicacies prepared by a dedicated team of qualified chefs using only the finest and freshest ingredients. In fact, the kitchen here is renowned locally for the quality of the produce it uses, much of which is organic and comes from the surrounding estate.

Last but not least, there's the hotel's purpose-built spa. Opening in the February 2008, it will offer an array of treatments, including massages that use honey, lavender or natural oils prepared from its own kitchen garden. Together with a jacuzzi, hydrotherapy pool and a relax area with a fireplace, the spa will offer total relaxation amid its tranquil Umbrian setting.

A host of other activities can also be found within easy driving range, such as golf, horse riding and, of course, all of the other attractions that make Umbria such a wonderful destination in the first place.

ROOMS
12

FOOD
Umbrian

DRINK
wine cellar

FEATURES
outdoor pool • snooker room • jogging track • mountain biking • cookery lessons • Botanical Garden

NEARBY
Allerona • Orvieto • Pienza • Monte Ruffeno Natural Park • Lake Trasimeno • Todi

CONTACT
Vocabolo Monticchio 34, 05011 Allerona, Umbria • telephone: +39.763 628 365 • facsimile: +39.763 629 569 • email: info@monticchio.com • website: www.monticchio.com

regina hotel baglioni

On entering the hotel, guests will be enveloped in an opulence of regal proportions.

Perhaps Rome's greatest charm is that 2,000 years of Italy's cultural and social history can be traced through its monumental landmarks and artistic treasures. No trip to the Eternal City would be complete without a visit to the awe-inspiring Roman Forums, the Emperors' residences on the Palatine, the Pantheon and the glorious Colosseum. Yet it is perhaps the Renaissance and Baroque treasures such as the Basilica of St. Peter and its sublime Sistine Chapel that are most celebrated. It was when the great city became capital of Italy in 1870 that the glorious Via Veneto came into its own as a lavish residential area. It is here, in the heart of Rome, where the Regina Hotel Baglioni—one of the city's finest luxury hotels—was built in 1904.

Housed in a Liberty-style palace, this exquisite boutique hotel stands a stone's throw from some of Rome's most important sights. The elegant period façade, complete with colourful blooms and charming balconies, offers a prelude to the grandeur of the hotel's interiors; the Regina Baglioni is truly in a league of its own when it comes to classical sophistication.

On entering the hotel, guests will be enveloped in an opulence of regal proportions. Polished, marble floors covered with ornate rugs combine with drapes in rich brocades and matching tapestry wallpapers, giving an overwhelmingly palatial feel. Elaborate Murano chandeliers and wall sconces illuminate delicate period paintings and mirrors in gilt frames, while antiques from the Art Deco era add a majestic quality.

Rooms are luxurious beyond compare and with some offering panoramic views over the rooftops of Rome, guests will find themselves resisting any temptation to leave the hotel. But for those who manage it, a walk through the Borghese Gardens and a visit to the spectacular Borghese Museum to see the works of Bernini and Caravaggio are highly recommended.

End a perfect day with an enchanting evening at the hotel's restaurant. Frequented as much by Romans as by visiting guests, the newly refurbished Brunello Lounge & Restaurant is one of the trendiest restaurants in the capital city. Blending modern and traditional styles for a cosy setting, diners are treated to superb Mediterranean cuisine cleverly crafted from local ingredients.

With attentive staff who are always there when needed but otherwise unobtrusive, the Regina Hotel Baglioni takes great pride in its flawless service and it comes as no surprise that it is a favourite among celebrities and dignitaries alike. In addition, the hotel offers specialised tours to the Roman Castle region, itineraries for wine and culinary enthusiasts, as well as guided tours—complete with a personal shopper—to the city's finest boutiques. Clearly there is nothing and no one that the Regina Hotel Baglioni hasn't taken into account.

THIS PAGE: *Regina Hotel Baglioni's majestic charm is evident from the fine furnishings in its lobby.*

OPPOSITE (ANTI-CLOCKWISE FROM TOP): *The Junior Suite's appeal lies in its classical yet luxurious interior; enjoy an exciting range of cocktails in the sohpisticated atmosphere of Brunello Lounge; silk tapestry provides a soft touch to the Deluxe Room.*

ROOMS
112

FOOD
Brunello Lounge & Restaurant: Mediterranean •
Caffè Baglioni: light snacks

DRINK
Brunello Lounge & Restaurant •
Caffè Baglioni

FEATURES
wireless Internet access • satellite TV •
specialised tours • babysitter on request

BUSINESS
conference rooms

NEARBY
Spanish Steps • Via Condotti •
Borghese Gardens • Borghese Museum

CONTACT
Via Veneto 72, 00187 Rome •
telephone: +39.06.421 111 •
facsimile: +39.06.4201 2130 •
email: reservations.reginaroma@
baglionihotels.com •
website: www.baglionihotels.com

st. regis grand hotel, rome

...the classic, the culinary and the contemporary co-exist in perfect harmony...

THIS PAGE (FROM TOP): Rooms are eclectically designed in its own unique and lavish style; the luxurious St. Regis has hosted several distinguished guests over the years.

OPPOSITE (ANTI-CLOCKWISE FROM TOP): No expense is spared in creating an exquisite feel; enjoy contemporary cuisine in Vivendo's sophisticated setting; the hotel's classic décor gives it an air of refined opulence.

To discover what a $35 million renovation can do for an already prestigious five-star hotel, simply visit the aristocratic St. Regis Grand Hotel, Rome. With the world-renowned Colosseum and Spanish Steps within walking distance, it is the location from which to absorb the cosmopolitan delights of the Eternal City. Opened in 1894 by fêted hotelier César Ritz, this exclusive destination is a crossroads for the world's elite, its prestigious clientele including Queen Elizabeth. This gloriously revamped hotel was unveiled on the brink of the new millennium, and exudes an aura of calm confidence as only ultra-luxurious properties truly can.

This Starwood hotel cherry-picked the best of French and Italian design influences to recreate the atmosphere of a Roman palazzo. From commissioned ceiling frescoes to unique Oriental rugs on the floors, no chance to impress has been overlooked. Before heading upstairs, enjoy a pick-me-up in the relaxing Le Grand Bar, voted by *Newsweek* as the Best Bar in Rome.

In the lobby, a soft glow refracts through antique Murano chandeliers, echoing off the gleaming marble columns. As for the suites, beds adorned with silk and brocade spreads are overlooked by authentic period paintings. Beneath this regal veneer lie myriad modern conveniences, from high-speed Internet access and advanced telecommunications to the impeccable and personalised butler service.

The 138 guestrooms and 23 unique suites combine Empire, Regency and Louis XV influences, in deference to César Ritz's original design inspiration. Each room boasts its own hand-painted fresco, its bathroom stocked with premium products from Laura Tonatto and Acqua di Parma. For extreme elegance, indulge in the Royal Suite that includes a master bedroom, guestroom, grand piano and private wine cellar. Alternatively, soak up the splendour of the Designer Suite with its gilded ceilings, Bohemian crystal chandeliers and precious carpets. With such treasures on tap, visits to Rome's numerous museums barely seem necessary.

Fitness regimes may be maintained at the fitness centre, with its panoramic views over ancient Diocletian baths. High-flying executives needn't miss a beat either, with cutting-edge computing and video conferencing services. For the ultimate wedding or banqueting event, reserve Rome's original ballroom, the Salone Ritz, now returned to its former antique grandeur.

Vivendo is the hotel's sophisticated 1940s-styled restaurant, which has several design awards to its credit. Its world-class cuisine is fêted by the gastronomic bibles *Gambero Rosso*

and *Zagat*, where it rates among Europe's top restaurants. Small, exclusive parties might prefer the privacy of its intimate Champagnerie venue. Wine lovers will be seduced by the international list of over 600 wines available by the glass from premium Amarone and Ornellaia to Barolo, chosen by the restaurant manager and sommelier Federico Galligani. These bottles are stored in the vaulted di...Vino Private Wine Cellar, very much a distinctive dining venue. To experience a microcosm of Rome, where the classic, the culinary and the contemporary co-exist in perfect harmony, St. Regis is the ultimate destination.

ROOMS
161

FOOD
The Vivendo Restaurant: contemporary •
di...Vino Private Wine Cellar: regional and international

DRINK
di...Vino Private Wine Cellar •
Le Grand Bar

FEATURES
e-butler service • 24-hour butler service • hi-speed Internet access • wi-fi (public areas) • massages • pilates room • fitness and wellness centre • multilingual personal shopper

BUSINESS
business and communication centre

NEARBY
Colosseum • Piazza Navona • Spanish Steps • Via Condotti • Via Veneto

CONTACT
Via Vittorio Emanuele Orlando 3, 00185 Rome •
telephone: +39.06.47 091 •
facsimile: +39.06.474 7307 • email: StRegisGrandRome@stregis.com • website: www.stregisgrand.hotelin roma.com

the duke hotel

Blending the style of an English gentlemen's club with classical Italian designs...

THIS PAGE: The stylish and cosy ambience of the Polo Lounge encapsulates The Duke Hotel's grandeur and warm hospitality.

OPPOSITE (CLOCKWISE FROM TOP): Enjoy a mixture of innovative and traditional dishes at I Duchi; rooms offer comfort as well as the latest technology; classic décor provides suites with an exquisite charm.

In a city as frenetic as Rome, with bustling streets, crowded museums and cafes brimming over with tourists, it may be worth trading a centrally located hotel for a little peace and quiet. The upmarket Paroli residential district of Rome is home to a number of embassies and well-heeled Italian families and is flanked by the vast Villa Borghese and Villa Glori parks. Though only a short drive from the main attractions, this oasis of tranquillity is sufficiently removed from the city centre to allow visitors a bit of breathing space, yet with some of Rome's finest restaurants and boutiques, Paroli is the perfect compromise.

Rising from Paroli's elegant, tree-lined boulevards is The Duke Hotel, one of Rome's most charming retreats. Occupying an Italian rationalist building dating back to 1950, The Duke Hotel was formerly the glamorous Residence Palace, which played host to a slew of Hollywood

stars including Richard Burton and Elizabeth Taylor. Unsurprisingly, following its reopening as a boutique hotel in 2000, The Duke continues to attract international celebrities and discerning travellers drawn by its impeccable personal service and sumptuousness.

Blending the style of an English gentlemen's club with classical Italian designs, the stunning interiors give the hotel a sophisticated, cosmopolitan edge. Its centrepiece is the Polo Lounge, where a spectacular painted glass domed roof combines with antique artworks, luxurious armchairs and a marble fireplace for a refined and cosy atmosphere, ideal for a quiet evening drink or a refreshing afternoon tea.

The Duke's spacious rooms and suites leave nothing to be desired with regard to creature comforts and state-of-the-art technology. Filled with natural light and gracefully appointed with polished, wooden floors, rooms come with private balconies and lavish marble bathrooms.

Following a gruelling day's work or sightseeing, guests wanting to spend the evening in the privacy of their own room can enjoy satellite TV channels or browse the web with wireless Internet access. And with a sauna and fitness centre soon to be opened on the premises, relaxation and well-being will take on a whole new dimension at The Duke Hotel.

The I Duchi restaurant serves first-class regional Italian cuisine, complemented by a seasonal tasting menu that changes every two months. Evening dinners are made all the more amenable with live piano music, while subtle lighting and refined décor create an intimate setting. Younger guests are not forgotten either, as I Duchi offers a children's menu.

Staff here will go to any length to ensure that guests get the most out of their stay in Rome—a complimentary limousine service takes guests to the downtown area and remains on call around the clock. In addition, aside from organising the usual itineraries and tours, the concierge at The Duke also provides guests with access to some of the city's loveliest private homes and gardens that are not usually open for public viewing. Clearly, for those seeking a quieter approach to the Eternal City, there is only one place to stay.

ROOMS
78

FOOD
I Duchi: Italian

DRINK
Polo Lounge Bar

FEATURES
satellite TV • wireless Internet access • special itineraries • limousine • banquets

BUSINESS
business centre • conference facilities • meeting rooms

NEARBY
Gallery of Modern and Contemporary Art • Villa Glori park • Villa Borghese Museum and park • Spanish Steps • spa • golf • horse riding • jogging • fitness centre

CONTACT
Via Archimede 69, 00197 Rome • telephone: +39.06.367 221• facsimile: +39.06.3600 4104 • email: theduke@thedukehotel.com • website: www.thedukehotel.com

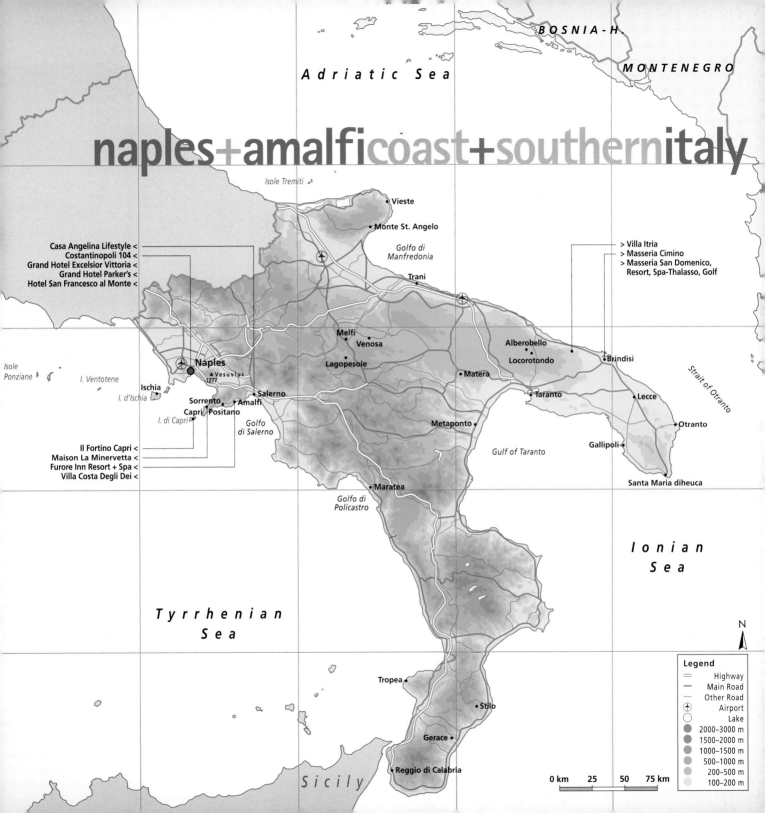

naples+amalficoast+southernitaly

BOSNIA-H

MONTENEGRO

A d r i a t i c   S e a

Isole Tremiti

• Vieste

• Monte St. Angelo

Golfo di Manfredonia

• Trani

Casa Angelina Lifestyle <
Costantinopoli 104 <
Grand Hotel Excelsior Vittoria <
Grand Hotel Parker's <
Hotel San Francesco al Monte <

> Villa Itria
> Masseria Cimino
> Masseria San Domenico,
   Resort, Spa-Thalasso, Golf

Isole Ponziane

I. Ventotene

Ischia
I. d'Ischia

Sorrento
Capri • Positano
I. di Capri

• Melfi
• Venosa

• Lagopesole

Naples
▲Vesuvius
1277

Salerno •
• Amalfi
Golfo di Salerno

• Matera

Alberobello •
Locorotondo •

• Brindisi

Strait of Otranto

• Taranto

• Lecce

Il Fortino Capri <
Maison La Minervetta <
Furore Inn Resort + Spa <
Villa Costa Degli Dei <

• Metaponto

• Gallipoli

• Otranto

• Maratea

Gulf of Taranto

Santa Maria diheuca

Golfo di Policastro

*I o n i a n
S e a*

*T y r r h e n i a n
S e a*

• Tropea

• Stilo

Gerace •

• Reggio di Calabria

S i c i l y

N

Legend
═══ Highway
─── Main Road
─── Other Road
⊕ Airport
◯ Lake
⬤ 2000–3000 m
⬤ 1500–2000 m
⬤ 1000–1500 m
⬤ 500–1000 m
⬤ 200–500 m
⬤ 100–200 m

0 km   25   50   75 km

naples + amalfi coast + southern italy

Sun-drenched Naples was adored by the Romans, who spent their holidays here in vast villa complexes facing the sea. Later, as capital of the Kingdom of Naples, it was one of the wealthiest cities in Europe, seized in turn by the Normans, the Aragonese and the Bourbons, all of whom built splendid palaces and gardens as well as churches. There's a wealth of art to see, such as finds from Pompeii and the Farnese marbles in the Archaeological Museum; the Farnese painting collection in the Capodimonte; and literally hundreds of churches, each hiding treasures within. Naples also has some of Italy's most startling design projects and contemporary art. There are shops dominated by artisans following time-honoured traditions and a new generation of forward-thinking youngsters. Times may be tough but the people's warmth and passion for life is infectious, and their food is some of Italy's simplest and best.

Twinkling tantalisingly in the bay are the islands of Capri, Ischia and Procida. Beyond the city, there's Vesuvius to climb or the Roman ruins of Pompeii, Erculano and Oplontis to explore. Resort Sorrento is also the gateway to the legendary Amalfi Coast while the Greek temples of Paestum and the beautiful forests and beaches of the Cilento lie south of Salerno towards Calabria, where the landscape becomes even more dramatic. To the east are the inland villages of unspoilt Basilicata, transfixed in the annals of time, while neighbour Puglia is hailed for its beautiful coastline and vast olive groves.

a naples to die for

Many people have a love-hate relationship with Naples. Many don't try to have one at all, rushing through the city as quickly as they can to get to Sorrento, the Amalfi Coast or Capri. But they're missing out—there's a lot more to the city than meets the eye. The centre of Naples is surprisingly compact. One of Europe's most densely inhabited cities, the streets and the traffic can be overwhelming at times and walking is really the best way to move around. Royal Naples commences around the busy sea port, with the austere Angevin Castel Nuovo. Curving round it meets the Teatro San Carlo and

PAGE 220: *This view from Capri is shared with a statue of Caesar Augustus in Anacapri.*

THIS PAGE (FROM TOP): *Naples' city sprawl seen from the Castel Sant'Elmo in Vomero; a gruesome death mask of a man who perished at Pompeii. Engulfed in volcanic ash the bodies left a permanent imprint, recreated in plaster cast when the ruins were excavated.*

OPPOSITE: *The Amalfi Coast.*

royal palace, which opens on to the central square of Piazza Plebescito. Downhill, to the left of the square, is the charming old quarter of Santa Lucia, complete with fishing boats and yachts clustered around the Castel dell'Ovo and more of those to-die-for views. On the corner of Piazza Plebescito and Via Chiaia is the grand old caffè of Gambrinus. This is the gateway to the stylish bars and restaurants off Piazza dei Martiri, as well as the luxury shops of Via dei Mille and Piazza Amedeo. It is from here that one of Naples' funiculars departs for Vomero, a well-to-do neighbourhood high over old Naples. Up in Vomero await the Castel Sant'Elmo and the Certosa di San Martino, both of which harbour ancient and modern art and some more stunning views over the city and across both bays. Via Roma leads up past the Galleria Umberto I (inspired by the Galleria in Milan) towards Piazza Dante and into the old heart of Naples, Spaccanapoli. Here the oldest, narrowest and perhaps most quintessentially Neapolitan streets await, as well as an important archaeological museum. The Museo Archeologico

Nazionale is filled with treasures from Pompeii, Herculaneum and other Roman sites. Highlights include the colossal marble sculptures of the Farnese collection, wall paintings from Pompeii, bronze sculptures from Herculaneum, the enchanting fresco of Spring from the Villa Stabia and a giant mosaic of Alexander the Great. There's also the Secret Cabinet, once a private room that was filled with ancient erotica. Nearby, Piazza Dante and Piazza Bellini have plenty of little cafés, perfect for sampling some Italian coffee.

Down from the museum is a bevy of worthy sights such as the grand Duomo of San Gennaro; one of Caravaggio's finest works, the *Seven Acts of Mercy*, in the Monte della Misericoridia; the beautiful Renaissance church of San Giovanni a Carbonara; and the chapel of Sansevero, with Sammartino's extraordinary sculpture *The Veiled Christ*.

Naples' passion for cutting-edge art, music and theatre has given rise to various projects which have transformed the city. MADRe is an art space set in the convent of Donna Regina. Adapted by Portuguese architect Alvaro Siza, it houses a collection of modern art including stars such as Damien Hurst and Anish Kapoor as well as Neapolitan painter Francesco Clemente. Tiny gallery space T293 on Via Tribunali 293 is another key arts venue. Over on Via dei Mille is the gallery PAN, which holds theatre-style events and shows art films as well as modern art. But again it's underground that even more is going on—seven new stations of the city's expanding metro system form backdrops to installations by artists from all over the world, with more in the pipeline.

High over Naples is the Villa Capodimonte, a royal hunting lodge and park, housing first-rate art. Underneath are acres of another underground Napoli—one of caves, tunnels, catacombs, secret passageways, air raid shelters and homes. There are several entrance points: one is beneath the church of San Paolo another is under Santa Maria della Sanità in the Vergini district. Near the church are the magnificent double-flight stairways of the Palazzo dello Spagnolo (which also houses the art gallery Fondazione Morra) and the Palazzo Sanfelice.

THIS PAGE: *Sorrento with Vesuvius looming beyond.*

OPPOSITE (FROM TOP): *Lemons, brought to Amalfi by the Arabs, are intrinsic to local cuisine. There are several varieties some so sweet locals like to eat them; swimming by the Galli Islands off Positano, the legendary home of Homer's Sirens and real-life home of the great ballet dancer, Rudolf Nureyev.*

big bad vesuvius

Vesuvius last erupted in 1944. Now almost a million people live on its fertile slopes. It's easy to climb to the summit and peering into the crater with its steaming fumaroles some 200 m (656 ft) below is a distinctly eerie sensation that is rewarded with superb views from the top. When Vesuvius erupted, Pompeii was scorched, squashed and shrouded in ash; Herculaneum was swallowed up in a torrent of mud, which hardened on reaching the sea, thus preserving it. Both sites are equally impressive in different ways. Pompeii is like a vast ghost town, with the impressive old enemy Vesuvius still looming in the near distance. It was rediscovered in 1600 but not excavated until over a hundred years later when many treasures vanished as the Grand Tour kicked in. Most of the best pieces are in the Museo Archeologico, but there are still plenty of frescoes and mosaics to hunt for. Highlights are the Villa dei Misteri, the House of the Vetti, the Lupinarium or brothel, and the house of the Golden Cupids. Herculaneum, smaller and more intact, is particularly famous for its mosaics. The Neptune and the Amphitrite Mosaics are a sight to behold, as are those of dolphins and other sea creatures in the bathhouses.

lemonsville + amalfi coast

Surrounded by lemon groves, Sorrento became popular with the English in the early 19th century and has stayed that way. Away from the frenzy of Naples, it is a useful place too: Pompeii, Capri and the Amalfi Coast are all within easy reach. Sorrento's pretty centre leads onto a cliff top giving fine views across the Bay of Naples, the pontoons below serving as a beach. The pretty fishing harbour, Marina Grande, is a step back in time and has some great restaurants, as does Massa Lubrense.

The Amalfi Coast is home to Italy's most beautiful coastline. Driving from one S-bend to another, dense vertical vegetation defiantly sprouts from limestone cliffs, precariously balanced villages tumble down ravines and the sky and the sea merge into one big breathless blue panorama. The town of Amalfi has a strong sense of its Saracen influences, which are evident not just in the lemons that grow all around, but in the tiled bell tower, Moorish cloister and lace-like arches of its cathedral. Set deep inside a ravine, carved by waterfalls, Amalfi's main industry was making paper.

Positano has a spectacular position perched above a strip of sand, its road snaking past pastel-coloured cube houses, all proudly facing out to sea. Stumbled upon by John Steinbeck after the war, it is now a bit of a battleground come high season, with tourists arriving in their hordes. The place remains exquisite, but the squash can be off-putting.

Other notables along this stretch of coast include Furore, Italy's only fjord, tucked out of sight between Amalfi and Positano. Ravello towers above Amalfi and has the most privileged views of all. Literally breathtaking are those from the Villa Cimbrone—where the Bloomsbury Set cavorted—or those from romantic Villa Rufolo, which hosts a summer music festival in its gardens. Ravello's cathedral is the most beautiful on the coast.

island chic

Not all beautiful places attract so many beautiful people, and that's part of Capri's attraction. Pristine white houses rouged with bougainvillea cluster around the Piazzetta and anyone who's anyone has sat here at some point. The Blue Grotto and the splendid shops are popular, but there's far more to the island. Strolling around the old meandering paths is what Capri is all about. Among a handful of things to stumble upon are Le Corbusier's Punta Tragara; the Villa Jovis or the Arco Naturale; the Villa Malaparte; and the pretty gardens of the Villa Krupp.

Beyond Capri town, Marina Piccola has great views of the Faraglioni as well as the island's best beach. Emilio Pucci's first shop opened here in 1949. Anacapri, the other town on the island is quieter and less manicured. Savour staggering views at the Villa Michele or the beautiful majolica Garden of Eden in San Michele. At sunset, the bars beside the Punta Carena lighthouse—not far from the Blue Grotto—are the perfect place for a drink. And exploring the island by boat is one of the best ways to see Capri, swimming by the Faraglioni is one of life's true pleasures.

Ischia is a lush and surprisingly large island. Towered by dormant Monte Epomeo, it is scattered with copious thermal pools. Crammed with vines, lemons and small farms, it is home to the beautiful gardens of La Mortella, which were created by William Walton and his wife

Susana. Ischia's beaches at Maronti, near trendy Sant'Angelo, and San Montano, in Forio are the best in the Bay. And, while Ischia Porto is the liveliest resort, Ischia Ponte should not be missed. Its castle, linked with a village by a causeway, is a gem. The island's top restaurants are around Forio.

Procida is a tiny island, famed for its lemons and used as backdrop in several films. Its colourful houses are dishevelled and unpretentious. The old fishing village of Corricella is the oldest part of the island; just opposite is the fine beach of Chiaia and its perfect trattoria.

step we gaily: heel for heel and toe for toe

Puglia is the high heel and spur of the Italian boot. The country's biggest producer of olive oil, the olive groves to the south and fertile plains to the north dominate Puglia's countryside. The spur is home to the Gargano Peninsula, where pretty little seaside towns perch on cliff tops and can only be reached by winding coastal drives or by the dark inland Foresta Umbra. The Isole Tremiti—an exquisite archipelago of five islands with legendary diving—are a short boat ride away. Vieste is easily the prettiest town on the peninsula; more inland it's Monte Sant'Angelo.

To the south, Lecce is renowned for its baroque architecture; the golden stone here is easy to carve. It was used to build the opulent Basilica di Santa Croce and the Piazza del Duomo, just two of master sculptor Giuseppe Zimbalo's masterpieces that appear in the town. Beyond Lecce are the scenic seaside towns of Otranto, Gallipoli and Santa Maria di Leuca—beautiful beaches, castles and a colourful history.

The trulli around Alberobello and Locorotondo are Puglia's biggest other draw. Quirky, beehive-shaped, single-roomed houses, in limestone blocks with grey tile roofs, clustered together as if for hobbits. Many of the houses have symbols with magical and pagan connotations painted on the roofs. Alberobello has unfortunately become somewhat touristy; Locorotondo is much less commercial.

THIS PAGE (FROM TOP): Alberobello's trulli, their conical roofs a distinctive feature of southern Puglian architecture; Zimbalo's elaborate façade of the Santa Croce.

OPPOSITE: Via Krupp Road in Capri. Despite her glossy appearance and any attempt to tame Capri, the island's enchantment derives from her dual personality—her glamour and her fiercely natural beauty.

Set in a great plain is the Castel del Monte near Bari; its vast proportions and perfect geometry have puzzled people for centuries. Designed by Frederick II Stupor Mundi in the mid-13th century as a hunting lodge, its octagonal form shows a strong Islamic influence.

The Normans established both Calabria and Basilicata in the 11th century. Eventually they became part of the Kingdom of Sicily, which stretched across the southern third of mainland Italy. In Matera between the 8th and 13th centuries, Byzantine monks inhabited many of its sassi (caves) that were gouged from the rock face. Inside the caves the monks created exquisitely tiny chiese rupestre (rock churches), making the town one of Basilicata's top attractions.

magna graecia

Around 800 BC the Greeks settled in southern Italy, building vast city-states along the high arch of Italy's boot. The ghostly ruins of these powerful places are all that remain of Rheggium, Locri, Croton, Sybaris, Heraclea, Metapontion and Taras. A wealth of artefacts survive, however, and are exhibited in the museums of Taranto and Reggio Calabria.

THIS PAGE (FROM TOP): A fresco from the church of Santa Maria d'Idris in Matera's Sasso Caveoso district, where Mel Gibson shot much of his film The Passion of the Christ; many of the cave dwellings are being transformed into smart hotels or restaurants revitalising the town of Matera.

OPPOSITE: The Castel del Monte near Bari is just one of several noble castles in the south.

Locri Epizephiri was home to Zaleucus, who wrote the first Greek code of law, the *Locrian Code*. He was a tough old cookie; adultery was punishable by blinding. But he was also quite sensible; no free woman was to be allowed more than one maid to follow her unless she was drunk. The legendary indulgers, the Sybarites, whose lifestyle entered the dictionary, were literally wiped out by next-door neighbour Croton in 510 BC. The Greeks thought it was divine justice—such was their arrogance, the Sybarites had even tried to set up a rival to the Olympic Games. Poseidonia, known better as Paestum, was established by wandering Sybarites in 600 BC. Abandoned in the Middle Ages, it vanished from sight. Rediscovered by royal road builders in the 18th century, Paestum soon became a firm favourite on the Grand Tour. It is the best preserved Magna Graecia sight of them all.

...its vast proportions and perfect geometry have puzzled people for centuries.

casa angelina lifestyle

...on a clifftop overlooking the picturesque village of Praiano on the Amalfi Coast...

An integral feature of any boutique hotel is that it should offer guests a degree of cutting-edge, minimalist design. The problem is quite a few of them overdo it, all but eliminating any sense of comfort, and the result can just be a little too sterile and soulless for the guests, reducing their stay to a kind of tedious routine instead of the pleasurable experience originally hoped for.

Not all boutique hotels are guilty of making this mistake, however, as some go out of their way to blend the best of innovative design and modern facilities with the more traditional virtues of friendly service and a luxurious ambience. As the name suggests, the Casa Angelina Lifestyle Hotel is one of these. It is a home as much as it is a hotel, and a place where traditional Italian hospitality and first-class service are as important as the chic décor and wide-ranging facilities.

Enjoying a spectacular setting high on a clifftop overlooking the picturesque village of Praiano on the Amalfi Coast, Casa Angelina boasts 41 beautifully designed bedrooms and suites, all of which are as stylish as any to be found in Italy. Here, contemporary furnishings and artefacts—including Sosabravo sculptures, Philippe Starck lamps, Gervasoni sofas and Murano glass masterpieces—have been skilfully introduced to create an über-cool yet tranquil environment that is as pleasing to the senses as it is to the soul. The wonderful sense of style and romance engendered would be remarkable even without the added benefit of the stunning views of the Gulf of Salerno that all rooms share, not to mention the satellite plasma TVs, spacious en suite bathrooms, air conditioning and 24-hour room service.

Equally exceptional are the hotel's other attractions, starting with the main restaurant, Un Piano nel Cielo, where guests can simultaneously enjoy gourmet classic Italian cuisine—a delectable mix of the flavours of the Mediterranean and the Amalfi Coast—and the magnificent coastline from the large sea view terrace. Locally sourced fish and shellfish dishes are the

THIS PAGE (FROM TOP): Casa Angelina mixes avant-garde and modern comfort to great effect; rooms are minimalist yet stylish.

OPPOSITE (FROM TOP): Stunning Murano glass artwork is very much part of the hotel's décor; sit back and enjoy the warmth of the the Amalfi Coast sun; or head indoors for a relaxing swim in the heated pool.

ROOMS
41

FOOD
Un Piano nel Cielo: Mediterranean

DRINK
Marrakech Bar

FEATURES
indoor pool • outdoor pool • jacuzzi • gym • sauna • spa

NEARBY
Amalfi • Capri • Pompeii • Positano • Ravello • Sorrento • Vietri

CONTACT
Via G. Capriglione 147, 84010 Praiano, Salerno • telephone: +39.089.813 1333 • facsimile: +39.089.874 266 • email: reservations@casangelina.com • website: www.casangelina.com

highlights here, all of which can be accompanied by an extensive selection of Italian and international wines. In addition, there are a few stylish bars, including the Cigar Room that features an award-winning selection of the finest cigars, rums and grappas.

Last but not least, Casa Angelina also has its own private beach, though the real winner probably lies in its small fleet of exquisite Sea Gem boats—classic boats powered by modern technology—that make day-trips to such places as Positano, Naples, Capri and Sorrento an effortless pleasure. Then there are the three swimming pools, and a 150-sq-m (1,615-sq-ft) spa complex that specialises in a wide variety of exercise routines based on the Pilates Method and includes a jacuzzi, sauna and gym. All in all, it's a combination of style, comfort, setting and amenities that other hotels in the region would not find easy to emulate.

costantinopoli 104

...ideally located in the heart of the city's historic centre...

In the shadow of Mount Vesuvius, the city of Naples lies around the beautiful bay sharing its name in the Campania region of southern Italy. Famed as much for its noisy streets as it is for its piazzas, ebullient character and spectacular sights, the city that invented the pizza offers a colourful alternative to the pristine cities of the north. And with some of the Mediterranean's most spectacular beaches close by along the Amalfi Coast, Naples offers an array of attractions to suit all tastes.

Vibrancy abounds in Naples with crowded, narrow streets bursting with cars, Vespas and vendors, yet it all seems to contribute to its lively charm. Visitors to the city, however, will always appreciate a little calm at the end of the day and the place to find it is in the gracious setting of the hotel Constantinopoli 104, whose origins can be traced back to the late 19th century.

This tastefully adapted Art Nouveau villa is ideally located in the heart of the city's historic centre, just a few blocks from the National Anthropological Musuem housing the legendary treasures of Vesuvius and Herculaneum. An oasis of calm, the hotel is nestled in a quiet courtyard, where a swimming pool, gardens and exotic palms create a serene countryside feel despite the urban surrounds.

THIS PAGE (FROM TOP): Illuminated by the warm lighting, the pool looks particularly inviting at night; suites at the hotel have parquet flooring and a four-poster bed for an exquisite feel.

OPPOSITE (CLOCKWISE FROM TOP LEFT): Warm colour tones and a spacious interior make rooms a comfortable retreat; Costantinopoli 104 welcomes guests to its 19th-century home; the hotel's period paintings typify its old world charm.

Much of the original architectural styling of the hotel remains intact, including the stunning stained-glass windows, marble balustrades and elaborate floor tiling. Interiors are classically elegant, while polished wooden floors, period antiques and prints, and a cosy fireplace welcome guests in the living room. Rooms are spacious and luxurious, opening out to the garden on the ground floor or to terraces on the upper level. Suites, on the other hand, come with sumptuous marble jacuzzis, the perfect antidote after a full day in the bustling city.

Exquisite details such as bowls of fresh fruit and bouquets of flowers decorate the interior, making guests feel that they are in a home away from home. Furthermore, the friendly, attentive,

multilingual staff ensure that guests are able to completely relax and make the most of their visit to Naples.

Following a delectable breakfast at the hotel, guests could take a stroll in the streets near the hotel and find themselves watching as craftsmen restore antique musical instruments. They could also wander into one of the many remarkable baroque churches such as San Domenico Maggiore or the stunning Duomo itself. There is no shortage of irresistible trattorias in the area close to Constantinopoli either, ideal for savouring Naples' very own specialty dish, the pizza. Constantinopoli 104 is the antithesis of the rumbustious city that it stands in, a haven of tranquillity and a sumptuous retreat.

ROOMS
19

FOOD
meals on request

DRINK
wine list

FEATURES
excursions to Pompeii and Herculaneum • pool • satellite TV • jacuzzi • CD and DVD players • multi-functional space

NEARBY
National Archeological Museum • historic centre • Sansevero Chapel • Museum of Contemporary Art Donnaregina of Naples

CONTACT
Via S Maria Constantinopoli 104, 80138 Naples •
telephone: +39.081.557 1035 •
facsimile: +39.081.557 1051 •
email: info@constantinopoli104.it •
website: www.constantinopoli104.com

furore inn resort + spa

...the complete Amalfi Coast experience in one exquisitely neat little package.

Some parts of the world are so heartbreakingly beautiful that it's hard for the visitor to find a hotel to match the quality and splendour of the surroundings. The Amalfi Coast is one such area and the task is rendered doubly difficult by the fact that the spectacular terrain is so rugged and precipitous that hotels of any sort are notoriously hard to come by. All the more reason then guests should be grateful for the existence of the classy, super-swish, five-star Furore Inn Resort and Spa. Among the cognoscenti, it is the only place to stay on the Amalfi Coast.

Of course, such a lack of any real competition might lead to a culture of complacency—but not at the Furore Inn. Here, the pursuit of excellence is a never-ending goal, as the uncompromising and unstinting levels of service and attention to detail continually testify. The result is a resort that not only sets the standard by which other resorts in the region should be judged upon, but one which also offers the complete Amalfi Coast experience in one exquisitely neat little package.

Spread over seven terraces high on a hillside overlooking the charming town of the same name and the Mediterranean Sea itself, this wonderful boutique hotel could not be better positioned. Furthermore, its small size means that guests are ensured the undivided attention of the cheerful and friendly staff throughout their stay.

All 22 rooms and suites are light, bright and spacious, seamlessly blending stylish furnishings with the latest modern amenities to create a luxurious and comfortable environment of the highest standard. Although no two rooms are alike, they all have one notable quality in common—each offers one of the most romantic and visually stunning backdrops imaginable.

But it's not just the stunning vistas that have drawn people to the Amalfi Coast over the years. No visit to the region would be complete without an equally magnificent culinary experience, and in this respect the Furore Inn doesn't disappoint. There are two restaurants to choose from. The innovative Italian Touch marries Mediterranean and international flavours in elegant surroundings and has justly earned an impressive reputation

THIS PAGE (FROM TOP): Guestrooms at Furore Inn provide a dazzling view of the sea; enjoy an espresso in the quiet ambience of Caffé dell'Affresco.

OPPOSITE (FROM TOP): The spa offers a wide range of treatments for total rejuvenation; take a dip in the gorgeous pool that appears as part of the Mediterranean Sea; resting on the hill of Crevano away from the hustle of Amalfi Drive, the resort is a peaceful retreat for both mind and body.

ROOMS
22

FOOD
Italian Touch: Mediterranean and international • Fishing Vixen: Italian

DRINK
American Bar • Caffè dell'Affresco • wine cellar

FEATURES
outdoor pools • Beauty Furore Spa • hydro-massage jacuzzi • parking • tennis court • satellite TV

BUSINESS
meeting room

NEARBY
Amalfi Coast • Capri • Pompeii • Positano • Ravello • Sorrento • Vietri

CONTACT
Via dell'Amore, Piazza Sant'Elia 1, 84010 Furore, Amalfi Coast • telephone: +39.089.830 4711 • facsimile: +39.089.830 4777 • email: information@furoreinn.it • website: www.furoreinn.it

as a gourmet restaurant of the highest order. The Fishing Vixen, on the other hand, offers traditional fare in a more casual environment, with two terraces on which diners can simultaneously savour both the brilliant view and cuisine. Locally sourced ingredients, in particluar seafood, feature prominently and a wide array of local and international wines is available to accompany every course.

In addition, the hotel offers three spectacular outdoor swimming pools, an extensive health and beauty centre, open-air jacuzzi and tennis court. So all in all, it's not hard to see why this hotel is regularly rated as one of Italy's top ten boutique hotels.

grand hotel excelsior vittoria

...history can be felt in every corner of the Vittoria.

THIS PAGE (FROM TOP): *The Pompei Suite's luxurious décor allows guests to relive the opulent lifestyle of Imperial Rome; the Aurora Suite impresses with its beautiful ceiling fresco and old world charm.*

OPPOSITE (FROM TOP): *Enjoy a relaxing swim in the peaceful surrounds of the hotel's gardens; indulge in a wide range of beauty treatments at the spa.*

Sorrento has beguiled the world for centuries, lying between the azure sky and the shimmering waters of the Bay of Naples. A member of The Leading Small Hotels of the World, the five-star Grand Hotel Excelsior Vittoria has hosted Pavarotti, Sophia Loren and countless members of royalty. Featured on *Condé Nast Traveller*'s Gold List, Excelsior Vittoria is the ideal base from which to explore the cultural riches of this diverse region.

From the Art Nouveau Winter Garden to the authentic, handcrafted furniture of the Belle Époque Music Room, history can be felt in every corner of the Vittoria. Renowned contemporary artists have created exclusive trompe l'œils and tapestries to enhance the

romance and atmosphere of this characterful property, which is itself recognised as a heritage site of much cultural significance. The 98 luxuriously appointed rooms and suites are located in adjoining buildings which together form the hotel complex. The Pompei Suite offers loft sleeping, two marble bathrooms and breathtaking sea views, while the Princess Margaret Suite has a stunning neo-Renaissance ceiling and a locally-hewn red marble bathroom. Masterpieces grace the walls, with Louis XVI and Biedermeier furniture adding to the hotel's timeless style.

The private terraces survey the Neapolitan Riviera, 2 hectares (5 acres) of verdant gardens or the hotel's bright orange groves. Fragrant bougainvillea and tropical palms surround the Trani marble pool with its invigorating water massage area.

The adjacent La Serra holistic centre, designed by British architect Colin Gold, offers a multitude of indulgent spa products. The tempting menu of detoxifying and well-being rituals is delivered in a private or couples only suite. The Orange Garden is a highly recommended signature treatment. Shiatsu, Ayurvedic and Swedish massage are also available, as well as beauty treatments using the finest Salin de Biosel and Organic Pharmacy labels to enhance this deliciously pure spa experience.

Splendid fin de siècle frescoes, gleaming marble panelling and waxed parquet flooring furnish the Vittoria's elegant restaurant. Its windows frame the panoramic views outside, with picturesque islands dappling the middle distance. Chef Vincenzo Galano revels in producing

the freshest Mediterranean cuisine to satisfy the most demanding of gastronomes. In summer, the Bosquet provides a more intimate environment, its sun terrace overlooking the soaring Mount Vesuvius. For a pleasurable diversion, remember to browse through the chic boutiques of this exclusive destination. Naples, Mount Vesuvius, the dramatic cliff-clinging towns of Amalfi and the archaeological sites at Pompeii and Herculaneum too are within easy day-tripping distance. The Vittoria's multi-faceted destination means a busy holiday or a relaxing escape and one that can be enjoyed at any time of the year.

ROOMS
98

FOOD
Ristorante Vittoria: Mediterranean •
Terrazza Bosquet: Mediterranean •
Pool restaurant: Neapolitan

DRINK
Bar Vittoria • Pool Bar

FEATURES
satellite TV • minibar • safe •
La Serra Holistic Centre •
outdoor pool • jacuzzi • Internet •
babysitter on request

BUSINESS
conference rooms

NEARBY
Amalfi • Capri • Pompeii

CONTACT
Piazza Tasso 34,
80067 Sorrento, Napoli •
telephone: +39.081.877 7111 •
facsimile: +39.081.877 1206 •
email: exvitt@exvitt.it •
website: www.exvitt.it

grand hotel parker's

...explicitly designed to provide hospitality and service of the highest order.

THIS PAGE (FROM TOP): *The hotel's spectacular façade at night; the extravagant ballroom; dine outdoors and take in the magnificent view of the bay.*

OPPOSITE (ANTI-CLOCKWISE FROM TOP): *Bright and spacious guestrooms; the Day Light spa offers a wide range of programmes; at George's Restaurant, enjoy a romantic candlelight dinner overlooking the Bay of Naples.*

There are some hotels that are so perfect and welcoming that at some point during their stay, guests cannot help but dream of buying the place outright, making it their home and staying there for the rest of their lives. English gentleman and connoisseur George Parker Bidder's fantasy came true when he checked into the Hotel Tramontana-Beaurivage in Naples back in the late 1880s. Here, he was so enamoured with the hospitality and surroundings that he decided to make the dream a reality and the result is known today as the Grand Hotel Parker's.

And who can blame him for his decision? The Grand Hotel Parker's is everything anyone could ever hope for, with all the facilities and attractions of a luxurious hotel and the comforts and intimacy of a home. Situated on a hillside overlooking the glorious Bay of Naples, it not only enjoys one of the city's finest locations but also the inherited grandeur and sophistication

of one of its finest buildings—a magnificent six-storey landmark in the Art Nouveau style with plenty of spacious salons, all exquisitely furnished with gilt-trimmed Empire bureaus, 19th-century paintings, bronze and marble sculptures, shimmering chandeliers and fluted pilasters—a visual feast for guests. The accommodation, consisting of 73 spacious rooms and 9 superlative suites, is equally impressive. All come with spectacular views of the bay on one side, or of the vibrant city on the other. The rooms feature antiques from the eras of Charles X, Louis XIV and the Empire, not to mention marble en suite bathrooms, and an impressive array of modern conveniences such as air conditioning, satellite TV and high-speed Internet access.

While Naples has some of the finest cuisine in Italy, guests will find the food at the hotel's rooftop restaurant, George's Restaurant, more than a match for the best that the city has to offer. Here, Neapolitan Executive Chef Baciòt oversees a dedicated team in the preparation of delightfully imaginative dishes reflecting the region's rich culinary heritage. Also, as wine producers, the hotel owns Villa Matilde in the region of Campania where guests can embark on a tour of the vineyard, complete with wine tasting sessions.

In addition, there are the two bars, Le Muse and Il Bidder's, which share the panoramic views. Guests looking to indulge in some cigars, whisky and cognac can head for the Cigar Corner. The wonderful state-of-the-art Day Light spa features every conceivable treatment and therapy, while an atmospheric and well-stocked library ensures an enjoyable afternoon of relaxing reading. Then again, guests should perhaps look forward to the mother of all treats—the opportunity to go on-board Mataibis II, the hotel's private speedboat, for trips over to the outlying islands.

Originally built to cater to the nascent international tourist trade, the hotel was explicitly designed to provide hospitality and service of the highest order. It is a tradition that continues well into the modern age, as the long list of illustrious guests who have stayed here over the decades amply testifies.

ROOMS
82

FOOD
George's Restaurant: Mediterranean

DRINK
Bidder Bar • The Muses Terrace • Cigar Corner

FEATURES
private parking • health centre • private speedboat • gym • ballrooms

BUSINESS
meeting rooms • wi-fi • high speed Internet access

NEARBY
Piazza Plebiscito • Royal Palace • San Carlo Theatre • Capri Ischia • Sorrento • Pompeii • Amalfi coast • Villa Matilde • Campania

CONTACT
Corso Vittorio Emanuele 135, 80121 Naples • telephone: +39.081.761 2474 • facsimile: +39.081.663 527 • email: info@grandhotelparkers.it • website: www.grandhotelparkers.it

hotel san francesco al monte

...medieval works of art and frescoes adorn the walls beneath cavernous, vaulted roofs...

As Italy's third largest metropolis, Naples has much to offer. Having been once dominated by the Romans and various groups of people such as the Byzantines and the revolutionary French in a history that dates back to the 6th and 7th centuries BCE, the city that invented the pizza has a gritty side to it. But this is far outweighed by its liveliness, its intriguing past, its piazzas and cobbled streets and the magnificent bay that it stands on. In addition, the city offers a gateway to the beauties of the Amalfi Coast and has the antiquities of Pompeii on its doorstep.

Commanding breathtaking views over the Bay of Naples and bursting with character, the Hotel San Francesco al Monte is a must for those visiting the city. It was formerly a 16th-century Franciscan monastery founded by Friar Agostino da Miglionico, a monk of the Order of Friars Minor Conventual, otherwise known as Barbanti for their flowing beards. This exquisite boutique hotel has been painstakingly restored to create the perfect marriage between absolute luxury and comfort on the one hand, and old world grandeur and grace on the other.

Authentic, medieval works of art and frescoes adorn the walls beneath cavernous, vaulted roofs, while open-air, cloistered walkways frame tranquil patios to create a truly atmospheric interior. Rooms have been tastefully converted into havens of refined elegance, all with panoramic views over the Bay to Mount Vesuvius and the island of Capri. With polished, tiled floors, pastel hues and antique features such as leaded rosette windows, they are a cool, yet cosy retreat. Modern amenities such as satellite TV abound amid classic furnishings, and the jacuzzi tub in each room simply adds to their splendour.

The proprietors of San Francesco al Monte have done their utmost to preserve as much of the original monastery as

THIS PAGE (FROM TOP): The monks' former quarters, where the old world charm has been retained; luxurious bathrooms come with either a bathtub or jacuzzi; relax and have a quiet read or chat with friends within the serene atmosphere of the hotel.
OPPOSITE (FROM TOP): Relive medieval times while enjoying a traditional feast in the majestic interior of the restaurant; the hotel's gorgeous pool on the green hill of San Martino.

ROOMS
45

FOOD
La Terrazza dei Barbanti: Italian •
The Cloister: afternoon tea •
The Vineyard: Italian light lunch

DRINK
La Cantinetta dei Barbanti •
Lounge Bar • The Cloister • wine cellar

FEATURES
minibar • pool • hanging gardens •
roof terrace • satellite TV • jacuzzi •
wedding facilities • sightseeing tours

NEARBY
funicular railway • city centre •
Pompeii • Amalfi Coast

CONTACT
Corso Vittorio Emanuele 328,
80135 Naples •
telephone: +39.081.423 9111 •
facsimile: +39.081.251 2485 •
email: info@hotelsanfrancesco.it •
website: www.hotelsanfrancesco.it

possible, and the extraordinary hanging gardens are no exception. With footpaths criss-crossing the verdant mountainside, through cultivated vegetable gardens, vineyards and pergolas, guests will get a genuine taste of the countryside in the heart of the city.

Contiguous to the gardens is the rooftop terrace, featuring a stunning swimming pool dug into the cliff-face, complete with an equally splendid view over the Bay of Naples. Surely, there is no better way to end the day than sipping a cocktail on the terrace bar and watching the sun go down over one of the most glorious bays in the Mediterranean.

If staying at the former monastery is a near heavenly experience, then dining here is the stuff of angels. The elegant La Terrazza dei Barbanti restaurant offers some of the finest Mediterranean food in Naples, along with awe-inspiring vistas. For guests who want to enjoy some fresh air, a delicious, light lunch can be enjoyed al fresco in the vineyard itself. Wine aficionados will relish the prospect of an evening spent in La Cantinetta dei Barbanti, the wine cellar. The original convent cellar, this classic bar houses over 350 wines from Italian and international wineries, the icing on the cake of this gem of a hotel.

maison la minervetta

...a masterpiece in contemporary design...

THIS PAGE (FROM TOP): The dynamic interior of the kitchen inspires culinary excellence; intricate ornaments decorate the rooms, giving them a stylish and unique look; bathrooms are just as vibrant.

OPPOSITE (FROM TOP): The terrace offers the ideal spot to take in the magnificent Bay of Naples; enjoy the sea view from the comfort of the room.

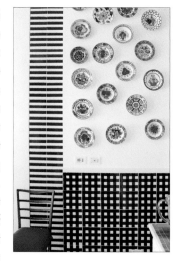

When Adda Cacace and her son Marco renovated La Minervetta, their objective was not simply to convert it into one of the most remarkable hotels on the Amalfi Coast. Rather, it was to restore the prestige established by Adda's father—La Minervetta's founder Don Giovanni Cacace—some 30 years ago. With Marco's experience as an interior designer and Adda's eye for modern comforts, they have created an impressive boutique hotel, bursting with character, which is as original as it is enchanting.

Perched on a high cliff-face overlooking the Bay of Naples, with a picturesque fishing village of Marina Grande directly beneath it and Mount Vesuvius rising majestically to one side, the location of La Minervetta could not be more spectacular. And with the glorious town of Sorrento 500 m (550 yds) away, guests can enjoy the best of both worlds—a soothing seaside vacation on the one hand, and cultural attractions and lively restaurants on the other.

Reopened in 2005, La Minervetta is a masterpiece in contemporary design and yet maintains an informal and distinctly Mediterranean feel. Vibrant colours, vintage objets d'art and an extensive collection of art books characterise the living room, which opens out onto a stunning terrace with panoramic sea views. It is here that a mouth-watering breakfast is served in the shade of the colourful umbrellas.

Lounging on the classic, teak deck furniture before the sleek lap pool, guests could while away an entire afternoon watching the inhabitants of Marina Grande quietly go about their routine, while the fishing boats moored there feel almost close enough to touch.

Like the rest of the hotel, the 12 rooms are impeccably decorated and are filled with charming details. Antique wooden chests and tables befit the nautical setting and complement the natural wood framed windows, which fold away completely to convert rooms into terrace-like spaces. Crisp, white walls contrast with the bold navies, reds or oranges of the cosy bedspreads and armchairs, while bathrooms dazzle with hand-painted striped tiles or bright, Mediterranean colours for a fresh, invigorating effect.

ROOMS
12

FOOD
breakfast

DRINK
cocktails • wine list

FEATURES
wi-fi • satellite TV • open-air jacuzzi • solarium • terrace • excursions • guided tours • sporting activities • car, scooter and boat rental • babysitter on request • massage and beauty services on request

NEARBY
wellness and thermal centre • beaches • Marina Grande • Sorrento

CONTACT
Via Capo 25,
80067 Sorrento, Naples •
telephone: +39.081.877 4455 •
facsimile: +39.081.878 4601 •
email: info@laminervetta.com •
website: www.laminervetta.com

After a long day viewing the sights in Sorrento or down at the beach—accessible from the hotel via a private staircase—guests can unwind with a cocktail on the terrace and take in the sunset. Those seeking a little more privacy, however, might want to curl up in bed and tune in to their flat-screen satellite TV before succumbing to a perfect night's sleep—the soundproof walls will take care of that.

La Minervetta is the kind of boutique hotel in which every corner, room and detail are worthy of a photograph—and it's not difficult to see why. A luxury hotel with a lot of extra charm, it is sure to exceed all expectations.

masseria cimino

...beautiful blend of old and new.

Up until a few years ago, anyone drawing up a shortlist of golfing holiday destinations would have included places like the Algarve, Spain, Scotland, Ireland and Florida. Not many people would have suggested Italy. Italy was where you went for food and wine, culture and history, and if there happened to be a golf course nearby, it probably wasn't up to the standards expected by the true golfing aficionado anyway. In recent years all that has changed. Today, Italy has some of the most beautiful and challenging golf courses in Europe, one of the most impressive being the San Domenico Golf Course, located about halfway between Bari and Brindisi on the beautiful southern Adriatic coastline. And lying right alongside the 9th hole is the equally impressive Masseria Cimino Guest House.

It may overlook the course, but the Masseria Cimino is anything but your typical golfing hotel. Like its sister hotel, the neighbouring Masseria San Domenico, the Masseria Cimino is family-owned, and is based around a series of historic 18th-century watchtowers and farmhouse buildings that were originally home to the legendary Knights of Malta. Using traditional materials and methods of construction, these have been painstakingly renovated over a five-year period and the result is an astonishingly beautiful blend of old and new.

There are only 15 rooms, each individually furnished in a clean, fresh Mediterranean style featuring neutral tones and minimalist finishes. Some come with a beautiful open fireplace, while others have a balcony overlooking the golf course and the sea. All come equipped with flat-screen TVs, and the marble-clad bathrooms with their travertine stone basins are a special treat. Unsurprisingly, the overall effect is an atmosphere of refined luxury and romance, one that brings to mind Giorgio Armani's famous dictum, 'eliminate the superfluous, emphasise the comfortable and acknowledge the elegance of the uncomplicated'.

THIS PAGE (FROM TOP): **The Suite del Massaro exudes a relaxing Mediterranean charm with its refreshing colour tones; luxurious, marble bathrooms are found in every room.**

OPPOSITE (CLOCKWISE FROM TOP): **Modern décor is also part of Masseria Cimino's style; head for a round of golf on the superb greens of the San Domenico Golf Course; guests can relax and enjoy regional cuisine in the cosy atmosphere of the restaurant.**

ROOMS
15

FOOD
regional

DRINK
bar • lounge

FEATURES
boat rental • pool • bicycles •
18-hole golf course

NEARBY
Alberobello • Bari • Brindisi • Lecce

CONTACT
Contrada Masciola,
72010 Savelletri di Fasano, Brindisi •
telephone: +39.080.482 7886 •
facsimile: +39.080.482 7950 •
email: info@masseriacimino.com •
website: www.masseriacimino.com

For those who are able to tear themselves away from their room, there are other treats in store. There's the stunning outdoor pool, for example, and a little jewel of a restaurant that serves simple but expertly prepared dishes typical of the Apulia region. All of these can be accompanied by one of the many bottles of wine on offer; and a lounge-style bar provides the perfect environment in which to relax or socialise before or after a meal.

Last but not least, there's the star of the show—the magnificent 18-hole, par-72 golf course right on the doorstep. With greens that conform to USGA specifications, this world-class course comes with its own clubhouse, pro shop, dressing rooms, restaurant and steam bath, all set against the stunning backdrop of the Adriatic Sea. This is golfing heaven, Italian style.

masseria san domenico,
resort, spa-thalasso, golf

...tastefully furnished in a traditional style...

THIS PAGE (FROM LEFT): Intricately styled, guestrooms combine modern comfort with a splendid view of the historic surroundings; the hotel façade at night.

OPPOSITE (FROM TOP): The old watchtower looks resplendent in its whitewash appearance; Masseria San Domenico's location near the sea makes it an ideal place to enjoy some Thalassotherapeutic treatments; indulge in a relaxing swim in the luxurious indoor pool.

First settled by the ancient Egnathians in the 5th century BCE, the beautiful stretch of coastline halfway between Bari and Brindisi has been successively fought over and occupied by the Romans, Normans and Turks, to name but a few. Today, however, there is little to show for all this activity except a collection of wonderfully atmospheric watchtowers and farmhouses that were built in the 15th century and are a legacy of the legendary Knights of Malta.

These buildings, idyllically set amid 100 hectares (247 acres) of historic olive groves and orchards, have recently been converted into one of the most dramatic boutique hotels to be found on the Adriatic Coast—the Masseria San Domenico, Resort, Spa-Thalasso, Golf, a five-star hotel that was recently described by Frommer's as the 'finest and most refined hotel in Apulia'.

Using traditional materials and methods of construction, the renovation took over five years to complete and the attention to detail throughout is impressive. This is especially true of the 48 rooms and suites, all of which have been tastefully furnished in a traditional style and enjoy stunning views of the surrounding estate, with the blue waters of the Adriatic in the distance.

The food and drink at the Masseria San Domenico constitute another highlight. There are two bars, and the San Domenico Restaurant—with its 18th-century vaulted ceiling and open fireplace—is as impressive as the food is delicious. Using homegrown products and ingredients

from the hotel's estate, in addition to seafood from the Adriatic Coast, the dishes at this restaurant reflect the various tastes and flavours of the region. To top it off, they are offered together with a vast selection of the finest local and national wines.

The facilities here are no less exceptional, including a fully-equipped gym, a private beach and an indoor pool. In addition, the hotel has one of Italy's best Thalassotherapy spas, which utilises locally sourced seaweed and heated seawater in conjunction with a wide variety of treatments and therapies to ensure complete and total rejuvenation. The centrepiece, however, has to be the large, irregularly shaped outdoor pool. Encircled by rocks and foliage and fed with naturally filtered seawater, it must rank as one of the most beautiful of its kind in the world.

Last but by no means least, lying next door to the hotel and alongside the sea, is a superbly landscaped, 18-hole, par-72 golf course that was opened in the year 2000 and has already established itself as one of the best in the area. Add to this the fact that the hotel is family-owned and run, and that the levels of service leave nothing to be desired, you have what is, quite simply, a world-class destination.

ROOMS
48

FOOD
Pool Grill: buffet • San Domenico Restaurant: Mediterranean

DRINK
Pool Bar • San Domenico Bar

FEATURES
18-hole golf course • tennis courts • Thalassotherapy spa • gym • outdoor seawater pool • indoor pool • private beach • wi-fi

BUSINESS
meeting rooms

NEARBY
Alberobello • Bari • Brindisi • Lecce

CONTACT
Strada Litoranea 379, 72010 Savellatri di Fasano, Brindisi • telephone: +39.080.482 7769 • facsimile: +39.080.482 7978 • email: info@masseriasandomenico.com website:www.masseriasan domenico.com

villa costa degli dei + Il fortino capri

...exude the glamour of Italian chic...

It's easy to see why the world's famous jetsetters and holidaymakers frequent the fabled Amalfi Coast and island of Capri. Both destinations are filled with stunning views, fine beaches, vibrant town centres, culinary treasures and rich history—all that makes for a great vacation.

The Villa Book's Villa Costa Degli Dei in the Amalfi Coast and Il Fortino on the island of Capri couldn't have been better positioned. Both luxury properties sit on prime sites that provide visitors with a taste of Italian paradise and plenty of opportunity to enjoy the fabulous outdoors. Guests are also pampered by the discreet service of the staff during their stay.

Villa Costa Degli Dei is a true gem situated on a cliff in Furore, a Mediterranean fjord cut deep into the Amalfi Coast and only two minutes from Praiano. With the property spread over three levels, visitors can enjoy a refreshing walk in the gardens and relax on the large outdoor terrace. There's also the choice of taking a dip in the seawater swimming pool or in the ocean, which is accessible by a private path. Indoors, old world charm is palpable with the antique furnishings and the grand living room's original Vietri ceramic tiled floor. The villa houses nine bedrooms, all on the upper floor, while

THIS PAGE (FROM TOP): Villa Costa Degli Dei offers stunning views from the top of the cliff; and also of the boundless ocean from the seawater pool.

OPPOSITE (FROM TOP): Steps leading to Il Fortino Capri; from which guests can enjoy a bird's eye view of the town; a relaxed theme for the room.

the fully-equipped kitchen opens up to the terrace and outdoor dining area, ideal for a quiet dinner or party. The adventurous traveller will welcome a drive along the Amalfi Coast to the villages nearby, including Positano, Amalfi and Ravello.

On the island of Capri, just a few minutes walk from the lively main square of the town's La Piazzetta, is Il Fortino. Access this vast and secluded property by walking up 164 steps, and catch panoramic views of the town and the Bay of Marina Piccola. The gardens, spread over four levels, are beautifully landscaped with fruit trees, olive trees and flowers. Featuring antiques, as well as paintings by the famous German artist Diefenbach, the villa's décor is one exquisite showcase of art. While each room offers gorgeous views, the place to be has got to be the 1,208-sq-m (13,000-sq-ft) outdoor terrace, where spectacular views and sea air can be enjoyed.

With their distinctive style and character, Villa Costa Degli Dei and Il Fortino exude the glamour of Italian chic and will not be easily forgotten.

Villa Costa Degli Dei

ROOMS
9

FOOD
in-house chef on request

DRINK
wine list

FEATURES
seawater pool • private beach

NEARBY
Praiano • Positan • Amalfi • Ravello

Il Fortino Capri

ROOMS
5

FOOD
in-house chef on request

DRINK
wine list

FEATURES
outdoor terrace

NEARBY
Capri town • La Piazzetta • San Giacomo • La Fontelina • Marina Piccola

CONTACT
12 Venetian House, 47 Warrington Crescent, London W9 1EJ • telephone: +44.845.500 2000 • facsimile: +44.845.500 2001 • email: info@thevillabook.com • website: www.thevillabook.com

villa itria

...lacks for nothing in terms of setting, style and sophistication.

Based in London it may be, but property rental company The Villa Book has a truly global reach. Representing hundreds of properties on three continents they're never at a loss for suggestions when it comes to matching a client's needs. Add to this a depth of experience based on almost 30 years in the sector and a team of specialists as knowledgeable and efficient as any in the industry, and it's easy to see why so many people turn to them when it comes to organising their holidays.

The Villa Book take particular pride in the range of properties they represent in Italy, up to and including the region of Puglia in the south of the country. With its beautiful landscapes, charming towns and villages, and wide-ranging inventory of cultural and outdoor activities, this largely undiscovered area is fast earning a reputation for being one of the hottest new destinations for holidaymakers. This is especially true for those looking to break away from the more traditional tourist enclaves such as Tuscany and the Amalfi Coast.

Although they represent dozens of properties in the region, one of The Villa Book's most prestigious and exclusive destinations there has to be the Villa Itria. Located between the towns of Cisternino and Ostuni—about a 20-minute drive from the Adriatic Sea and 40 minutes from the Ionia—it offers the idyllic rural lifestyle for which Italy is famous, while enjoying the added benefit of easy access to the sandy beaches and other seaside attractions without which no Italian villa holiday would be complete.

The property itself consists of a recently renovated Puglian 'trulli' house—a distinctive 18th-century white cone-shaped dwelling typical of the region—and lacks for nothing in terms of setting, style and sophistication. The interior, for example, with its three

double bedrooms, has been luxuriously furnished in a blend of modern minimalist glamour and the more traditional North African influences that once held sway over the area. Much use has been made of cool neutral tones, stone floors and exposed walls, creating a light, airy and refreshing environment that is as relaxing as it is functional.

All of this is set within 1 hectare (2½ acres) of olive groves, with sublime views over the surrounding countryside. But without question the Villa Itria's finest feature is the divine 12-m (39-ft) outdoor swimming pool. Themed along the lines of a desert oasis, it features underwater lighting and a chemical-free filtration system, and comes complete with its own outdoor kitchen and dining room. Together with deep built-in seating, plump cushions and a westerly orientation, it's the perfect place to enjoy an evening while watching the sun as it sets.

ROOMS
3

FOOD
in-house chef on request

DRINK
wine list

FEATURES
pool • outdoor kitchen

NEARBY
Ostuni • Brindisi • Cisternino

CONTACT
12 Venetian House, 47 Warrington Crescent, London W9 1EJ •
telephone: +44.845.500 2000 •
facsimile: +44.845.500 2001 •
email: info@thevillabook.com •
website: www.thevillabook.com

FRANCE

Isola Maddalena

Santa Teresa di Gallura   La Maddalena
    Porto Cervo

Isola Asinara

> Hotel Pitrizza
> Hotel Capo d'Orso Thalasso + Spa
> La Coluccia
> Resort Valle dell'Erica Thalasso + Spa
> Hotel Marinedda Thalasso + Spa

S a r d i n i a

Nuoro   Orosei
Dorgali
Oliena   Cala Luna
Tiscali

Monti del Gennargentu

Oristano

Barumini

Fluminimaggiore

> Chia Laguna Villas
> Le Meridien Chia Laguna
> Cala Caterina

Iglesias

Isola di San Pietro

Isola di Sant' Antioco

Cagliari   Villasimius

island italy

Isola di Ustica

Aeolian Islands   Isola Stromboli
Salina
Isola Lipari

Hotel Signum <
Falconara <
Santa Teresa <

Mondello
San Vito lo Capo   Palermo   Cefalù
Trapani   Scopello   Bagheria
Isole Egadi
Mozia   Taormina
Marsala
Selinunte   S i c i l y   3323 Monte Etna
Sciacca   Stretta di Messina
Agrigento   Piazza Armerina
Butera   Caltagirone
Gela   Syracuse
Ragusa
Modica   Noto
Scicli

TUNISIA

Isola di Pantelleria

MALTA

Isola di Linosa

I s o l e   P e l a g i e

Isola di Lampedusa

N

Legend
≡ Highway
— Main Road
| Other Road
⊕ Airport
○ Lake
3000–4000 m
2000–3000 m
1500–2000 m
1000–1500 m
500–1000 m
200–500 m
100–200 m

0 km   25   50   75 km

island italy

Goethe once wrote, 'To have seen Italy without having seen Sicily, is not to have seen Italy at all'. He never made it to Sardinia, nor did the Greeks for that matter. And while Sicily will seem immediately familiar as quintessential Italy, Sardinia remains an unknown entity, its inscrutable quality intact. Both have wonderful cuisines, friendly inhabitants and complex, deep-seated traditions. And historically both have been sidelined, underestimated and exploited by their Italian mainland neighbours. Overrun by invading civilisations, Sicilian resistance came stealthily in the creation of the Mafia; while in Sardinia the Nuraghic chieftains fought the good fight, a melancholy permeating the island when they lost. Though poor, as is most of the Italian South, both peoples have a proud, intransigent and admirable nature. Equally beautiful in different ways, either island will claim your heart.

sicilian passion

Palermo is a noble, gracious city. Second to Syracuse under the Greeks, it became the capital of Sicily under the Saracens. For over 200 years, it was at the heart of the empire. Christians, Jews and Muslims lived side by side in peace, and Palermo achieved great wealth from trade, and the arts flourished. Nowadays this unique fusion of Arabic, Norman, Spanish baroque and Italian art nouveau creates a beautiful, vibrant city. The 12th-century cathedral, changed from basilica to mosque to cathedral and still shows details of all three phases. The Arab palace became the Norman parliament, and contains the Palatine Chapel with its exquisite Byzantine mosaics. Around the Vucciria and Ballarò markets are some of the city's finest chapels and churches. Go to the Oratorio di Santa Zita to admire the beautiful stucco work of Giacomo Serpotta and hunt out the Oratorio del Rosario di San Domenico, two of the city's masterpieces.

Near the Royal Palace is San Giovanni degli Eremiti. Once a mosque, its red Moorish domes and Arab gardens are all that remain. Further out are the Zisa, a summer residence, and the Cuba, a former pleasure palace where the Emir once

PAGE 254: *The Fontana dell'Amenano, in gleaming white Carrara marble, in Catania's Piazza Duomo.*

THIS PAGE: *Palermo's Cappella Palatina, built between 1132 and 1143 by enlightened King Roger II. Combining Norman, Byzantine and Arab influences, stars are arranged on the ceiling in the form of a cross.*

OPPOSITE: *The well-preserved Temple of Concord, part of Agrigento's Valley of the Temples, was built in 440 BC.*

entertained his harem. The Kalsa, a typically Arab residential area, retains much of its old atmosphere. After lengthy restoration work, trendy galleries and restaurants have sprung up. The Palazzo Abatellis, housing the Galleria Regionale di Sicilia, is also in this area as are the botanical gardens on Via Lincoln.

Palermo shows off her neoclassical and art nouveau architecture around Piazza Politeama and Piazza Verdi where the main theatre and opera house are based, along with more shops and bars. The Galleria d'Arte Moderna is set in the magnificent convent of Sant'Anna della Misericoridia near Piazza Castelnuovo, while the Archaeological Museum on Piazza Olivella sits between several boutiques and nightspots.

Outside Palermo, the elegant bathing resort of Mondello, offers some of the city's best restaurants. Bagheria, the residential quarter of the city's elite in the 17th century, has two attractions—the Villa Palagonia and Villa Cattolica. The first is also known as the Monster's Villa, due to its grotesque stone statues; the second houses a modern art gallery. Monreale's Norman cathedral complex has exquisite medieval mosaics and an enchanting cloister. Cefalù to the east has a long sandy beach, a charming old quarter and another fine Norman cathedral.

THIS PAGE: Glorious Baroque architecture at Palazzo Biscari, Catania, built after the devastating earthquake of 1693. Goethe wrote about the palace a century later.

OPPOSITE: Only volcanologists can get this close to Etna when in full flow. When things aren't too lively jeep trips or walking tours show visitors the way.

decadent vice town faces volcanic wrath

Taormina was founded as Tauromenium in 304 BC by the Greeks. Its narrow streets, lined with designer boutiques and chi-chi meeting places, are beautifully tended. Walk up the Salita Castello to the town's summit for the best views or go by cable car (the walk is only for die-hard masochists) down to the beach at Mazzarò opposite the tiny Isola Bella. At night take part in the obligatory passeggiata up and down the Corso Umberto I and wine and dine in some of the island's most exclusive restaurants. A pilgrimage to the Wunderbar, beloved of Liz Taylor and Richard Burton, is a must. The annual Taormina International Film Festival in June draws the glitterati. Films are shown in the Greek theatre, where concerts are held in summer.

Taormina became known to the outside world courtesy of the Grand Tourists. Word spread and the town began competing with Capri as the top Mediterranean haunt. After the war, Taormina attracted the Hollywood set. Marlene Dietrich and Rita Hayworth came as well as writers Truman Capote, Tennessee Williams and Somerset Maugham, who named it the Disneyland of Sin. It was the stiff upper lip of the prudish Brits that pulled the resort back into the mainstream. Many were saddened at the end of an era.

Etna, Europe's largest volcano (three times the size of Vesuvius) and its most active, is a do-able day-trip. The constant stream of sulphuric gases and regular eruptions are a sight to behold and in winter, when snow caps the summit, you can even ski down. On the eastern slope is an ancient chestnut tree, the Castagno dei Cento Cavalli, one of the oldest and largest trees in the world. Beyond Etna lie the Nebrodi Reserve and the Madonie Mountains, fertile pastureland strewn with wildflowers and dense forests.

syracuse: magna graecia's powerbase

Syracuse was once the wealthiest and most powerful city-state in the entire Greek empire. Governed by the great and the good, it was a hotbed of political intrigue and a mecca for the biggest names in the arts, sciences and philosophy. Ortygia, by far the prettiest part of the city, is also the oldest; Neapolis, the 'newer' town, is where the archaeological park lies. Tourists flock to Syracuse for the park and the Museo Archeologico Paolo Orsi with its incredible array of Greek treasures. Many of Aeschylus' finest tragedies had their first night in the city's 5th-century-BC Teatro Greco, which at 15,000 capacity was the largest theatre in Sicily. Don't miss the eerie quarry, the Latomia del Paradiso, and the vast cave nicknamed Orecchio di Dionisio (Ear of Dionysius), where the tyrant Dionysius kept his prisoners, and where the acoustics allowed him to eavesdrop on their conversations. The fortified 4th-century-BC Castello di Euralio on the tip of Ortygia was stomping ground for local lad Archimedes, the genius mathematician, inventor and military theorist. Sunny Ortygia has stayed at the heart of city with its pretty fishing fleet, excellent restaurants and lively nightlife radiating around its beautiful Baroque architecture. Stroll along Via Maestranza for the city's best shops and trattoria or head for the old Jewish ghetto between via della Giudecca and Via Alagona.

THIS PAGE: *Every even-numbered year a summer festival of Greek drama is held at Syracuse's Teatro Greco.*

OPPOSITE (FROM TOP): *The Easter Sunday procession in Caltagirone begins with a large statue of Saint Peter who seeks out a statue of the Virgin Mary. After meeting with Mary, Peter seeks out Jesus. After Peter bows to Jesus, the figures of Mary and Jesus are united; exhibits at Agrigento's superb archaeological museum.*

flights of fancy

Nowadays, little rocks the sleepy, butterscotch-hued towns of the Val di Noto and Val di Catania. But some 300 years ago, no fewer than 45 cities in southeastern Sicily were devastated in the tumultuous earthquake of 1693, a disaster that killed 60,000. Two-thirds of Catania's inhabitants perished. Eight of the rebuilt cities—Caltagirone, Militello Val di Catania, Catania, Modica, Noto, Palazzolo, Ragusa and Scicli—are now UNESCO World Heritage sites (Sicily is the proud possessor of no less than five). Each of these cities was rebuilt in a uniquely Sicilian Baroque style. The architecture and art exemplify the wealth and creative brilliance of the period, as well as the typically robust Sicilian response to calamity. Sumptuous, ornate architectural reliefs and dramatic stone façades; vast, spiralling staircases that lead from one part of town to another, often stretching over gorges; the bleached terracotta and gold of the towns' churches, cathedrals and palazzi will leave you breathless, in more ways than one. Fortunately, the towns offer some of the island's finest food, there's always a trattoria around the corner and a sympathetic smile from the locals, used to huffing and puffing their own way around.

Originally called Akragas by its Greek founders, the city-state of Agrigento was an ally of the mighty Syracuse, its people renowned for their horsemanship (riders from here frequently won events in the Olympic Games). The Romans who seized the city in a bitter battle with the Carthaginians renamed it Agrigentus and lived side by side with the Greeks.

Backed by a turquoise sea, the temples are best seen in springtime when blossoming almond trees dance around the noble white Doric columns. The almost intact Temple of Concord dates to 430 BC, while the oldest temple, to Herakles, was built in 500 BC. The nearby archaeological museum holds a wealth of excavated material from both here and nearby Gela. Particularly impressive is the reconstructed gigante (or giant), one of 38, which once supported the entablature of the Temple of Olympian Zeus.

Modern Agrigento has few obvious charms. A region blighted by the infamous Sicilian Mafia and poverty, it does command deep loyalty and it's also the birthplace of some of Italy's best writing talent. Leonard Sciascia, author of *The Day of the Owl* labelled his homeland a wicked stepmother. He never managed to leave her. Fellow writer Luigi Pirandello, who dealt with schizophrenia in his work and in his personal life, was born in the nearby town of Caos (chaos) a century earlier—the irony was not lost on him. Tomasi di Lampedusa, who wrote *The Leopard*, based a large part of his novel on his ancestral town of Palma di Montechiaro, not far from Agrigento.

Beyond the city, just outside Sciacca, is an outpouring of creative folly by outsider artist Filippo Bentivegna, a peasant who headed home after his new life in America turned sour. Discovered by surrealist artist Jean Dubuffet, Bentivegna's work earned pride of place in the Gallerie d'Art Brut in Lausanne. Set in an Arcadian scene of olive and almond trees he sculpted 3,000 faces from lava and olive wood. Disturbing, fascinating and moving in equal parts, his very personal enchanted castle is well worth a visit.

THIS PAGE: Filippo Bentivegna's sculptures outside Sciacca, a town known for its thermal waters and muds.

OPPOSITE: The sun sets over Cala Grande on Favignana.

mosaic maidens + tales of bloodshed

Perfectly preserved by a vast mudslide in the 12th-centruy, Villa Romana del Casale sits in hazel woodland in Piazza Armerina. Dating from 3 AD, the Roman hunting lodge contains 40 rooms, each with lavish mosaic masterpieces that were probably created by a North African master. The highlight is a mosaic of ten bikini-clad athletes in competition. The winner is shown parading a flowered crown in her hair and wielding a palm sceptre. Beside her with looks that could kill is one of her rivals. It's just like Miss World, only better. Selinunte is the westernmost temple complex on the island and one of Sicily's biggest. It remained unfinished after the city was sacked by Hannibal in 409 BC. The finest surviving stonework is in the Archaeological Museum at Palermo.

Marsala was founded in 397 BC by the Carthaginians who controlled the area until it fell to the Romans. Cut to a millennia and a half later in 1773, when Englishman John Woodhouse established huge demand in England for his fortified dessert wine. Woodhouse never lost his passion for his product, and liked to run naked through his vineyards after drinking vast amounts, presumably for quality control.

A short boat ride away lie the Egadi Islands of Levanzo, Favignana and Marettimo complete with kingfisher seas to swim in. Levanzo is home to one of Italy's best-kept secrets, the Grotta del Genovese, a cave containing 10,000-year-old paintings discovered in 1949. Favignana hosts the annual mattanza, a bloody event in which thousands of giant tuna fish meet their death in an ancient fishing rite established by the Arabs. Back on Sicily's north coast between Scopello and San Vito lo Capo is the Zingaro Reserve, the only stretch of untamed Sicilian coastline with no road alongside, a privileged place of pilgrimage for those in the know. Almost in North Africa, the exotic island of Pantelleria, part of Trapani province, has many Arabic customs. The

typical houses, called dammusi, are white low-roofed cubes that keep the heat and cold out. Black volcanic outcrops of rock covered with citrus groves and vineyards, Pantelleria was a Phoenician trading post. Today it's an exclusive resort with volcanic waters and mud baths, deliciously secluded coves and dozens of shipwrecks to explore.

casting your cares to the wind

Aeolus, the ruler of the winds in Greek mythology, gave Odysseus a bag of westerly Zephyrus' breath to take him home to Ithaca when he found himself stranded on the beautiful archipelago of the Aeolian Islands. You may be surprised he ever wanted to leave, but he was hurrying back to his beloved Penelope. It took him 20 years. Nowadays, it takes just three hours via motorboat from Naples or Milazzo.

The vulcanic septet of islands—Lipari, Vulcano, Salina, Stromboli, Filicudi, Alicudi and Panarea—were depopulated after battles between the French and the Spanish in the mid 1500s. Today's islanders are comparative 'newcomers' from mainland Italy, Sicily and Spain. Extremes are the islands' essence: intense sunlight, dark sands and crystalline seas. On Lipari, the pumice dust on the seabed creates dazzling light refraction, producing particularly turquoise-emerald seas. Tastebuds are also subject to dramatic sensations here—from the sour capers to the sweet Malvasia wine. Vulcano Island is black and jagged, with pungent sulphur emerging from the ground tinting nearby rocks lurid yellows and fiery reds. Salina has white meringue-like rock formations and seas brimming with marine life. Salina's Pollara beach is accessible only by boat and has legendary snorkelling. Panarea, the smallest and most exclusive island, has the Bronze Age settlement of Punta Milazzese and some of the best nightlife. Alicudi and Filicudi, a little out on a limb to the west, are pretty and quiet; the wail of the wind is the only distraction. Meanwhile, noisy showman Stromboli, rumbling with chronic indigestion for some two millennia, spews up sparks and red-hot rocks to crowd-pleasing effect.

sardinia's emerald isles

The Aga Khan, who created the brightly coloured resort of Costa Smeralda in 1962, brought Sardinia to the attention of the jet-set, and they've made a beeline for it ever since. There are emerald seas, white sands and untouched wildernesses to discover and, with many other people trying to do the same, a yacht helps to escape the crowds. Much of the maquis, tiny hamlets, fishing fleets and grazing cattle have made way for stylish luxury hotels, glitzy high-tech marinas and bronzed sun worshippers on a quest for their very own Xanadu. The Costa Smeralda is one of the Mediterranean's ultimate party capitals. Regattas, speed racing and golf events are the envy of the world; the finest architects and designers flock to show off their work, and the who's who guide to the rich or beautiful pack the beaches and spend in the designer boutiques. Porto Cervo is the heart and soul of the Costa Smeralda.

THIS PAGE: *Porto Cervo is renowned for its regattas. The Maxi Yacht Rolex Cup, held every September since 1980, is unquestionably the most prestigious event.*

OPPOSITE: *An aerial view over Lipari, the largest of the Aeolian Islands. Though its volcano last erupted in 5 AD, its main by-products, obsidian and pumice, are big business here.*

Olbia is a bustling port with excellent restaurants and great beaches; just opposite is the island of Tavolara. Once Italy's smallest kingdom, it's famous for its moufflon breed of sheep. Sassari is the regional capital. A lively elegant city, it has a beautiful baroque cathedral, one of the island's best archaeological museums and some divine old bars and cake shops on the Piazza d'Italia, a regal square where concerts are held in summer.

crème catalane

Established by the noble Doria family from Genoa in the 1100s, along with nearby Castelsardo, Alghero on the northwestern coast became a Catalan enclave on Sardinia in the power struggles that followed. A colourful fishing port, it is almost a home from home for visitors from Barcelona. Street signs are written in Catalan, and the locals understand and even speak it. The food's heavily influenced too—the lobster Catalana is particularly good. The famous winery Sella e Mosca is located just outside the town. Meandering around the ancient fortified quarter, flitting from boutique to bar, will easily fill a morning. All around the town the medieval ramparts and noble watch towers, a popular place for the evening stroll, afford beautiful views over the sea.

Beaches abound—one of the best, Bombarde, is just to the north of the town. Due south, head for the gorgeous artistic town and resort of Bosa, famed for its goldsmiths, and well worth a visit en route to the ancient Phoenician site of Tharros. At nearby Arutas the sand is of quartz, set against a backdrop of pineforest. The Sale Porcus Reserve, temporary home to 10,000 flamingos and hundreds of other bird species is not far away. Oristano, the regional capital, renowned for its carnival celebrations, has a Lombard cathedral with majolica tiles, onion dome and bronze doors. The fertile plains all around are home to vineyards producing the delicious white Vernaccia wine. Inland, at Sedilo, there's a horse race around the early Christian sanctuary of Santu Antine in July, which gives the Palio at Siena a serious run for its money.

THIS PAGE: *Sardinia's liveliest carnival takes place at La Sartiglia in Oristano, famed for its displays of horsemanship, parades and street parties. Participants wear masks and medieval costumes.*

OPPOSITE: *Cagliari's pretty harbour overlooked by the old city above. A new Museum of Nuragic and Contemporary Art, designed by Zaha Hadid, is in the pipeline.*

digging for gold

Though often ignored by tourists stampeding their way to the Costa Smeralda or the Alghero coastline, Sardinia's southern province is full of hidden treasure. Pretty fishing villages, some of the island's best beaches, ancient nuraghe and temple sites as well as a lively capital city await. The Cagliari province has for thousands of years been the island's economic backbone due to its wealth of precious ores. Copper, silver, zinc and even gold were mined here from 5000 BC up until the 1970s.

   The city of Cagliari has its own beaches and beautiful salt marshes to the east, which are home to thousands of flamingos over the winter. Poetto, the marina, is a lively nightspot with excellent bars and restaurants. There's plenty to see here, from the Roman amphitheatre, which was flooded to re-enact naval victories, to the Castle district. Constructed by the Pisans in the 11th and 12th centuries, the splendid castle is home to a fine museum complex housing ancient and modern art. There is also a

cathedral and some pretty shops around Via la Marmora. The elegant 18th-century boulevard Via Roma offers designer shopping down to the picturesque old port where fishermen's homes have become antique shops and osterias. High at the Bastione San Remy there's a lively weekly flea market. Exma, the former municipal slaughterhouse, is now a funky arts centre that's well worth checking out.

mountain passes + popular impasses

The Golfo di Orosei, the Parco Nazionale del Gennargentu and the Barbagia are the least invaded regions due to their inaccessibility. The coast is all cliffs and coves, only reachable by boat or foot. The mountains are similarly untamed where the roads are tortuous affairs and are surrounded by wild landscapes. It is a land that time forgot, a million miles from the polished Costa Smeralda and for many the real Sardinia. Throughout time, the people of the Barbagia have had a reputation of being proud and ruthlessly self-sufficient. In the face of rough treatment by successive governments they were resistant to change, and certainly resistant to meddling. Orgosolo is now as famous for its fascinating murals, started in the 1960s, as it once was for its hard-man past—there are even bullet holes in the town sign. Oliena is a beautiful market town not far away, as are the enchanting ravines of Su Gorroppu and the Su Gologone spring. Nuoro, the main town, has a fascinating ethnographic museum showing many of the ancient festivals and rites peculiar to the Barbagia. Some of the masks are pretty scary.

For those inclined, a walk down the Valley of the Moon from the Supramonte takes you to the sea, where you can swim at Cala Luna. Further south, Artizo is renowned for its horseback riding and rodeos as well as its tradition of handmade wooden furniture, especially wedding chests. The good news is you can get there by car. Back on the coast, heart-stopping beaches await around the pretty towns of Orosei and Dorgali, home to a rare species of monk seal. Boats will take you to tiny coves. At Muravera and Villasimius, in the Sarrabus, there are more accessible beaches and a bird sanctuary on the marshland at Notteri, where yet more thousands of flamingos gather in the winter.

...a land that time forgot, a million miles from the polished Costa Smeralda and for many the real Sardinia.

cala caterina

...ideal destination from which to experience the manifold attractions of this island.

THIS PAGE (FROM TOP): *Cala Caterina blends in perfectly with its natural surroundings; guestrooms are bright and airy, ensuring a relaxing stay.*

OPPOSITE (FROM TOP): *The Piano Bar overlooks the pool and garden; the inviting pool beckons; take a leisurely stroll through the lawns to the beach.*

The unspoilt island of Sardinia is the second largest in the entire Mediterranean Sea, exceeded in size only by Sicily. This magical destination lies just south of the French island of Corsica, with the coasts of Italy, Spain and Tunisia its closest neighbours.

Fashioned in the traditional Mediterranean style, the four-star Hotel Cala Caterina is located in a splendid nook in Sardinia's southeastern corner. Secluded, tranquil and enjoying a breathtakingly beautiful setting, it is a few minutes from the typical Sardinian fishing village of Villasimius. With long stretches of pristine white beaches and unpolluted waters, this charming resort is renowned for its photogenic harbour, bustling cafés and well-equipped tourist marina, not to mention its vibrant nightlife.

Cala Caterina is the ideal destination from which to experience the manifold attractions of this island. Its grounds are lapped on one side by the cobalt blue of the Mediterranean Sea, with the lush green of the hinterland bordering the other. The two-storey building complements rather than compromises this textbook backdrop, with cool peach-coloured arches and cloistered colonnades offering a welcome interlude from the heat of the blazing Mediterranean sun. The hotel boasts a spacious lobby and an elegant restaurant that serves an appetising

blend of local and internationally-inspired dishes. The stylish bar has a terrace overlooking the pool while on summer evenings, mellow notes from the Piano Bar escape across the sculpted lawns, melding into the hypnotic blue of the ocean.

The aromatic gardens provide generous sun-bathing opportunities or ample shaded retreat from the heat of the day, in the lee of the fragrant pine trees. The lawns continue seawards and open out into a pristine, granite-edged sandy bay, where courtesy beach umbrellas and towels are provided. Cala Caterina also has an exclusive beauty centre during the summer months, proposing an extensive palette of indulgent treatments.

Cala Caterina's accommodation comprises 48 air-conditioned rooms, each of which encapsulates the quintessence of Sardinian style. The colourways are in gentle pastel shades, with gleaming marble-topped tables and hand-painted wooden furniture. Each room is en suite, and is equipped with satellite TV, direct-dial telephone, minibar and safe. To top it off, the superior rooms all possess incomparable sea views.

Exploring the region's secluded coves, picturesque ports and natural terrain is facilitated by the rental of a car, mountain bike or scooter, which Cala Caterina's staff will be more than happy to organise. Adrenaline junkies will welcome the numerous activities available a short walk away in Porto Giunco, which include fishing, diving, tennis, water skiing and horse riding. To experience the marine life teeming beneath the glittering surface of the Mediterranean, chartered excursions to the protected island reserves of Serpentara and Cavoli are highly recommended.

Sardinia is not Italy's most obvious vacation spot, simply because it is not part of the sailing fraternity. Yet, it is precisely for this reason alone that the island retains its exclusivity, helping it to exude an effortless Italian chic.

ROOMS
48

FOOD
Sardinian, Italian and international

DRINK
Piano Bar

FEATURES
patio • sun terrace • satellite TV • minibar • safe • beauty centre • pool • boat rental • water sports • diving • horse riding • tennis courts

NEARBY
Cagliari • Villasimius

CONTACT
Via Lago Maggiore 32, 09049 Villasimius, Sardinia • telephone: +39.070.797 410 • facsimile: +39.070.797 473 • email: calacaterina@mobygest.it website: www.mobygest.it • www.hotelphilosophy.net

chia laguna villas

...the sun-drenched south of this mysterious island remains reassuringly undiscovered.

THIS PAGE (FROM TOP): Fine air and countryside are the attractions of the villas; take a refreshing dip in one of the three private pools.

OPPOSITE (CLOCKWISE FROM TOP): The beautiful Bay of Chia and its sandy beaches; wake up to a splendid view; in the evenings, sit back, relax and enjoy the sea view.

The alluring Italian island of Sardinia has an enviable Mediterranean location a mere 161 km (100 miles) from the African coastline of Tunisia. Despite having a beautiful climate well into November, a fabulous coastline and myriad archaeological sites of interest, the sun-drenched south of this mysterious island remains reassuringly undiscovered.

For an escape to this paradise, plot a course for Chia, on Sardina's southern extremity.

Sardinia brims with intriguing cultural sites, pink flamingo-dotted lagoons and championship golf courses at Is Molas and Sa Tanca. Chia offers some of the most magnificent inlets and spectacular diving reefs; its breathtaking beaches have cobalt waters reminiscent of the Caribbean and creamy white dunes, shaded by wise, old juniper trees. Chia Villas captures the island's essence, with 29 privately-owned luxury properties in this uncrowded dream destination.

With evocative names like Casa Laguna, Paradiso and Orchidea, each home in Chia's impressive portfolio was sensitively designed by local architects. These air-conditioned retreats have up to three bedrooms, and exclusive access to private or communal swimming pools.

The discreet staff at Chia Villas understand each guest's unique requirements. Each villa is personally maintained and furnished to the highest standards of comfort and convenience.

They can be rented independently—with full service—or on a five-star basis, with the use of the private beach, concierge service and the Penguin Club, in addition to the wide range of services available at the nearby world-renowned Hotel Le Meridien Chia Laguna, part of the Chia Laguna Resort that also hosts the Chia Village, the Hotel Laguna and the Baia Chia Hotel. Cocktail parties aside, the Hotel Le Meridien Chia Laguna offers preferential treatment to Villa Chia guests in its restaurants, and this warm welcome extends to its pristine beach. The coastline teems with activities, from scuba-diving and sailing, to fishing and boat excursions.

Grandly presiding over the stunning Golfo degli Angeli, the island capital of Cagliari is about an hour away. With numerous fine wining and dining options to be found everywhere, and a plethora of characterful cafés that dot the streets, going hungry is simply not an option in this stylish Mediterranean haven. Although discovering a favourite culinary spot by accident is often the highlight of a trip to Cagliari, Chia Villas will happily recommend an eatery to suit any palate. Excellent local restaurants that accept Villa dwellers' Special Guest Card include Le Dune Restaurant, the Steak House and Pizzeria in the piazza, or the elegant Luna, a brand-new dining and nightclub venue.

Chia Villas presents a unique way of enjoying Sardinia. From the languorous and relaxing pastime of the contemporary beach holiday to the adrenaline-fuelled scrambles through history at the lost Phoenician city of Nora, Chia has pre-empted every possible holiday requirement. With its world-class hospitality experience, Chia Villas' menu of diversions will entertain the most discerning and demanding of travellers.

VILLAS
29

FOOD
Bouganville Restaurant: Mediterranean and international • La Terrazza: Mediterranean and international • Art à la Carte Restaurant: global fusion • Le Dune Restaurant • Pizzeria • Steak House

DRINK
Bar Rondini • Bar Bollicine • Bar Piscina • Bar Dune • Bar Piazza degli Ulivi • Wine Bar • Luna

FEATURES
room climate control • pools • Penguin Club for children • Special Guest Card • catering services • babysitter on request

NEARBY
Pula • Nora • Cagliari • golf course at Is Mola • Chia Golf Club • Hotel Le Meridien Chia Laguna • diving • sailing

CONTACT
Località Chia, 09010 Domus de Maria, Cagliari, Sardinia • telephone: +39.070.9239 3431 • facsimile: +39.070.923 0144 • email: info@chialagunaresort.com • website: www.chialagunaresort.com

falconara

...merges seamlessly with its environment to create an elegant setting...

Sicily, just off the southwestern coast of Italy, is a complex and intriguing entity. It is an island that veils one of Europe's richest and most cosmopolitan heritage, having been ruled by Asia, Africa and Europe at various points in its history. From this dramatic past comes a fascinating present, with an impressive and multicultural display of art, folklore and cuisine. The religious architecture alone spans the Romanesque, the Gothic and the Baroque as Greek temples, Roman amphitheatres and Norman Arab castles dot its breathtaking coastline.

Falconara House and Resort is an exciting new member of the Design Hotels, situated within the grounds of Butera's atmospheric Castello di Falconara. It overlooks the eternal lapping of the Mediterranean Sea from a rocky promontory of Sicily's southeastern coast. Originally built in Norman times to quell the Moorish invasions, this medieval castle now enchants visitors with its considerable charm.

Much thought has been put into the design of Falconara House, which is evident from the way its unique setting has been fully harnessed. Constructed from authentic local materials, the hotel merges seamlessly with its environment to create an elegant setting with a welcoming, natural ambience. The long flagstone corridors weave their way beneath smooth stone arches, with grills protecting the windows as they would have done in ancient times.

The Falconara's Club House is just 200 m (219 yd) from the delicious blue depths of the Mediterranean. It is home to the resort's lobby, bars, restaurant and boutique, in addition to 35 double rooms

THIS PAGE: **Soft lighting and a comfortable canopy bed combine for a warm ambience.**
OPPOSITE: **Arched walkways, exquisite décor and antique furnishings all add to Falconara's rustic appeal.**

and four suites on two levels. The complex also boasts a swimming pool and tennis courts. Its Space Comfort Zone spa and beauty centre has an extensive massage menu, invigorating Turkish bath and high adrenaline workout options. To take the sea air, a pleasurable stroll through the gardens leads to a quiet bay with a smooth and sandy beach, where sun loungers, umbrellas and beach towels are all provided for guests.

The charming suites feature spacious bedrooms and living areas with showers or rejuvenating hydro-massage bathtubs in each private bathroom. Guestrooms on the ground floor enjoy their own patio, while first-floor suites boast private balconies from which to absorb the stunning vistas across ever-changing land- and seascapes. Each room is equipped with a private telephone, satellite TV, minibar and safe, deftly juxtaposing the history-saturated atmosphere with every modern convenience. The premier La Fattoria annex houses a further 10 superior suites, each

evocatively named after one of the castle's former owners. These noble personages include Martino d'Aragona, Conte Wilding and the Principe di Butera.

For guests who want a glimpse of the island's colourful past, enriching day-trip possibilities include Agrigento's renowned Valley of the Temples, Villa del Casale's splendid mosaics and the superb ceramics and majolica pots from the craftsmen of Caltagirone.

Prepare to fall in love with the Falconara and with Sicily, the island that delivers all the culture and style of Europe, Africa and Asia in one unforgettable package.

ROOMS
65

FOOD
Sicilian, Italian and international

DRINK
pool bar

FEATURES
satellite TV • direct-dial telephone • minibar • safe • Internet • pool • gym • spa and beauty centre • tennis courts • boutique

BUSINESS
meeting room

NEARBY
Falconara Castle • Agrigento • Catania • Licata • Palermo

CONTACT
Località Falconara, Butera, 93011 Sicily • telephone: +39.0934.349 012 • facsimile: +39.0934.349 015 • email: falconara@mobygest.it • website: www.mobygest.it • www.hotelphilosophy.net

hotel capo d'orso thalasso + spa

...located in the heart of an intimate and lovingly maintained estate...

THIS PAGE: Capo d'Orso Hotel overlooks the Cala Capra bay.

OPPOSITE (FROM TOP): Play a game of golf with the sea in full view; take a dip in the pool or enjoy a tan on the wooden deck; every guestroom exudes an unmistakable Sardinian charm while providing the most lavish of comforts.

For the experience of bathing in a new aquamarine paradise every single day, Sardinia's benchmark Capo d'Orso Hotel is the ultimate point of departure. Located within Cala Capra's pristine bay, this distinctive five-star hotel is the epitome of Sardinian style, its natural charm and elegance permeating every aspect of its beautiful, shore-side setting. Just 4 km (2½ miles) from the quaint seaside resort of Palau and an hour from Olbia, this chic and recently expanded hotel overlooks the glimmering islets of the Archipelago of La Maddalena, a protected marine environment and ideal boat-trip destination.

This romantic hideaway is located in the heart of an intimate and lovingly maintained estate, whose wild olive groves and juniper trees are redolent with the evocative scents of the Mediterranean. The curvaceous outdoor pool is framed by this richly verdant backdrop, encircled by a sun-warmed wooden walkway. At the meeting of ocean and shore is an attractive marina, where the hotel's private boat fleet is moored. To steep in the radiant sunshine, choose between the creamy white beaches of Cala Capra and Cala Selvaggia or one of the five hardwood solaria that stretch out indolently over Sardinia's famously clear waters.

Maximising the benefits of the mineral-rich Mediterranean is L'incantu, Capo d'Orso's impressive Thalasso & Spa Centre. It houses upmarket guest suites, three heated seawater pools, professional massages and invigorating Turkish baths. Essential oils derived from the region's unique plants ensure that the true essence of Sardinia penetrates every pore, after just one indulgent pampering session.

For its adrenaline-seeking guests, Capo d'Orso ably offers an exclusive golfing green and an outdoor fitness centre that surveys the colourful reef. Sailing, tennis and horse riding too are just a stone's throw away.

ROOMS
84

FOOD
Il Paguro: Mediterranean and regional • Gli Olivastri: Mediterranean and regional

DRINK
L'Approdo Bar & Pizzeria • piano bar

FEATURES
L'incantu Thalasso & Spa Centre • pitch and putt golf course • outdoor fitness centre • tennis court • private harbour • solariums • air conditioning • seawater pool • veranda • terrace • satellite and Sky TV • minibar • safe • beaches • scooter rental • car rental • boat charter • boat trips toArchipelago of La Maddalena

BUSINESS
conference room

NEARBY
Palau • Olbia • diving centre • boat charter • horse riding • sailing boat trips to Archipelago of La Maddalena

CONTACT
Località Cala Capra, 07020 Palau, Sardinia • telephone: +39.0789.790 018 • facsimile: +39.0789.790 058 • email: info@delphina.it • website: www.delphina.it

Hotel Capo d'Orso provides 84 completely modernised rooms and suites, each with a balcony or veranda and private bathroom. The interior design is informed by classic Sardinian style influences, and was conceptualised by renowned interior decorators. While escaping from it all on this heavenly island sanctuary, guests can also choose to remain connected with the outside world via in-room satellite TV and telephone links.

The resort is part of Italy's prestigious Delphina hotels group, which boasts an impeccable reputation for seamless service, unparalleled locations and tremendous cuisine, and the Capo d'Orso restaurants convey this ethos effortlessly. Delicate harp music accompanies the pastry and fruit-laden breakfast table, which can be enjoyed in the shaded olive groves. Authentic Mediterranean and Sardinian fruits de mer are served at Il Paguro, which faces the sea. And then there's the Gli Olivastri restaurant that occupies a romantic terrace setting beneath the garden's revered, age-old trees.

Italy is renowned as the romantic and cultural centre of the world, and island living is the quintessential form of modern escapism. Combine the two with a flawless sojourn at Capo d'Orso on the breathtaking Italian island of Sardinia.

hotel marinedda thalasso + spa

...authentic wooden boats and an Aragonese tower add to the unique touch...

THIS PAGE: *Marinedda's stunning pool is the quintessence of unrivalled beauty in which the resort is immersed.*

OPPOSITE (FROM TOP): *Enjoy fine dining with the sea in full view; the sunny paradise that is Marinedda's beach; the canopy bed typifies the luxury and Mediterranean charm in the Presidential Suite.*

The manifold wonders of Sardinia are succinctly captured in *Sea and Sardinia*, an evocative work by British author D.H. Lawrence. To experience the essence of this magical Mediterranean island first-hand, pencil in the Hotel Marinedda as the first port of call.

A member of the Delphina hotels group, the Marinedda occupies a premier location mere metres from its namesake beach in the north of Sardinia. Its immaculate bay effortlessly explains why Sardinia's crystal clear waters and unadulterated coastline are renowned throughout the world for their timeless, unspoilt beauty.

The Marinedda is situated about an hour's drive from the coastal towns of Olbia and Alghero. The picturesque fishing village of Isola Rossa is just 1 km (½ mile) away, its coastline dotted with multi-hued shells, and red granite rocks, authentic wooden boats and an Aragonese tower add to the unique touch of this beautiful spot.

The hotel's beach complex provides sunbeds for the ideal tan, and offers sailing lessons for the nautically inclined. There is a lively piano bar with regular art exhibitions and two pools, both with bar service—one is overlooked by panoramic terraces upon which freshly-prepared breakfast or Mediterranean brunch is served. Closer to the sea is the Petra Ruja split-level restaurant, which offers mesmerising seascapes at sunset, with a fine array of international cuisine.

L'Elicriso Thalasso & Spa Centre is the undisputed centre of attraction in this resort, standing as one of the most prestigious spa destinations in the Mediterranean. Its myriad treatments and tonics are just waiting to relax, tone or rejuvenate its pampered guests, using beneficial salts, minerals and health-giving products derived from the sea itself. Essential oils originating from Sardinia's indigenous plants also contribute to the Marinedda's distinctive spa experience. In addition, L'Elicriso features a cardio-fitness area, a heated seawater pool, an elegant sauna and Turkish bath and exclusive treatment cabins.

The Marinedda's 195 en suite guestrooms include standard and superior rooms, a relaxation room with a refreshing outdoor shower, and there's the Presidential Suite—any honeymooner's dream. Each room is beautifully appointed and has satellite TV and a private veranda or terrace from which to appreciate the Sardinian sunset in its full glory. The décor is inimitably Mediterranean, constructed with gleaming chestnut timber and local stone.

The menu of daily diversions teems with possibility, from visiting the artisanal craftsmen at Castelsardo to hiking the rugged mountains of the island's interior or sampling a new water sport. In all, Sardinia is the ideal destination for families with children, culture-conscious independent travellers or couples seeking a little island romance. The Marinedda's sole intention is to make each of their experiences as memorable and enjoyable as possible.

ROOMS
195

FOOD
Petra Ruja: Mediterranean and regional • Li Canneddi: Mediterranean and regional • Tramonto Rosso: Mediterranean and regional

DRINK
2 bars

FEATURES
L'Elicriso Thalasso & Spa Centre • tennis court • five-a-side football pitch • Mini Club • pools • boat excursions • air conditioning • satellite TV • hairdryer • minibar • safe • veranda • terrace • boat charter • beaches

CONTACT
07038 Isola Rossa, Sardinia • telephone: +39.0789.790 018 • facsimile: +39.0789.790 058 • email: info@delphina.it • website: www.delphina.it

hotel pitrizza

...discreet grass-topped villas scattered amid flowering gardens and manicured lawns...

The Costa Smeralda on the northeastern coast of Sardinia has to be one of the best preserved and most beautiful stretches of coastline in the Mediterranean. Striking rocky outcrops shelter pristine, white sandy coves enveloped by shimmering seas of vivid turquoise, deep indigo and a dazzling emerald hue. Since it was first developed as a tourist destination in the 1960s, great care has been taken to ensure that this part of the island remains virtually untouched and that any new constructions are in harmony with the environment and surrounding scenery.

One of the first hotels to be built in this glorious enclave was the Hotel Pitrizza, a distinguished member of the prestigious Starwood Hotels and Resorts group that brings together all the prerequisites for a truly spectacular holiday. Built in 1963 and completely renovated in 1990, this charming hotel still retains the modernist architecture typical of the era with vast spaces and floor-to-ceiling windows, ideal for beach locations. Occupying the end of a small peninsula and flanked by private beaches, the Pitrizza consists of discreet grass-topped villas scattered amid flowering gardens and manicured lawns, all with ample terraces and

breathtaking views. Interiors are luxurious with a fresh, exotic feel. Cool, white walls and decorative, handcrafted furnishings contrast with splashes of bright turquoise or burnt red and the green fronds of indoor plants.

Guests really looking to escape from the stresses of everyday life will relish the prospect of a suite with a private pool or beach, while the state-of-the-art gym and fitness facilities ensure that even the most overworked will leave completely relaxed and renewed.

Sporting types will not be disappointed. Although the hotel offers the perfect opportunity to soak up the sun on the beach or by the spectacular saltwater pool carved out of granite rock, one of the world's top golf courses at the Pevero Club occupies the neighbouring property. In addition, water skiing, tennis and windsurfing are also available.

The perfect complement to this sublime seaside haven is the fine food served at the Hotel Pitrizza. At lunch time, the Ristorante Pitrizza by the pool proffers welcome shade and yet

manages to maintain an al fresco atmosphere, while at night, incurable romantics will love the candlelit dining under the stars. The tantalising menu of fresh seafood and aromatic Mediterranean dishes will satisfy even the most discerning palate.

In addition to the gourmet cuisine at the Pitrizza, guests on full board can also enjoy the exceptional food served at the nearby Cala di Volpe, Cervo and Romazzino hotels—fellow members of the Starwood collection located on the Costa Smeralda—at no additional cost.

The Costa Smeralda is a must for any visitors to Sardinia, and those lucky enough to stay at the Pitrizza will be in for an unforgettable experience.

ROOMS
55

FOOD
Ristorante Pitrizza: international

DRINK
Pitrizza Bar

FEATURES
babysitter on request • satellite TV • beauty and fitness centre • terraces • water skiing • windsurfing • wireless Internet access

BUSINESS
business centre • conferences at nearby Hotel Cervo

NEARBY
Pevero Club • tennis club • Porto Cervo village

CONTACT
07020 Porto Cervo, Costa Smeralda, Sardinia • telephone: +39.0789.930 111 • facsimile: +39.0789.930 611 • email: pitizza@luxurycollection.com • website: luxurycollection.com/ hotelpitrizza

hotel signum

...the volcanic island backdrop of Stromboli and Panarea visible from the terraces...

The UNESCO World Heritage Site of Salina is the lushest and most verdant island in the breathtaking Aeolian archipelago. Rising dramatically from the surface of the Mediterranean just north of Sicily with striking volcanic twin peaks, this island with its geologically tumultuous history is today famed for its exquisite coastline, mouth-watering capers and the sweet Malvasia wines produces on its mineral-rich slopes.

Opened in 1988 in the hometown of husband and wife team Clara Rametta and Michele Caruso, the couple's dream retreat very nearly didn't materialise as they were originally handed a sigillo—or seal—by villagers unwilling to see a hotel open its doors to outsiders in the midst of their beloved hamlet. Fortunately there was a change of heart, and this charming boutique hotel was thus born, its owners playfully naming it after the Latin root for sigillo—Hotel Signum.

Mere metres from the hotel is the pristine Pollara Bay, the setting for Michael Radford's seductive film *Il Postino*. The farmhouse-styled Hotel Signum is every bit as memorable and romantic as the Pablo Neruda poems featured in this poignant love story.

This exclusive island hotel has garnered rave reviews from the prestigious travel press. *Condé Nast Traveller* is greatly impressed by its unique setting and traditional wrought ironwork, not to mention the authentic touches such as embroidered bedlinen in the quaint guest suites. With the volcanic island backdrop of Stromboli and Panarea visible from the terraces, this is one jasmine-scented destination that should not be missed.

With considerable taste and an eye for detail, Clara and Michele have created an authentic Aeolian atmosphere in their lovingly decorated hotel. Each unique room features handcrafted, artisanal furniture and is personalised further with the artwork of local painters and creators. Select a suite by its evocative name alone—the Acanto, Bougainvillea, Cappero, Ginestra or Malva suites—to name a few.

The Classic, Superior and Deluxe Rooms boast every luxurious feature as befits a four-star hotel, from climate control and satellite TV to private telephones and Internet access. The minibar is also thoughtfully stocked with an appetising array of typical Aeolian drinks and snacks.

Immersed amid heavenly-scented jasmine plantations, the Hotel Signum offers an elegant library and reading room as well, complete with antique sofas for guests to while away an afternoon. Alternatively, head to the solarium, impeccably maintained gardens or the tempting infinity-edge pool—the ideal spot from which to witness the beautiful rising and setting of the sun.

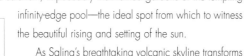

As Salina's breathtaking volcanic skyline transforms into an awe-inspiring silhouette, enjoy an aperitif or secluded candlelit dinner on the terrace. Michele's renowned tasting menu of Aeolian specialities is simply unsurpassable. His inspired culinary touch extends to freshly-caught fish, homemade pasta and light Mediterranean dishes. Round off the meal and a wonderful day with a glass of Malvasia, the locally produced dessert wine.

ROOMS
30

FOOD
Signum: Aeolian and Mediterranean

DRINK
wine cellar

FEATURES
satellite TV • reading room • library • infinity-edge pool with hydro-massage • solarium • massage • Vespa rental • excursion booking service

BUSINESS
meeting facilities

NEARBY
diving • sailing • Monte Porri • Monte Fossa Delle Felci • Stromboli • Pollara Bay

CONTACT
Via Scalo 15, 98050 Malfa, Salina, Aeolian Islands • telephone: +39.909.844 222 • facsimile: +39.909.844 102 • email: salina@hotelsignum.it • website: www.hotelsignum.it

la coluccia

...rooms blend a distinctly contemporary style with an underlying timeless elegance...

No tour of Italy is complete without a visit to one of its splendid Mediterranean islands, with destinations such as Sardinia offering the ultimate in sea-encircled escapism. The flowing architectural forms of Hotel La Coluccia create one such exclusive getaway. A favourite haunt of discerning travellers since its opening in 2003, it is the ideal base from which to experience Sardinia's myriad attractions including visits to the Gennargentu National Park or scuba diving near the wonderful marine reserve of Tavolara Island.

This sleek and secluded designer hotel is situated on the northern coast of Sardinia, a mountainous paradise noted for the extraordinary rock formations of its numerous bays, plateaus and caves. The complex proffers expansive views across to the hazy shores of Spargi Island, and boasts a superb setting at the start of a pristine, 4-km- (2-mile-) long bay.

Set in landscaped grounds, Hotel La Coluccia is separated from its exclusive, granite-edged beach by a fresh-scented pine forest. With comfortable sunbeds, towels and beach umbrellas provided by the hotel, a chilled fruit juice and riveting bestseller are the only other prerequisites necessary for a perfect morning right on the sea's edge.

With this intimate and luxurious beach retreat, architect Julio César Ayllòn has tangibly succeeded in his quest to fuse art and fashion with interior design. The 45 air-conditioned rooms blend a distinctly contemporary style with an underlying timeless elegance, a philosophy reinforced by the materials that have been used—polished cement, rich dark woods, deep leather furnishings and luxurious fabrics.

With finishings that are of the highest standards, each en suite room is also equipped with a satellite TV, direct-dial telephone, minibar and safe. The warm palette choice of chocolate and cream creates a calming contrast to the bright sapphire of the sea and the verdant green of the gardens, as viewed from the curvaceous private balconies.

The wave-like formation of the hotel's undulating roof forms a striking silhouette, and this free-flowing theme continues with

THIS PAGE (FROM TOP): Guestrooms contain slick furnishings befitting of a top class hotel; enjoy a stroll on the beautifully lit piazza in the evenings.

OPPOSITE (FROM TOP): A sunny vacation on the island of Sardinia beckons; La Coluccia's modern lobby is typical of its avant-garde style; take a swim, or relax by the hotel's equally stylish pool.

ROOMS
45

FOOD
Terrace Restaurant: Sardinian,
Italian and international

FEATURES
satellite TV • direct-dial telephone •
minibar • safe • pool • gym •
spa • Turkish bath • relaxation area •
pedaloes • boats and bikes rental

BUSINESS
conference room

NEARBY
water sports • horse riding •
golf at the Pevero Club • Olbia airport

CONTACT
Gallura, Località Conca Verde,
07028 Santa Teresa Gallura, Sardinia •
telephone: +39.0789.758 004 •
facsimile: +39.0789.758 007 •
email: lacoluccia@mobygest.it •
website: www.mobygest.it •
www.hotelphilosophy.net

the contours of the naturally heated outdoor pool, forming an impressive backdrop for the hotel's restaurant that serves both local and international cuisines. Even if guests are only here for a brief sojourn, the restaurant's four-course tasting menu of Sardinian specialities is an essential culinary experience. To work up an appetite for such a gastronomic indulgence, the well-equipped gym is located in La Collucia's cutting-edge Space Comfort Zone. This ultra-modern spa complex also features massage rooms, Turkish bath and a serene relaxation area that help maintain physical and spiritual equilibrium.

For a chance to fully enjoy the attractive environs, sailing, horse riding and golf are all within a short drive of the hotel, as are boat trips to the neighbouring French island of Corsica. From experience, however, the desire to leave this luxurious designer hotel is rarely felt by the guests of La Coluccia, Sardinia's most stylish new arrival. Its magnetism awaits.

le meridien chia laguna

...everything guests could hope for in a hotel, all set in exquisitely beautiful grounds.

In a perfect world, all hotels would offer wonderful service, stylish accommodation, the best facilities and a glorious setting. The reality, of course, is altogether different, with many an establishment failing to live up to these expectations. Unless, that is, the hotel in question happens to belong to the renowned Le Meridien group.

With more than 120 luxury and upscale hotels in over 50 countries around the world, Le Meridien has a peerless and long-standing reputation for excellence in every aspect of the hospitality it provides. Located within the Chia Laguna Resort, at the southern end of Sardinia on one of the Mediterranean's largest and most unspoilt white sand beaches, Le Meridien Chia Laguna is one such hotel.

Designed to provide comfort at the highest level, Le Meridien Chia Laguna offers two types of accommodation, providing everything guests could hope for in a hotel, all set in exquisitely beautiful grounds. The Hotel Laguna offers 72 rooms that are recently refurbished, many of which enjoy a private balcony or terrace and stunning views of the nearby lagoon and the sea beyond.

For guests who want something unique, the cottage rooms at Chia Village combine contemporary and vintage designs. All rooms are luxuriously appointed, with standard features including Internet access, flat-screen TV, air conditioning and en suite bathrooms. It goes without saying too that Le Meriden's hallmark touches of quality, thoughtfulness and style are prominent throughout.

This uncompromising attention to detail is also evident in the hotel's extensive public areas and facilities, which must be the envy of every other hotel in Sardinia. Apart from tennis courts, an 18-hole pitch and putt golf course,

a driving range and several swimming pools, the hotel has a superbly-equipped Beauty Centre and gym. In addition, it offers exclusive access to one of the most spectacular beaches in the region, and also has one of the island's leading convention centres—the Congress Centre is capable of hosting up to 1,200 people at any one time.

Those who have chosen this destination in order to experience some of Italy's legendary cuisine will not be disappointed as there is a wide variety of cuisine for guests to choose from. Because hotel guests have access to the facilities at the Baia Chia Village—part of the Chia Laguna Resort as well—there's no shortage of restaurants and bars to choose from, including a classic Italian pizzeria and one that is romantically nestled among the dunes. Foremost among them, however, has to be the La Terrazza restaurant, which offers gourmet dining on a shaded patio with panoramic views of the magnificent Chia Bay, and with a twist—the executive chef demonstrates his culinary skills right in front of guests. There's also the Bar Bollicine, where aperitifs and champagne can be savoured in equally sumptuous surroundings. Traditional Italian, Sardinian and Mediterranean dishes feature strongly on all the menus, and an extensive wine list contributes to the perfect dining experience. In a perfect world all hotels would be just like this one.

ROOMS
72

FOOD
Bouganville Restaurant: Mediterranean and international • La Terrazza: Mediterranean and international • Art à la Carte Restaurant: global fusion • Le Dune Restaurant • Steak House

DRINK
Bar Rondini • Bar Bollicine • Bar Piscina • Bar Dune • Bar Piazza degli Ulivi • Wine Bar • Luna

FEATURES
gym • Beauty Centre • private beach • pools • tennis courts • five-a-side football pitch • 18-hole pitch and putt golf course • babysitter on request

BUSINESS
auditorium • Congress Centre • exhibition area

NEARBY
Chia • Bithia archaeological site • Nora archaeological site • Pula

CONTACT
Località Chia, 09010 Domus De Maria, Cagliari, Sardinia • telephone: +39.070.92 391 • facsimile: +39.070.923 0141 • email: info@hotelchialaguna.com • website: www.lemeridien-chialaguna.com

resort valle dell'erica thalasso + spa

...sink into the luxury of a suite retreat or explore the island's rhythms...

Sardinia is separated from Corsica by the Straits of Bonifacio. Scattered throughout this cobalt blue stretch of the Mediterranean is an archipelago of seven wonderful islands and islets named after the chain's only inhabited island, La Maddalena. It is a brief boat trip from Palau, a seaside resort on the mainland's northern coast. The secluded enclave of Resort Valle dell'Erica extends its warm welcome from a prime location upon La Maddalena, itself a Marine National Park. The island's jagged coastline is punctuated by red, wind-sculpted rocks that shield an endless selection of bathing coves.

Situated just 100 m (109 yd) from the coast, dedicated water babies will revel in Valle dell'Erica's exclusive beach as well as its two splendid seawater swimming pools. Replete with relaxing sunbeds and attentive bar service, one boasts breathtaking vistas over a pearl-white bay to the island-specked horizon, while the other is reassuringly child-friendly. This family-friendly resort even has a dedicated children's restaurant, Capitan Uncino.

Delphina resorts are renowned for their high calibre culinary provision. Valle dell'Erica's Nautilus, Il Grecale, La Prua and Li Zini restaurants are as impressive as their stunning, waterside settings. The inspired chefs are equally adept at creating casual poolside snacks as impeccable candlelight dinners that showcase fresh, locally caught seafood. As twilight melds into night, either sink into the luxury of a suite retreat or explore the island's rhythms courtesy of the live music coming from the hotel's vibrant night scene.

THIS PAGE (FROM TOP): Valle dell'Erica's stylishly laid-back character is evident in the relaxing colour tones and atmosphere of its interior; a panoramic view of the resort.

OPPOSITE (FROM TOP): Golfing enthusiasts can improve their handicap on the chipping greens of Valle dell'Erica; indulge in the seawater pools at the Thalasso & Spa Centre; Li Zini offers the ideal spot for a relaxing meal outdoors, complete with a hammock.

After going through a revamp in 2005, this stylish hotel now has 140 ground-level rooms and suites. Most rooms include gorgeous sea views, and each has a shaded verandah for an indulgent afternoon nap. The rooms are designed with comfort, convenience and communication as the main objectives, as amenities include satellite and Sky TV and minibar. The cool interiors are oases of elegance and romance, emanating the very essence of the relaxed Mediterranean.

For guests who want to experience the ultimate luxury, the prestigious Presidential Suite comprises a spacious living area, a panoramic verandah and a second bathroom with an invigorating hydro-massage tub. Designed with relaxation in mind, the five Wellness Centre rooms provide direct access to the hotel's cutting-edge spa facility.

The Le Thermae Thalasso & Spa Centre benefits from an incredible natural granite setting. As befits a spa of such stature, it boasts four outdoor seawater pools, 13 private treatment cabins, a Turkish bath, sauna, relaxation area and a well-equipped cardio-fitness room. Aromatic essential oils from Sardinia's unique plants are also used to heighten the multi-sensory experience of its plethora of body and soul-inspiring treatments.

A favourite haunt of royalty and celebrities alike since 1958, this luxuriously renovated property retains the same elegance and exclusivity as it did when originally constructed back then, as part of Sardinia's first-ever holiday resort. Enjoy it today as it carves its own distinctive niche into the new millennium.

ROOMS
140

FOOD
Li Zini: seafood • Nautilus: Mediterranean and regional • La Prua: Mediterranean and regional • Il Grecale: Mediterranean breakfast and brunch • Capitan Uncino: Mediterranean (for children)

DRINK
3 bars

FEATURES
Le Thermae Thalasso & Spa Centre • pitch and putt golf course • driving range • beaches • boat excursions • satellite and Sky TV • minibar • safe • verandah • terrace • pools • air conditioning • Mini and Junior Club

NEARBY
Santa Teresa Gallura • horse riding • sailing • diving

CONTACT
07028 Santa Teresa Gallura, Sardinia • telephone: +39.0789.790 018 • facsimile: +39.0789.790 058 • email: info@delphina.it • website: www.delphina.it

santa teresa

...a bastion of untainted beauty.

The exquisite island of Pantelleria is the largest of Sicily's dramatic islands, with its rugged landscape evoking memories of authentic, inventive island wandering. Almost equidistant from the African coastline and the Sicilian mainland, the island's volcanic past is evident in its mineral-rich black rocks, creating a stunning contrast with the cobalt blue and glinting emerald tones of the sea that laps the shores of Pantelleria's spectacular swimming coves.

The Santa Teresa resort is located in the island's principal village, standing as a bastion of untainted beauty. While a distinguished member of the prestigious Design Hotels group, Santa Teresa remains completely original, exuding a rustic charm of its own.

Revolving round Santa Teresa's 40-hectare (99-acre) organic farm, the resort's low stone lodges are in complete harmony with their surroundings which comprise olive trees, Nero d'Avola—often regarded as 'the most important red wine grape in Sicily'—Merlot and

THIS PAGE (FROM TOP): Santa Teresa offers a unique holiday with its beautifully rugged surroundings; the clear blue waters of the pool blend perfectly with the natural splendour that surrounds it.

OPPOSITE (FROM LEFT): Lodges have a simple yet stylish décor; the historic dammusi provides modern comfort and luxury.

Cabernet grape vines and countless beds of aromatic herbs. A helping hand with the grape harvest in September is always welcomed, not to mention all the wine tasting that follows.

Known as 'dammusi', Santa Teresa's lodges are in fact clusters of ancient stone hideaways that have been exquisitely restructured and host up to four guests in simple, refined luxury. Sibà houses the reception area and eight dammusi, along with a flourishing Arabian garden, a golf practice area and an outdoor swimming pool. Another four lodges are located at the nearby Fra Diavolo, profiting from an exclusive solarium and sun-warmed pool.

Inside, the cool, air-conditioned dammusi are tastefully decorated, each maintaining its own unique style. The walls are a crisp white, with smooth Moorish archways and inviting beds tucked into secluded niches. The refreshingly simple interiors utilise natural materials, with rattan and wonderful examples of locally handcrafted wooden furniture throughout. In the nearby Monastero Valley are two more collections of dammusi. This casual scattering of its lodges makes Santa Teresa ideal for either total escapism, or for couples travelling together who cherish the idea of retreating to a romantic hideaway at the end of the day.

Excursion opportunities include mountain biking, fishing and hikes along the marked walking paths to the Parco della Riserva, which begin at Sibà. Hiring a car will open up further options, with breezy harbours and shingle beaches beckoning. For the adventurous, the exotic coast of Africa can be spied on a clear day from the summit of Montagna Grande at 836 m (2,743 ft) above sea level. On this self-sufficient island enclave, even the most luxurious beauty spas are made redundant, with soothing mud baths readily available at Lake Venus, courtesy of Pantelleria's natural thermal zones.

At sunset, join other guests in Sibà's aromatic Arabian garden for a refreshing aperitif before sampling the mouth-watering local delicacies of pesto Pantelleria, spicy couscous and fresh fish at the many welcoming local restaurants. For authentic souvenirs to remember this truly unique destination, Santa Teresa sells a wide range of its own organic produce, spanning wine and olive oil, sauces, confectionery and themed gifts.

ROOMS
18 dammusi lodges

FOOD
Arabian gardens: breakfast

DRINK
Cantina

FEATURES
air conditioning • car rental • pool • golf club • kitchenette • mountain bikes • private boats

NEARBY
Parco della Riserva • Piana di Sabà • Pantelleria village • Venere Lake • Valle di Monastero

CONTACT
C. da Monastero Alto, Sibà, 91010 Scauri Siculo, Pantelleria Egadi Islands, Sicily • telephone: +39.092.391 6389 • facsimile: +39.092.391 6666 • email: santateresa@mobygest.it • website: www.mobygest.it www.hotelphilosophy.net

index

index

picturecredits+acknowledgements

The publisher would like to thank the following for permission to reproduce their photographs:

A + L Sinibaldi/Getty Images back cover (below right), 191
Adler Thermae Spa + Wellness Resort 130, 140–41
Alan Copson/Photolibrary 35
Alessandro Rizzi/Getty Images 193
Alessandro Saffo/Corbis 198, 258, 263
Alois Weber/Photolibrary 51 (top)
Andrea Pistolesi/Getty Images 49, 52
Andrew Pini/Photolibrary 34 (top right)
Anthony Blake/Photolibrary 36, 99 (top)
Arper 21, 23 (centre 2)
Baglioni Hotels 148–49, 214–15
Bauer Il Palazzo 102–3
Bauer Palladio Hotel + Spa 104–5
Benjamin Rondel/Photolibrary 30 (below)
Billy Hustace/Getty Images front cover (below left), 14 (below)
Bob Sacha/Corbis 34 (top left), 98, 261 (top)
Bruce Forster/Getty Images 44
Bulgari Milan Hotel 38 (top + below)
Ca Maria Adele front cover (top right), 106–7
Ca'Pisani 108–9
Cala Caterina 270–71
Casa Angelina lifestyle 22, 232–33
Charles + Josette Lenars/Corbis 268 (left)
Charles Bowman/Getty Images 40
Charming House DD.724 back flap (bed), 110–11
Chia Laguna Villas 272–73
Chris Moore/Getty Images 19 (top left)
Claudio Peri/epa/Corbis 194 (below)
Colin Dutton/Corbis back cover (painting), 92, 93
Corbis/Photolibrary 97
Corrado Poli/Photolibrary 59
Cosmo Condina/Getty Images 84
Costantinopoli 104 234–35
Cracco 5
Dallas + John Heaton/Corbis 41 (Dolomites)
David Madison/Getty Images 196
David Noton/Getty Images 41 (trulli houses)
David Sutherland/Corbis 266
David Tomlinson/Getty Images 127 (top)
DEA/L. Romano/Getty Images 41 (Villa San Michele)
DeA Picture Library/Getty Images 268 (right), 269
DEA/Pubbli Aer Foto/Getty Images 264
DEA/R. Felderer/Photolibrary 60
Delphina Hotels + Resorts 276–77, 278–79, 288–89
Dietmar Fritze 89 (below)
Douglas Kirkland/Corbis 13
Elisabetta Villa/Getty Images 19 (Valentino exhibition)
Ernst Haas/Getty Images 88
Falconara 274–75

Filippo Monteforte/Getty Images 17 (top right + centre), 199
Fornasetti 23 (top 2)
Franco Cogoli/Corbis 58
Frumm John/Photolibrary 12
Fulvio Roiter/Corbis 200
Furore Inn Resort + Spa 236–37
Gaetan Bally/epa/Corbis 9
Gallia Palace Hotel 142–43
Gary Yeowell/Getty Images 54, 86, 126
Gian Berto Vanni/Corbis 96 (below)
Gina Martin/Getty Images 37 (top right)
Giuseppe Cacace/Getty Images 17 (top left)
Glenn Beanland/Getty Images 187 (below)
Grand Hotel et de Milan 62–3
Grand Hotel Excelsior Vittoria 238–39
Grand Hotel Firenze 144–45
Grand Hotel Parker's 240–41
Grand Tour/Corbis back cover (below left), 42, 137
Guenter Rossenbach/zefa/Corbis 231
Guido Baviera/Corbis 29 (top), 53 (below), 96 (top)
Guido Cozzi/Corbis 197 (top), 201
Hauke Dressler/Getty Images 45, 47 (top)
Hotel de Russie front cover (martini), 33 (below), 206–7
Hotel Giardino back cover (dish), 64–5
Hotel Gritti Palace back cover (top left), 144–45
Hotel Milano Alpen Resort, Meeting + Spa 66–7
Hotel Monaco + Grand Canal 116–17
Hotel Pitrizza 280–81
Hotel Principe di Savoia front cover (below right), 4
Hotel San Francesco al Monte 242–43
Hotel Santa Maria Novella 152–53
Hotel Savoy 154–55
Hotel Signum 282–83
Hotel Villa del Quar 118–19
Ian Cumming/Photolibrary 195
I Casali Di Monticchio 210–214
Il Canto 26 (top)
Il Pellicano 158–59
James Leynse/Corbis 19 (Gucci handbag)
Jean-Bernard Carillet/Getty Images 223 (top)
Jeff Spielman/Getty Images front cover (staircase), 189 (below)
Jeremy Horner/Corbis 228
Jeremy Woodhouse/Getty Images 55
Joe Beynon/Getty Images 187 (top)
Joe Murador/Getty Images 33 (top)
John Brown/Getty Images 8–9
John Miller/Getty Images 267
Jon Hicks/Corbis 46
Jonathan Blair/Corbis 227 (below)
Jörg Sundermann back cover (spa treatment), 39

José Fuste Raga/zefa/Corbis 256
JTB Photo/Photolibrary 101, 131
Jupiterimages/Photolibrary back cover (café), 34 (below)
Kazuyoshi Nomachi/Corbis 190
Keith Miller 41 (Tuscan Hills), 127 (below)
Kim Sayer/Getty Images 129 (below)
K.M. Westermann/Corbis 262
Kos Picture Source/Getty Images 265
L'Albereta front flap (top and below), 68–9
L'Andana 1, 160–61
La Coluccia 284–85
Le Meridien Chia Laguna 286–87
Locanda Mongreno 25 (top left)
Louis-Laurent Grandadam/Getty Images 254
Lucy Davies/Getty Images 222
Macduff Everton/Corbis 194 (top)
Madonnina del Pescatore 27 (top)
Maison La Minervetta 244–45
Marco Cristofori/Corbis 50
Marco Di Lauro/Getty Images 89 (top)
Marco Scataglini/Photolibrary 230 (below)
Marcos Delgado/epa/Corbis 99 (below)
Maren Caruso/Photolibrary 51 (below)
Mario Cipollini/Getty Images 259
Mark Bolton/Corbis 2
Mark Jenkinson/Corbis 14 (top)
Martin Moos/Getty Images 133
Masseria Cimino 246–47
Masseria San Domenico, Resort, Spa-Thalasso, Golf 248–49
Massimo Listri/Corbis 48 (top), 53 (top), 192
Massimo Borchi/Corbis 139, 224, 225 (below)
Matteo Brogi 26 (below left + below right)
Melisa Teo front cover (dish), 24
Michael S. Yamashita/Corbis 18 (top)
Mike King/Corbis 100
Mimmo Jodice/Corbis 260
ML Sinibaldi/Corbis 220
Moritz Steiger/Getty Images 186
Neil Emmerson/Getty Images 124
Paco Serinelli/Getty Images 29 (below)
Palace Merano Espace Henri Chenot 70–1
Palazzo Arzaga Hotel Spa + Golf Resort 72–3
Palazzo Viviani back flap (top), 120–21
Panoramic Images/Getty Images 188–89
Park Hyatt Milan back cover (top right), 32, 74–5
Pascal Le Segretain/Getty Images 19 (below)
PatitucciPhoto/Getty Images 37 (top left)
Piazza Duomo 25 (top right)
Peter Poulides/Getty Images 28
Poltrona Frau 20
Prada 17 (below)

Principe di Piemonte 162–166
Puku/Grand Tour/Corbis 136
Rainer Hackenberg/zefa/Corbis 138
Randy Belice/NBAE/Getty Images 95 (top)
Raul Touzon/Getty Images 47 (below)
Relais La Suvera 166–71
Relais Santa Croce 172–73
Rieger Bertrand/Photolibrary 91
Richard Ross/Getty Images 261 (below)
Ristorante Duomo 27 (centre + below)
Rogan Macdonald/Photolibrary 227 (top)
Roger Antrobus/Corbis front cover (Tuscan hills), 134
Salvatore Ferragamo 30 (top), 129 (top)
Salvatore Laporta/Getty Images 225 (top)
San Clemente Palace Hotel + Resort 122–23
Sandro Vannini/Corbis 197 (below)
Santa Teresa 290–91
Seamas Culligan/ZUMA/Corbis 223 (below)
Seiser Alm Urthaler 76–7
Sergio Pitamitz/Getty Images 56
Sergio Pitamitz/zefa/Corbis 135
Sheila Terry/Photolibrary 31 (top), 48 (below)
Silvia Otte/Getty Images 184
SINA Fine Italian Hotels front flap (centre), 78–9, 146–47, 204–5
St. Regis Grand Hotel, Rome 216–17
Stefano Amantini/Corbis 18 (below), 132, 229 (below)
Stefano Scatà/Grand Tour/Corbis 95 (below)
Steven Vidler/Eurasia Press/Corbis 61
Stuart Dee/Getty Images 87 (below)
Stuart Westmorland/Getty Images 87 (top)
Susie Cushner/Photolibrary 37 (below left + below right)
Terme di Saturnia Spa + Golf Resort 174–75
The Duke Hotel 218–19
The Straf 80–1
The Travel Library Limited/Photolibrary 57, 226
The Villa Book 82–3, 156–57, 182–83, 250–51, 252–53
Tim McGuire/Corbis 31 (below)
Todd Gipstein/National Geographic 94
Villa La Vedetta 176–77
Villa Mangiacane 178–79
Villa Olmi Resort 180–81
Vintage Hospitality 150–51, 202–3, 208–9
Virginia Farneti/epa/Corbis front cover (model), 16
Walter Bibikow/Getty Images front cover (chapel), 229 (top), 230 (top), 257
Walter Bibikow/Photolibrary 128
WireImage/Getty Images 15
Wowe/Le Calandre 25 (below)
Zucchetti 23 (below)

directory

HOTELS

155 Via Veneto Boutique Hotel
(page 202)
Via Veneto 155, 00187 Roma
telephone : +39.06.322 0404
facsimile : +39.06.322 0405
info@155viaveneto.com
www.155viaveneto.com

Adler Thermae Spa + Wellness Resort
(page 140)
1-53027 Bagno Vignoni, Tuscany
telephone : +39.0577.889 000
facsimile : +39.0577.889 999
toscana@adler-resorts.com
www.adler-resorts.com

Bauer Il Palazzo (page 102)
San Marco 1413/d, 30124 Venice
telephone : +39.041.520 7022
facsimile : +39.041.520 7557
marketing@bauervenezia.com
www.bauerhotels.com

Bauer Palladio Hotel + Spa (page 104)
Giudecca 33, 30133 Venice
telephone : +39.041.520 7022
facsimile : +39.041.520 7557
marketing@bauervenezia.com
www.bauerhotels.com

Brufani Palace Perugia (page 204)
Piazza Italia 12, 06121 Perugia
telephone : +39.075.573 2541
facsimile : +39.075.572 0210
brufanipalace@sinahotels.it
www.brufanipalace.it

Ca Maria Adele (page 106)
Rio Terà dei Catecumeni 111,
30123 Dorsoduro Venice
telephone : +39.041.520 3078
facsimile : +39.041.528 9013
info@camariaadele.it
www.camariaadele.it

Ca'Pisani (page 108)
Dorsoduro 979/a, 30123 Venice
telephone : +39.041.240 1411
facsimile : +39.041.277 1061
info@capisanihotel.it
www.capisanihotel.it

Cala Caterina (page 270)
Via Lago Maggiore 32,
09049 Villasimius, Sardinia
telephone : +39.070.797 410
facsimile : +39.070.797 473
calacaterina@mobygest.it
www.hotelphilosophy.net

Casa Angelina Lifestyle (page 232)
Via G. Capriglione 147,
84010 Praiano, Salerno
telephone : +39.089.813 1333
facsimile : +39.089.874 266
reservations@casangelina.com
www.casangelina.com

Charming House DD.724 (page 110)
Dorsoduro 724, 30123 Venice
telephone : +39.041.277 0262
facsimile : +39.041.296 0633
info@dd724.it
www.dd724.it

Chia Laguna Villas (page 272)
Località Chia, 09010 Domus de Maria,
Cagliari, Sardinia
telephone : +39.070.9239 3431
facsimile : +39.070.923 0144
info@chialagunaresort.com
www.chialagunaresort.com

Costantinopoli 104 (page 234)
Via S Maria Constantinopoli 104,
80138 Naples
telephone : +39.081.557 1035
facsimile : +39.081.557 1051
info@constantinopoli104.com
www.constantinopoli104.com

Falconara (page 274)
Località Falconara, Butera, 93011 Sicily
telephone : +39.0934.349 012
facsimile : +39.0934.349 015
falconara@mobygest.it
www.mobygest.it
www.hotelphilosophy.net

Furore Inn Resort + Spa (page 236)
Via dell'Amore, Piazza Sant'Elia 1,
84010 Furore, Amalfi Coast
telephone : +39.089.830 4711
facsimile : +39.089.830 4777
information@furoreinn.it
www.furoreinn.it

Gallia Palace Hotel (page 142)
58040 Punta Ala, Tuscany
telephone : +39.056.492 2022
facsimile : +39.056.492 0229
info@galliapalace.it
www.galliapalace.it

Grand Hotel Baglioni (page 112)
Via Indipendenza 8, 40121 Bologna
telephone : +39.051.225 445
facsimile : +39.051.234 840
reservations.ghbbologna@baglionihotels.com
www.baglionihotels.com

Grand Hotel Excelsior Vittoria
(page 238)
Piazza Tasso 34, 80067 Sorrento, Naples
telephone : +39.081.877 7111
facsimile : +39.081.877 1206
exvitt@exvitt.it
www.exvitt.it

Grand Hotel Firenze (page 144)
Piazza Ognissanti 1, 50123 Florence
telephone : +39.055.27 161
facsimile : +39.055.217 400
grandflorence@luxurycollection.com
www.luxurycollection.com/grandflorence

Grand Hotel Parker's (page 240)
Corso Vittorio Emanuele 135,
80121 Naples
telephone : +39.081.761 2474
facsimile : +39.081.663 527
info@grandhotelparkers.it
www.grandhotelparkers.it

Grand Hotel Villa Medici Florence
(page 146)
Via Il Prato 42, 50123 Florence
telephone : +39.055.277 171
facsimile : +39.055.238 1336
villa.medici@sinahotels.it
www.villamedicihotel.com

Hotel Bernini Palace (page 148)
Piazza San Firenze 29, 50122 Florence
telephone : +39.055.288 621
facsimile : +39.055.268 272
reservations.berninifirenze@baglionihotels.com
www.baglionihotels.com

Hotel Capo d'Orso Thalasso + Spa
(page 276)
Località Cala Capra,
07020 Palau, Sardinia
telephone : +39.0789.790 018
facsimile : +39.0789.790 058
info@delphina.it
www.delphina.it

Hotel de Russie (page 206)
Via del Babuino 9, 00187 Rome
telephone : +39.06.328 881
facsimile : +39.06.3288 8888
reservations.derussie@roccofortecollection.com
www.roccofortecollection.com

Hotel Giardino (page 64)
Via Segnale 10, CH-6612
Ascona, Switzerland
telephone : +41.91.785 8888
facsimile : +41.91.785 8899
welcome@giardino.ch
website: www.giardino.ch

Hotel Gritti Palace (page 114)
Campo Santa Maria del Giglio,
2467 Venice
telephone : +39.041.794 611
facsimile : +39.041.520 0942
grittipalace@luxurycollection.com
www.luxurycollection.com/grittipalace

Hotel Lord Byron (page 208)
Via Giuseppe De Notaris 5, 00197 Roma
telephone : +39.06.322 0404
facsimile : +39.06.322 0405
info@lordbyronhotel.com
www.lordbyronhotel.com

Hotel Marinedda Thalasso + Spa
(page 278)
07038 Isola Rossa, Sardinia
telephone : +39.0789.790 018
facsimile : +39.0789.790 058
info@delphina.it
www.delphina.it

Palace Merano Espace Henri Chenot
(page 70)
Via Cavour 2, 39012 Merano
telephone : +39.047.327 1000
facsimile : +39.047.327 1100
reservations@palace.it
www.palace.it
www.henrichenot.com

**Hotel Milano Alpen Resort,
Meeting + Spa** (page 66)
Via Silvio Pellico 3, 24020 Castione della
Presolana, Bratto
telephone : +39.0346.31211
facsimile : +39.0346.36236
info@hotelmilano.com
www.hotelmilano.com

Hotel Monaco + Grand Canal (page 116)
San Marco 1332, 30124 Venice
telephone : +39.041.520 0211
facsimile : +39.041.520 0501
mailbox@hotelmonaco.it
www.hotelmonaco.it

Hotel Pitrizza (page 280)
07020 Porto Cervo, Costa
Smeralda, Sardinia
telephone : +39.0789.930 111
facsimile : +39.0789.930 611
pitizza@luxurycollection.com
luxurycollection.com/hotelpitrizza

Hotel Regency Firenze (page 150)
Piazza M. D'Azeglio 3, 50121 Florence
telephone : +39.055.245 247
facsimile : +39.055.234 6735
info@regency-hotel.com
www.regency-hotel.com

Hotel San Francesco al Monte (page 242)
Corso Vittorio Emanuele 328,
80135 Naples
telephone : +39.081.423 9111
facsimile : +39.081.251 2485
info@hotelsanfrancesco.it
www.hotelsanfrancesco.it

Hotel Santa Maria Novella (page 152)
Piazza Santa Maria Novella 1,
50123 Florence
telephone : +39.055.271 840
facsimile : +39.055.2718 4199
info@hotelsantamarianovella.it
www.hotelsantamarianovella.it

Hotel Savoy (page 154)
Piazza della Repubblica 7,
50123 Florence
telephone : +39.055.273 5831
facsimile : +39.055.273 5888
reservations.savoy@roccofortecollection.com
www.roccofortecollection.com

Hotel Signum (page 282)
Via Scalo 15, 98050 Malfa, Salina,
Aeolian Islands
telephone : +39.909.844 222
facsimile : +39.909.844 102
salina@hotelsignum.it
www.hotelsignum.it

Hotel Villa del Quar (page 118)
Via Quar 12, 37020 Pedemonte, Verona
telephone : +39.045.680 0681
facsimile : +39.045.680 604
info@hotelvilladelquar.it
www.hotelvilladelquar.it

I Casali Di Monticchio (page 210)
Vocabolo Monticchio 34, 05011
Allerona, Umbria
telephone : +39.763.628 365
facsimile : +39.763.629 569
info@monticchio.it
www.monticchio.it

Il Pellicano (page 158)
Sbarcatello 1, 58018 Porto
Ercole, Tuscany
telephone : +39.056.485 8111
facsimile : +39.056.483 3418
info@pellicanohotel.com
www.pellicanohotel.com

L'Albereta (page 68)
Via Vittorio Emanuele II 23,
25030 Erbusco, Brescia
telephone : +39.030.776 0550
facsimile : +39.030.776 0573
info@albereta.it
www.albereta.it

L'Andana (page 160)
58043 Castiglione della,
Pescaia, Grosseto
telephone : +39.0564.944 800
facsimile : +39.0564.944 577
info@andana.it
www.andana.it

La Coluccia (page 284)
Gallura, Località Conca Verde,
07028 Santa Teresa Gallura, Sardinia
telephone : +39.0789.758 004
facsimile : +39.0789.758 007
lacoluccia@mobygest.it
www.hotelphilosophy.net

Le Meridien Chia Laguna
(page 286)
Località Chia, 09010 Domus De Maria,
Cagliari, Sardinia
telephone : +39.070.92391
facsimile : +39.070.923 0141
www.lemeridien-chialaguna.com

Maison La Minervetta (page 244)
Via Capo 25, 80067 Sorrento, Naples
telephone : +39.081.877 4455
facsimile : +39.081.878 4601
info@laminervetta.com
www.laminervetta.com

Masseria Cimino (page 246)
Contrada Masciola, 72010 Savelletri
di Fasano, Brindisi
telephone : +39.080.482 7886
facsimile : +39.080.482 7950
info@masseriacimino.com
www.masseriacimino.com

**Masseria San Domenico, Resort,
Spa-Thalasso, Golf** (page 248)
Strada Litoranea 379, 72010 Savelletri
di Fasano, Brindisi
telephone : +39.080.482 7769
facsimile : +39.080.482 7978
info@masseriasandomenico.com
www.masseriasandomenico.com

**Palazzo Arzaga Hotel Spa + Golf
Resort** (page 72)
Loc. Arzaga 25080, Carzago di
Calvagese della Riviera, Brescia
telephone : +39.030.680 600
facsimile : +39.030.680 270
arzaga@arzaga.it
www.palazzoarzaga.com

Palazzo Viviani (page 120)
Via Roma 38, 47837 Montegridolfo,
Emilia Romagna
telephone : +39.0541.855 350
facsimile : +39.0541.855 340
montegridolfo@mobygest.it
www.mobygest.it
www.hotelphilosophy.net

Park Hyatt Milan (page 74)
Via Tommaso Grossi 1, 20121 Milan
telephone : +39.02.8821 1234
facsimile : +39.02.8821 1235
milano@hyattintl.com
www.milan.park.hyatt.com

Principe di Piemonte (page 162)
Piazza G. Puccini 1, 55049
Viareggio, Lucca
telephone : +39.0584.4011
facsimile : +39.0584.401 803
info@principedipiemonte.com
www.principedipiemonte.com

Regina Hotel Baglioni (page 214)
Via Veneto 72, 00187 Rome
telephone : +39.06.421 111
facsimile : +39.06.4201 2130
reservations.reginaroma@baglionihotels.com
www.baglionihotels.com

Relais La Suvera (page 166)
53030 Pievescola, Siena
telephone : +39.577.960 300
facsimile : +39.577.960 220
reservations@lasuvera.it
www.lasuvera.it

Relais Santa Croce (page 172)
Via Ghibellina 87, 50122 Florence
telephone : +39.055.234 2230
facsimile : +39.055.234 1195
info@relaisantacroce.com
www.relaisantacroce.com

Resort Valle dell'Erica Thalasso + Spa
(page 288)
07028 Santa Teresa Gallura, Sardinia
telephone : +39.0789.790 018
facsimile : +39.0789.790 058
info@delphina.it
www.delphina.it

San Clemente Palace Hotel + Resort
(page 122)
Isola di San Clemente 1, San Marco,
30214 Venice
telephone : +39.041.244 5001
facsimile : +39.0.41.244 5800
sanclemente@thi.it
www.sanclemente.thi.it

Santa Teresa (page 290)
C. da Monastero Alto, Sibà,
91010 Scauri Siculo, Pantelleria
Egadi Islands, Sicily
telephone : +39.092.391 6389
facsimile : +39.092.391 6666
santateresa@mobygest.it
www.mobygest.it
www.hotelphilosophy.net

Seiser Alm Urthaler (page 76)
Fam. Urthaler, I-39040 Seiser Alm
telephone : +39.0471.727 919
facsimile : +39.0471.727 820
info@seiseralm.com
www.seiseralm.com

St. Regis Grand Hotel, Rome (page 216)
Via Vittorio Emanuele Orlando 3,
00185 Rome
telephone : +39.06.47 091
facsimile : +39.06.474 7307
StRegisGrandRome@stregis.com
www.stregisgrand.hotelinroma.com

Terme di Saturnia Spa + Golf Resort
(page 174)
58014 Saturnia, Grosseto
telephone : +39.0564.600 111
facsimile : +39.0564.601 266
info@termedisaturnia.it
www.termedisaturnia.it

The Duke Hotel (page 218)
Via Archimede 69, 00197 Rome
telephone : +39.06.367 221
facsimile : +39.06.3600 4104
theduke@thedukehotel.com
www.thedukehotel.com

The Gray Milano (page 78)
Via San Raffaele 6, 20121 Milan
telephone : +39.02.720 8951
facsimile : +39.02.866 526
info.thegray@sinahotels.it
www.hotelthegray.com

The Straf (page 80)
Via San Raffaele 3, 20121 Milan
telephone : +39.02.805 081
facsimile : +39.02.8909 5294
reservations@straf.it
www.straf.it

The Villa Book (pages 82, 156, 182,
250, 252)
12 Venetian House, 47 Warrington
Crescent, London W9 1EJ
telephone : +44.845.500 2000
facsimile : +44.845.500 2001
info@thevillabook.com
www.thevillabook.com

Villa La Vedetta (page 176)
Viale Michelangiolo 78, 50125 Florence
telephone : +39.055.681 631
facsimile : +39.055.658 2544
info@villalavedettahotel.com
www.concertohotels.com

Villa Mangiacane (page 178)
Via Faltignano 4, 50026 San
Casciano, Florence
telephone : +39.055.829 0123
facsimile : +39.055.829 0358
mangiacane@steinhotels.com
www.villamangiacane.com

Villa Olmi Resort (page 180)
Via degli Olmi 4/8, 50012 Bagno
a Ripoli, Florence
telephone : +39.055.637 710
facsimile : +39.055.6377 1600
reservations@villaolmiresort.com
www.villaolmiresort.com

MADE IN ITALY: FASHION

10 Corso Como
Corso Como 10, 20154 Milan
telephone : +39.02.2900 2674
info@10corsocomo.com
www.10corsocomo.com

244 Via Panisperna
Via Panisperna 244, 00184 Rome
telephone : +39.06.488 0598

Armani
Spazio Armani
Via Manzoni 31, 20121 Milan
telephone : +39.02.7231 8630
facsimile : +39.02.7231 8639
www.armani-viamanzoni31.it

Boutique Giorgio Armani Milano
Via Sant'Andrea 9, 20121 Milan
telephone : +39.02.7600 3234
facsimile : +39.02.7601 4926
www.armani.com

Barbaro
Galleria Umberto I 50, 80132 Naples
telephone : +39.081.410 041

Brioni
Via Veneto 129, 00187 Rome
telephone : +39.06.4782 2119
www.brioni.it

Bulgari
Via della Spiga 6, 20121 Milan
telephone : +39.02.7601 3448
facsimile : +39.02.7631 7143
www.bulgari.com

Via Condotti 10, 00187 Rome
telephone : +39.06.696 261
facsimile : +39.06.678 3419
www.bulgari.com

Degli Effetti
Piazza Capranica 75, 79, 93,
00186 Rome
telephone : +39.06.679 0202
info@deglieffetti.com
www.deglieffetti.com

Di Maria
Via F Bandiera 63, 90133 Palermo
telephone : +39.091.609 0395

Diesel
Milano Concept, Corso di Porta Ticinese
44, 20123 Milan
telephone : +39.02.8942 0916
www.diesel.com

Dolce + Gabbana
Via della Spiga 26a, 20129 Milan
telephone : +39.02.7600 1155
www.dolcegabbana.it

E. Marinella
Riviera di Chiaia 287, 80121 Naples
telephone : +39.081.764 4214
facsimile : +39.081.245 1182
marinella@marinellanapoli.it
www.marinellanapoli.it

Eddy Monetti
Via Dei Mille 45, 80121 Naples
telephone : +39.081.407 064
facsimile : +39.081.764 3744
info@eddymonetti.it
www.eddymonetti.it

Emilio Pucci
Palazzo Pucci
Via dei Pucci 6r, 50122 Florence
telephone : +39.055.261 841
facsimile : +39.055.280 451
www.emiliopucci.com

Via Camerelle 65, 80073 Capri
telephone : +39.081.838 8200
www.emiliopucci.com

Fendi
Via Sant'Andrea 16, 20121 Milan
telephone : +39.02.7602 1617
www.fendi.com

Via Borgognona 39, 00187 Rome
telephone : +39.06.696 661
www.fendi.com

Palazzo Fendi
Largo Goldoni 415-421, 00187 Rome
telephone : +39.06.334 501
www.fendi.com

Via Camerelle 8, 80073 Capri
telephone : +39.081.837 0871
www.fendi.com

Fratelli Rossetti
Via Montenapoleone 1, 20121 Milan
telephone : +39.02.7602 1650
www.rossetti.it

Furla
Corso Vittorio Emanuele 1, 20121 Milan
telephone : +39.02.88521
www.furla.com

Gianfranco Ferré
Via Sant'Andrea 15, 20121 Milan
telephone : +39.02.780 406
www.gianfrancoferre.com

Giusti
Galleria Cavour 9h, 40124 Bologna
telephone : +39.051.228 755

Gucci
Via Montenapoleone 5-7, 20121 Milan
telephone : +39.02.771 271
www.gucci.com

Galleria Cavour 9o, 40124 Bologna
telephone : +39.051.262 981
www.gucci.com

Via Tornabuoni 73r, 50123 Florence
telephone : +39.055.264 011
www.gucci.com

Via Roma 32r, 50123 Florence
telephone : +39.055.759 221
www.gucci.com

Via Camerelle 25-27, 80073 Capri
telephone : +39.081.837 0820
www.gucci.com

L'Arte del Sandalo Caprese
Via Orlandi 75, Anacapri,
80071 Capri
telephone : +39.081.837 3583

La Coppola Storta
Via dell'Orologio 25, 90134 Palermo
www.lacoppolastorta.com

La Parisienne
Piazza Umberto I 7, 80073 Capri
telephone : +39.081.837 0283

La Perla
Galleria Cavour 1, 40124 Bologna
telephone : +39.051.273 363
facsimile : +39.051.270 377
laperlainfo@laperla.com
www.laperla.com

Leam
Via Appia Nuova 26 and 32,
00178 Rome
telephone : +39.06.7720 7204
leam@leam.com
www.leam.com

Marella Ferrera
Viale XX Settembre 25/27,
95100 Catania
telephone : +39.095.446 751
www.marellaferrera.com

Max Mara
Piazza del Liberty 4, 20121 Milan
telephone : +39.02.777 921
facsimile : +39.02.7779 2801
ufficio.stampa@maxmara.it

Merolla e del'Ero
Via Calabritto 20, 80121 Naples
telephone : +39.081.764 3012

Miss Sixty
Via Torino 19, 20123 Milan
telephone : +39.08.715 891
facsimile : +39.08.7156 2496
misssixty@misssixty.com
www.misssixty.com

Moschino
Via Sant'Andrea 12, 20121 Milan
telephone : +39.02.7600 0832
www.moschino.it

Patrizia Pepe
Piazza san Giovanni 12r, 50123 Florence
telephone : +39.055.264 5056
info@patriziapepe.com
www.patriziapepe.com

Prada
Galleria Vittorio Emanuele II 63/65,
20121 Milan
telephone : +39.02.876 979
www.prada.com

Via Montenapoleone 8, 20121 Milan
telephone : +39.02.7602 0273
www.prada.com

Via Camerelle, Capri
www.prada.com

Roberta Lojacono
Via Turati 17, 90139 Palermo
info@robertalojacono.it
www.robertalojacono.it

Roberto Cavalli
Via dei Tornabuoni 83r, 50123 Florence
telephone : +39.055.239 6226
www.robertocavalli.it

Via Vittorio Emanuele 26, 80073 Capri
telephone : +39.081.837 7750
www.robertocavalli.it

Salvatore Ferragamo
Via Montenapoleone 3, 20121 Milan
telephone : +39.02.7600 0054
www.salvatoreferragamo.com

Via dei Tornabuoni 4r-14r,
50123 Florence
telephone : +39.055.292 123
facsimile : +39.055.336 0468
www.salvatoreferragamo.com

Via Vittorio Emanuele 21-29, 80073 Capri
telephone : +39.081.837 0499
facsimile : +39.081.837 6777
www.salvatoreferragamo.com

Spazio
Via Porta Rossa 107r, 50123 Florence
telephone : +39.055.212 995
spazioa.firenze@aeffe.com
www.aeffe.com

TAD
Via Del Babuino 155a, 00187 Rome
telephone : +39.06.3269 5131
roma@taditaly.com
www.taditaly.com

directory

Tod's
Galleria Vittorio Emanuele II, 20121 Milan
telephone: +39.02.877 977
www.tods.com

Trussardi
Via Sant'Andrea 3/5/7, 20121 Milan
telephone: +39.02.7602 0380
www.trussardi.com

Valentino
Via Montenapoleone 20, 20121 Milan
telephone: +39.02.7600 6182
facsimile : +39.02.780 437
www.valentino.it

Via Condotti 13, 00187 Rome
telephone: +39.06.679 5862
facsimile : +39.06.6994 0709
www.valentino.it

Via del Babuino 61, 00187 Rome
telephone: +39.06.3600 1906
facsimile : +39.06.3600 1930
www.valentino.it

Via Bocca di Leone 15, 00187 Rome
telephone: +39.06.678 3656
facsimile : +39.06.673 9394
www.valentino.it

Venetia Stadium
St. Mark's Square 2425, 30124 Venice
telephone: +39.041.523 6953
facsimile : +39.041.522 7353
info@venetiastudium.com
www.venetiastudium.com

Versace
Via Montenapoleone 11, 20121 Milan
telephone: +39.02.7600 8528
www.versace.com

Galleria Cavour 2n, 40124 Bologna
+39.051.221 016
www.versace.com

Vittorio Trois
Campo San Maurizio, San Marco 2666,
30124 Venice
telephone: +39.041.522 2905

MADE IN ITALY: DESIGN

Alessi
Via Privata Alessi 6, 28887 Crusinallo
Di Omegna
telephone: +39.0323.868 611
facsimile : +39.0323.641 605
www.alessi.com

Archimede Seguso
Via dei Due Macelli 56, 00187 Rome
telephone: +39.06.679 1781
info@aseguso.com
www.aseguso.com

Arclinea
Lungotevere de'Cenci 4b, 00186 Rome
telephone: +39.06.686 5104
info@arclinea-roma.com
www.arclinea-roma.com

Arper
Via Lombardia 16, 31050 Monastier
telephone: +39.0422.7918
facsimile : +39.0422.791 800
info@arperitalia.com
www.arper.com

Artemide
Via Bergamo 18, 20010 Pregnana
telephone: +39.02.935 181
facsimile : +39.02.9359 0254
info@artemide.com
www.artemide.com

B&B Italia
Via Durini 14, 20122 Milan
telephone: +39.02.764 441
facsimile : +39.02.7644 4222
store.milano@bebitalia.it
www.milano.bebitalia.com

Babuino Novecento
Via del Babuino 65, 00187 Rome
telephone: +39.06.3600 3853
bab900@tiscali.it
www.babuinonovecento.com

Benedetti
Via Marmorata 139/141, 00153 Rome
telephone: +39.06.574 6610
facsimile : +39.06.574 6357
info@benedettiarredamenti.eu
www.benedettiarredamenti.eu

Cappellini
Via Santa Cecilia 4, 20122 Milan
telephone: +39.02.7600 3889
facsimile : +39.02.7600 3676
s.cecilia@cappellini.it
www.cappellini.it

Via di Propaganda 8, 00187 Rome
telephone: +39.06.678 4383
facsimile : +39.06.6929 5447
cappellini.roma@cappellini.it
www.cappellini.it

Carlo Moretti
Fondamenta Manin 3,
30141 Murano, Venice
telephone: +39.041.736 588
facsimile : +39.041.736 282
info@carlomoretti.com
www.carlomoretti.com

Cassina
Via Durini 16, 20122 Milan
telephone: +39.02.7602 0745
facsimile : +39.02.7602 0758
showroom@cassina.it
www.cassina.com

Ceramica Flaminia
S.S. Flaminia Km 54, 630, 01033
Civita Castellana
telephone: +39.0761.542 030
facsimile : +39.0761.540 069
ceramicaflaminia@ceramicaflaminia.it
www.ceramicaflaminia.it

C.u.c.i.n.a
Via Mario d'Fiori 65, 00187 Rome
telephone: +39.06.679 1275

Danese
Piazza San Nazaro in Brolo 15,
20122 Milan
telephone: +39.02.5843 2104
facsimile : +39.02.5830 4150
www.danesemilano.it

Domus Vetri d'Arte
Fondamenta Vetrai 82,
30141 Murano, Venice
telephone: +39.041.739 215
domusvetri@hotmail.com

E De Padova
Corso Venezia 14, 20121 Milan
telephone: +39.02.777 201
facsimile : +39.02.7772 0270
negozio@depadova.it
www.depadova.it

Flos
Via Angelo Faini 2, 25073 Bovezzo
telephone: +39.0302.4381
facsimile : +39.0302.438 250
www.flos.com

Fornari + Fornari
Via Frattina 133, 00187 Rome
telephone: +39.06.678 0105
facsimile : +39.06.679 7464
www.fornari1905.com

Fornasetti
Via Manzoni 45, 20121 Milan
telephone: +39.02.659 2341
facsimile : +39.02.259 4288
info@fornasetti.com
www.fornasetti.com

Galleria MK
Via Pietro Maroncelli 2, 20154 Milan
telephone: +39.02.655 1035
info@galleriamk.com
www.galleriamk.com

Galleria Rossella Colombari
Via Pietro Maroncelli 10, 20154 Milan
telephone: +39.02.2900 1189

Gusto
Piazza Augusto Imperatore 9,
00100 Rome
telephone: +39.06.323 6363
www.gusto.it

High Tech d'Epoca
Piazza A. Capponi 7, 00193 Rome
telephone: +39.06.687 2147
www.htdepoca.it

Il Loft
Via Pegoraro 24, 21013 Gallarate
telephone: +39.0331.776 578
facsimile : +39.0331.776 579
info@illoft.com
www.illoft.com

Magazzini Associati
Corso del Rinascimento 7, 00186 Rome
telephone: +39.06.6813 5179

Maurizio de Nisi
Via Panisperna 51, 00184 Rome
telephone: +39.06.474 0732
info@mauriziodenisi.com
www.mauriziodenisi.com

Minotti
Via Indipendenza 152, 20036 Meda
telephone: +39.03.6234 3499
facsimile : +39.03.6234 0319
info@minotti.it
www.minotti.it

Murano Più
Corso del Rinascimento 43/45,
00186 Rome
telephone: +39.06.6880 8038
facsimile : +39.06.687 5116
muranopiu@muranopiu.com
www.muranopiumadeinitaly.com

Odorisio
Via Tomacelli 150, 00186 Rome
telephone: +39.06.687 8235
facsimile : +39.06.687 8322
info@ odorisio.it
www.odorisio.it

Pauly
Calle Larga San Marco,
4391A San Marco, Venice
telephone: +39.041.520 9899

Poltrona Frau
S.S. 77 Km 74,500, 62029 Tolentino
telephone: +39.0733.9091
facsimile : +39.0733.971 600
info@poltronafrau.com
www.poltronafrau.com

Retrò
Piazza del Fico 20-21, 00186 Rome
telephone: +39.06.6819 2746
info@retrodesign.it
www.retrodesign.it

Spazio Sette
Via dei Barbieri 7, 00186 Rome
telephone: +39.06.686 9747
facsimile : +39.06.6830 7139
www.spaziosette.com

Zucchetti
Via Molini di Resiga 29, 28024 Gozzano
telephone: +39.0322.954 700
facsimile : +39.0322.954 823
customer@zucchettidesign.it
www.zucchettionline.it

ITALY'S RESTAURANT SCENE

Antica Focacceria San Francesco
Via A Paternostro 58, 90100 Palermo
telephone: +39.091.320 264
facsimile : +39.091.612 8855
info@afsf.it
www.afsf.it

Baby dell'Aldrovandi Palace
Via Ulisse Aldrovandi 15, 00197 Rome
telephone: +39.06.321 6126
facsimile : +39.06.322 1435
baby@ aldrovandi.com
www.aldrovandi.com

Bottega del Vino
Via Scudo di Francia 3, 37121 Verona
telephone: +39.45.800 4535
facsimile : +39.45.801 2273
www.bottegavini.it

Caffè Groppi
Via Goffredo Mameli 20, 28069 Trecate
telephone: +39.0321.71154
facsimile : +39.0321.785 732
info@caffegroppi.it
www.caffegroppi.it

Caminetto d'Oro
Via de'Falegnami 4, 40121 Bologna
telephone: +39.051.263 494
facsimile : +39.051.656 1109
info@caminettodoro.it
www.caminettodoro.it

Castel Ringberg
San Giuseppe al Lago 1, 39052 Caldaro
telephone: +39.0471.960 010
facsimile : +39.0471.960 803
info@castel-ringberg.com
www.castel-ringberg.com

Castello Banfi
Loc. Sant'Angelo Scalo,
Castello di Poggio alle Mura, 53024
Montalcino
telephone: +39.0577.877 500
www.castellobanfi.com

Combal.Zero
Piazza Mafalda di Savoia,
10098 Rivoli
telephone: +39.011.956 5225
facsimile : +39.011.956 5248
combal.zero@combal.org
www.combalzero.it

Cracco
Via Victor Hugo 4, 20123 Milan
telephone: +39.02.876 774
facsimile : +39.02.861 040

Da Caino
Via Chiesa 4, 58050 Montemerano
telephone: +39.0564.602 817
facsimile : +39.0564.602 807
info@dacaino.it
www.dacaino.it

Da Michele
Via C Sersale 1/3, 80100 Naples
telephone: +39.081.553 9204
www.damichele.net

Dal Pescatore
Loc. Runate 17, 46013 Canneto
sull'Oglio
telephone: +39.0376.723 001
facsimile : +39.0376.70304
pescatore@relaischateaux.com
www.dalpescatore.it

Dolce Stil Novo
Via San Pietro 71/73, Loc. Devesi-Ciriè,
10073 Turin
telephone: +39.011.921 1110
dolcestilnovo@esanet.it
www.dolcestilnovo.com

Enoteca Ferrara
Piazza Trilussa 41, 00153 Rome
telephone: +39.06.5833 3920
facsimile : +39.06.580 3769
info@enotecaferrara.it
www.enotecaferrara.it

Enoteca Pinchiorri
Via Ghibellina 87, 50122 Florence
telephone: +39.055.242 757
facsimile : +39.055.244 983
ristorante@enotecapinchiorri.com
www.enotecapinchiorri.com

Gambero Rosso
Piazza della Vittoria 13, 57027
San Vincenzo
telephone: +39.0565.701 021
facsimile : +39.0565.704 542
www.ristorantegamberorosso.it

Il Canto
Hotel Certosa di Maggiano
Strada di Certosa 82, 53100 Siena
telephone: +39.0577.288 180
facsimile : +39.0577.288 189
info@certosadimaggiano.it
www.ilcanto.it

Il Latini
Via dei Palchetti 6r, 50123 Florence
telephone : +39.055.210 916
facsimile : +39.055.288 794
info@illatini.it
www.illatini.it

Il Vecio Fritolin
Calle della Regina, 2262 Venice
telephone : +39.041.522 2881
info@veciofritolin.it
www.veciofritolin.it

L'Olivo
Capri Palace Hotel + Spa
Via Capodimonte 2b,
80071 Anacapri
telephone : +39.081.978 0111
facsimile : +39.081.837 3191
info@capri-palace.com
www.capripalace.com

**La Pergola de l'Hotel Rome
Cavalieri Hilton**
Via A Cadlolo 101, 00136 Rome
telephone : +39.06.3509 2152
facsimile : +39.06.3509 2165
lapergolareservations.rome@hiltonint.com
www.cavalieri-hilton.it

La Pista
Via Nizza 262/294, Lingotto,
10126 Turin
telephone : +39.011.631 3523
www.lapista.to.it

La Terrazza dei Barbanti
Hotel San Francesco al Monte
Corso Vittorio Emanuele 328,
80135 Naples
telephone : +39.081.423 9111
facsimile : +39.081.251 2485
info@hotelsanfrancesco.it
www.hotelsanfrancesco.it

Laite
Via Hoffe 10, 32047 Sappada, Belluno
telephone : +39.0435.469 070
ristorantelaite@libero.it
www.ristorantelaite.com

Le Calandre
Loc. Sarmeola, Via Liguria 1,
35030 Rubano
telephone : +39.049.630 303
facsimile : +39.049.633 000
reception@calandre.com
www.calandre.com

Locanda dell'Isola Comacina
Ossuccio, 22010 Lago di Como
telephone : +39.0344.55083 or 56755
facsimile : +39.0344.57022
www.locanda-isola-comacina.com

Locanda Mongreno
Strada Comunale Mongreno 50,
10132 Turin
telephone : +39.011.898 0417
facsimile : +39.011.822 7345

Locanda nel Borgo Antico
Via Boschetti 4, 12060 Barolo
telephone : +39.0173.56355
facsimile : +39.0173.560 935
info@locandanelborgo.it
www.locandanelborgo.com

Madonnina del Pescatore
Lungomare Italia 11, 60017
Marzocca di Senigallia
telephone : +39.071.698 267
facsimile : +39.071.698 484
info@madonninadelpescatore.it
www.madonninadelpescatore.it

Met de l'Hotel Metropole
Riva degli Schiavoni Castello 4149,
30122 Venice
telephone : +39.041.520 5044
venice@hotelmetropole.com
www.hotelmetropole.com

Osteria La Francescana
Via Stella 22, 41100 Modena
telephone : +39.059.210 118
facsimile : +39.059.220 286

Osteria Sotto l'Arco
Corso Vittorio Emanuele II 71,
72012 Carovigno
telephone : +39.0831.996 286
facsimile : +39.0831.994 769
sottolarco@libero.it
www.giasottolarco.it

Palatium Enoteca Regionale
Via Frattina 94, 00187 Rome
telephone : +39.06.6920 2132
facsimile : +39.06.6938 0504
info@enotecapalatium.it
www.enotecapalatium.it

Paolo e Barbara
Via Roma 47, 18038 San Remo
telephone : +39.0184.531 653
facsimile : +39.0184.545 266
paolobarbara@libero.it
www.paolobarbara.it

Piazza Duomo
Piazza Risorgimento 4, 12051 Alba
telephone : +39.0173.366 167
info@piazzaduomoalba.it
www.piazzaduomoalba.it

Ristorante Duomo
Loc. Ibla, Via Capitano Bocchieri 31,
97100 Ragusa
telephone : +39.0932.651 265
info@ristoranteduomo.it
www.ristoranteduomo.it

Ristorante Sadler
Via Ascanio Sforza 77, 20100 Milan
telephone : +39.02.5810 4451
facsimile : +39.02.5811 2343
sadler@sadler.it
www.sadler.it

S'Apposentu
Via Sant'Alenixedda, Teatro Lirico,
09128 Cagliari
telephone : +39.0704.082 315
facsimile : +39.0704.525 308
sapposentu@tiscalinet.it
www.sapposentu.it

San Domenico
Via Gaspare Sacchi 1,
40026 Imola
telephone : +39.0542.29000
facsimile : +39.0542.39000
sandomenico@sandomenico.it
www.sandomenico.it

St. Hubertus de l'Hotel Rosa Alpina
Fraz. San Cassiano, Strada Micura de Rü
20, I-39030 San Cassiano in Badia
telephone : +39.0471.849 500
facsimile : +39.0471.849 377
info@rosalpina.it
www.rosalpina.it

Su Gologone
Loc. Su Gologone, 08025 Oliena
telephone : +39.0784.287 512
facsimile : +39.0784.287 668
gologone@tin.it
www.sugologone.it

Torre del Saracino
Loc. Marina di Seiano, Via Torretta 9,
80069 Vico Equense
telephone : +39.081.802 8555
info@torredelsaracino.it
www.torredelsaracino.it

Villa Crespi
Via G. Fava 18, 28016 Orta San Giulio
telephone : +39.0322.911 902
facsimile : +39.0322.911 919
info@hotelvillacrespi.it
www.hotelvillacrespi.it

Villa Fiordaliso
Corso Zanardelli 132, 25083
Gardone Riviera
telephone : +39.0365.20158
facsimile : +39.0365.290 014
info@villafiordaliso.it
www.villafiordaliso.it

Vissani
Fraz. Civitella del Lago, 05023 Baschi
telephone : +39.0744.950 206
facsimile : +39.0744.950 186

THE TREASURES OF ITALY

Accademia
Campo della Carita
Dorsoduro n.1050, 30130 Venezia
telephone : +39.041.520 0345
www.gallerieaccademia.org

Archeological Museum
Piazza Museo Nazionale 19,
80135 Naples
telephone : +39.081.292 823
www.archeona.arti.beniculturali.it

Bargello
Via del Proconsolo 4, 50122 Florence
telephone : +39.055.294 883
www.polomuseale.firenze.it/musei/bargello

**Ca'Pesaro International Gallery of
Modern Art**
Santa Croce 2070, 30125 Venice
telephone : +39.041.721 127
facsimile : +39.041.524 1075
www.museicivicivenezioni.it

Capitoline Museums
Piazza del Campidoglio 1, 00186 Rome
telephone : +39.06.8205 9127
www.museicapitolini.org

Centrale Montemartini
Via Ostiense 106, 00154 Rome
telephone : +39.06.575 4207
museo.centrale.montemartini@comune.roma.it
www.centralemontemartini.org

Cittadella dei Musei
Piazza Arsenale, I-09100 Cagliari
telephone : +39.070.655 911

Fondazione Sandretto Re Rebaudengo
Via Modane 16, 10141 Turin
telephone : +39.011.379 7601
www.fondsrr.org

Galleria Borghese
Piazzale Scipione Borghese 5,
00197 Rome
telephone : +39.06.32810
www.galleriaborghese.it

Galleria dell'Accademia
Via Ricasoli 58-60, 50122 Florence
telephone : +39.055.294 883
www.polomuseale.firenze.it/accademia
www.polomuseale.firenze.it

Galleria Nazionale d'Arte Moderna
Viale delle Belle Arti 131,
00196 Rome
telephone : +39.06.322 981
www.gnam.arti.beniculturali.it

Galleria Nazionale Umbria
Corso Vannucci 1, Perugia,
06100 Umbria
telephone : +39.075.574 1247
info@gallerianazionaleumbria.it
www.gallerianazionaleumbria.it

International Museum of Ceramics
Viale Baccarini 19, I-48018 Faenza
telephone : +39.0546.697 311
www.micfaenza.org

Lo Scrigno
Pinacoteca Giovanni e Marella Agnelli
Lingotto, Via Nizza 230, 10126 Turin
telephone : +39.011.006 2008
www.pinacoteca-agnelli.it

MADre
Via Settembrini 79, 80139 Naples
telephone : +39.081.1931 3016
www.museomadre.it

MAMbo
Museo d'Arte Moderna di Bologna
Via Don Minzoni 14, 40121 Bologna
telephone : +39.051.649 6611
facsimile : +39.051.649 6600
info@mambo-bologna.org
www.mambo-bologna.org

MART
Corso Bettini 43, 38068 Rovereto
telephone : +39.0424.600 435
www.mart.trento.it

Milan Triennale
Triennale di Milano
Viale Alemagna 6, 20121 Milan
telephone : +39.02.875 441
www.triennale.it

Museo Archeologico Regionale
Piazza Olivella 24, 90100 Palermo
telephone : +39.091.611 6805

Museo del Mare
Calata de Mari 1, Darsena-Via Gramsci,
16126 Genoa
telephone : +39.010.234 5655
info@galatamuseoedelmare.it
www.galatamuseodelmare.it

Museo dell'Automobile
Corso Unita d'Italia 40, 10126 Turin
telephone : +39.011.677 666
facsimile : +39.011.664 7148
www.museoauto.it

**Museo della Vita e delle Tradizioni
Popolari Sarde**
Via Mereu 56, 08100 Nuoro
telephone : +39.0784.242 900

Museo di Arte Contemporanea
Castello di Rivoli
Piazza Mafalda di Savoia,
10098 Rivoli, Turin
telephone : +39.011.956 5222
facsimile : +39.011.956 5230
info@castellodirivoli.org
www.castellodirivoli.it

Museo Morandi
Piazza Maggiore 6, 40124 Bologna
www.museomorandi.it

Museo Nazionale di Capodimonte
Parco di Capodimonte
Via Miano 2, 80131 Naples
telephone : +39.081.749 9111
facsimile : +39.081.744 5032
capodimonte.spmn.remuna.org

Museo Salvatore Ferragamo
Piazza Santa Trinita 5r,
50123 Florence
telephone : +39.055.336 0456
facsimile : +39.055.336 0475
www.salvatoreferragamo.it

Museum of Cinema
Via Montebello 20, 10124 Turin
telephone : +39.011.813 8560
www.museonazionaledelcinema.it

Palazzo dei Diamanti
Corso Ercole d'Este 21, 44100 Ferrara
telephone : +39.0532.244 949
diamanti@comune.fe.it
www.palazzodiamanti.it
www.artecultura.fe.it

Palazzo Doria Pamphilj
Piazza del Collegio Romano 2,
I-00186 Rome
telephone : +39.06.679 7323
facsimile : +39.06.678 0939
arti.rm@doriapamphilj.it
www.doriapamphilj.it

Palazzo Fortuny
San Marco 3780, 30124 Venice
telephone : +39.041.520 0995
facsimile : +39.041.522 3088
www.museicivicivenezioni.it

Palazzo Massari
Corso Porta Mare 9, 44100 Ferrara
telephone : +39.0532.243 415
facsimile : +39.0532.205 035
artemoderna@comune.fe.it
www.palazzodiamanti.it
www.artecultura.fe.it

Palazzo Pantaleo
Corso Vittorio Emanuele II,
74100 Taranto
telephone : +39.099.458 1715
www.museotaranto.it

directory

Peggy Guggenheim Collection
Palazzo Venier dei Leoni
Dorsoduro 704, I-30123 Venice
telephone : +39.041.240 5411
facsimile : +39.041.520 6885
info@guggenheim-venice.it
www.guggenheim-venice.it

Pinacoteca di Brera
Via Brera 28, 20121 Milan
telephone : +39.02.722 631
www.brera.beniculturali.it

Pinacoteca Nazionale
Via delle Belle Arti 56, I-40100 Bologna
telephone : +39.051.420 9411
www.pinacotecabologna.it

Studio Museo Achille Castiglione
Piazza Castello 27, 20121 Milan
telephone : +39.02.805 3606
www.triennale.it

Uffizi Gallery
Loggiato degli Uffizi 6, 50121 Florence
telephone : +39.055.294 883
www.uffizi.firenze.it

Vatican Museums
Viale Vaticano, 00120 Vatican City
telephone : +39.06.6988 3333
www.vatican.va

ITALY'S CAFÉ SOCIETY

Alle Logge di Piazza
Piazza del Popolo 1, 53024
Montalcino, Tuscany
telephone : +39.057.784 6186

Antico Caffè
Piazza Costituzione 10/11, 09100
Cagliari, Sardinia
telephone : +39.070.658 206
info@anticocaffe1855.it
www.anticocaffe1855.it

Armani Privé
Via Alessandro Manzoni 31,
20121 Milan
telephone : +39.02.6321 2655
www.giorgioarmani.com

Bacaro Jazz
San Marco 5546, 30124 Venice
telephone : +39.041.528 5249
info@bacarojazz.com
www.bacarojazz.com

Bar Dandolo
Hotel Daniele
Riva degli Schiavoni 4196, 30122 Venice
telephone : +39.041.782 782
www.danieli.hotelinvenice.com

Bar Mexico
Piazza Dante 86, 80135 Naples
telephone : +39.081.549 9330

Baratti + Milano
Piazza Castello 27, 10124 Turin
telephone : +39.011.440 7138

Bibli
Via dei Fienaroli 28, Trastevere,
00153 Rome
telephone : +39.06.581 4534
www.bibli.it

Buddha del Mar
Villagio Gallura 2, San Teodoro,
08020 Sardinia
info@buddhadelmar.it
www.buddhadelmar.it

Café du Port
Molo Vecchio, 07020 Porto
Cervo, Sardinia
telephone : +39.0789.92348

Caffè Al Bicerin
Piazza della Consolata 5, 10122 Turin
telephone : +39.011.436 9325
bicerin@bicerin.it
www.bicerin.it

Caffè Cibreo
Via del Verrocchio 5r, 50122 Florence
telephone : +39.055.234 5853

Caffè Florian
Piazza San Marco 56, 30124 Venice
telephone : +39.041.520 5641
facsimile : +39.041.522 4409
info@caffeflorian.com
www.caffeflorian.com

Caffè Latino
Bastioni Magellano 10, 07041
Alghero, Sardinia
telephone : +39.079.976 541
facsimile : +39.079.984 795

Caffè Marconi
Corso Marconi 3, 10124 Turin
telephone : +39.011.650 5151

Caffè Pansa
Piazza Duomo 40, 84011 Amalfi
telephone : +39.089.871 065
www.pasticceriapansa.it

Caffè Sicilia
Corso Vittorio Emanuele 125,
96017 Noto, Sicily
telephone : +39.0931.835 013
www.paginegialle.it/caffesicilia

Caffè Zucca
Galleria Vittorio Emanuele II
Piazza del Duomo 21, 20121 Milan
telephone : +39.02.8646 4435

Caffeteria Leonardo
Via A Saffi 7, 20121 Milan
telephone : +39.02.439 0302

Ciak Bar
Museum of Cinema
Via Montebello 20, 10124 Turin
telephone : +39.011.839 5711
info@museocinema.it
www.museonazionaledelcinema.org

Coffee Design
Triennale di Milano
Viale Alemagna 6, 20121 Milan
telephone : +39.02.875 441
www.triennale.it

Cova
Via Montenapoleone 8, 20121 Milan
telephone : +39.02.7600 5599

Culti Spa Café
Via Carlo Poerio 47-47/b, 80121 Naples
telephone : +39.081.764 4619
www.culti.it

Dal Pescatore
Piazzetta Sant'Angelo
Loc. Sant'Angelo, 80070 Ischia
telephone : +39.081.999 206

Donatello Bar
The Westin Excelsior, Florence
Piazza Ognissanti 3, 50123 Florence
telephone : +39.055.27151
facsimile : +39.055.210 278
www.starwoodhotels.com/westin

Fiat Café
Triennale di Milano
Viale Alemagna 6, 20121 Milan
telephone : +39.02.875 441
www.triennale.it

Freni + Frizioni
Via del Politeama 4-6, Trastevere,
00153 Rome
telephone : +39.06.5833 4210
info@frenifrizioni.com
www.frenifrizioni.com

Giubbe Rosse
Piazza della Repubblica 13/14r,
50123 Florence
telephone : +39.055.212 280
facsimile : +39.055.290 052
info@giubberosse.it
www.giubberosse.it

Gran Caffè Cimmino
Via Filangieri Riccardo 12, 80121 Naples
Via Petrarca 147, 80122 Naples

Gran Caffè Gambrinus
Via Chiaia 1-2, 80132 Naples
telephone : +39.081.417 582
www.caffegambrinus.com

Kursaal Kalesa
Foro Umberto I 21, 90133 Palermo, Sicily
telephone : +39.091.616 2111
info@kursaalkalhesa.it
www.kursaalkalhesa.it

Martini Bar
Corso Venezia 15, 20121 Milan
telephone : +39.02.7601 1154

Mulassano
Piazza Castello 15, 10124 Turin
telephone : +39.011.547 990

Museo Atelier Canova Tadolini
Via del Babuino 150a/b, 00187 Rome
telephone : +39.06.3211 0702
facsimile : +39.06.3262 9336

Negroni
Via de'Renai 17r, 50125 Florence
telephone : +39.055.245 647
www.negronibar.com

Ojster's Bar
Villagio Poltu Quatu, 07020 Porto
Cervo, Sardinia
telephone : +39.0789.99460

Pasticceria Di Pasquale
Corso Vittorio Veneto 104,
97100 Ragusa, Sicily
telephone : +39.0932.624 635
facsimile : +39.0932.627 709
info@pasticceriadipasquale.com
www.pasticceriadipasquale.com

Peck Bar
Via Spadari 9, 20121 Milan
telephone : +39.02.802 3161

Quisi Bar
Grand Hotel Quisisana
Via Camerelle 2, 80073 Capri, Campania
telephone : +39.081.837 0788
facsimile : +39.081.837 6080
info@quisi.com
www.quisi.it

Ristorante Gran Caffè Quadri
Piazza San Marco 121, 30124 Venice
telephone : +39.041.522 2105
facsimile : +39.041.520 8041
www.quadrivenice.com

Spinnato Antico Caffè
Via Principe di Belmonte 107/115,
90139 Palermo, Sicily
telephone : +39.091.329 220

Supperclub
Via dei Nari 14, 00186 Rome
telephone : +39.06.6880 7207
www.supperclub.com

Tazio Champagnerie
Hotel Exedra
Piazza della Republica 47, 00185 Rome
telephone : +39.06.489 381
facsimile : +39.06.4893 8000
www.boscolohotels.com

Tazza d'Oro
Via degli Orfani 84, 00186 Rome
telephone : +39.06.678 9792
facsimile : +39.06.679 8131
info@tazzadorocoffeeshop.com
www.tazzadorocoffeeshop.com

The Fusion Bar
Gallery Hotel Art
Vicolo dell'Oro 5, 50123 Florence
telephone : +39.055.283 054
www.glahotels.com

ITALIAN INDULGENCE

Acanto Spa
Via Rondanini 30, 00186 Rome
telephone : +39.06.6813 6602
info@acantospa.it
www.acantospa.it

Bagni di Bormio Spa Resort
Via Bagni Nuovi 7, 23038
Valdidentro, Sondrio
telephone : +39.0342.910 131
facsimile : +39.0342.918 511
www.bagnidibormio.it

Borgo La Bagnaia
Strada Statale 223,
Siena Grosseto Km 12, 53016
Localita Bagnaia, Siena
telephone : +39.0577.813 000
facsimile : +39.0577.817 464
www.borgolabagnaia.com

Bulgari Hotel Spa
Bulgari Hotels + Resorts Milano
Via Privata Fratelli Gabba 7b,
20121 Milan
telephone : +39.02.805 8051
facsimile : +39.02.8058 05222
www.bulgarihotels.com

Capri Beauty Farm
Capri Palace Hotel + Spa
Via Capodimonte 2b, 80071 Anacapri
telephone : +39.081.978 0111
facsimile : +39.081.837 3191
info@capri-palace.com
www.capripalace.com

Casanova Spa
Hotel Cipriani
Giudecca 10, 30133 Venice
telephone : +39.041.520 7744
facsimile : +39.041.520 3930
info@hotelcipriani.it
www.hotelcipriani.it

Daniela Steiner Beauty Spa
Kempinski Hotel Giardino di Costanza Sicily
Via Salemi Km 7, 100,
91026 Mazara del Vallo
telephone : +39.0923.675 000
facsimile : +39.0923.675 876
info.mazara@kempinski.com
www.kempinski-sicily.com

ESPA at Castello del Nero
Castello del Nero Hotel + Spa
Strada Spicciano 7,
50028 Tavarnelle Val di Pesa
telephone : +39.055.806 470
facsimile : +39.055.8064 7777
reservations@castellodelnero.com
www.castello-del-nero.com

Grand Hotel Tombolo
Via del Corallo 3, 57022 Marina di
Castagneto Carducci
telephone : +39.0565.74530
facsimile : +39.0565.744 052
info@tombolotalasso.it
www.grandhoteltombolo.com

Spa at Mezzatorre
Mezzatorre Resort + Spa
Via Mezzatorre 23, 80075 Forio D'Ischia
telephone : +39.081.986 111
facsimile : +39.081.986 015
info@mezzatorre.it
www.mezzatorre.it

Terme Merano
Piazza Terme 9, I-39012 Merano
telephone : +39.0473.252 000
facsimile : +39.0473.252 022
info@termemerano.it
www.termemerano.it

Terme Pré-Saint-Didier
Allée des Thermes Pré-Saint-Didier,
11010 Terme di Pré-Saint-Didier
telephone : +39.0165.867 272
facsimile : +39.0165.867 726
info@termedipre.it
www.termedipre.it

Vigilius Resort
Vigiljoch Mountain, I-39011 Lana
telephone : +39.0473.556 600
facsimile : +39.0473.556 699
info@vigilius.it
www.vigilius.it

Villa del Parco + Spa
Le Méridien's Forte Village Resort
Santa Margherita di Pula, I-09010
Cagliari, Sardinia
telephone : +39.070.921 516
facsimile : +39.070.921 246
forte.village@fortevillage.com
www.fortevillage.com